WORLD BANK WORKING PAPER NO. 79

# Growth and Poverty Reduction

## *Case Studies from West Africa*

*Edited by Quentin Wodon*

**THE WORLD BANK**
Washington, D.C.

ISBN-10: 0-8213-6629-7          ISBN-13: 978-0-8213-6629-5
eISBN: 0-8213-6630-0
ISSN: 1726-5878                  DOI: 10.1596/978-0-8213-6629-5

Quentin Wodon is Lead Poverty Specialist in the Poverty Reduction and Economic Management office of the Africa Region at the World Bank.

Library of Congress Cataloging-in-Publication Data.

Growth and poverty reduction : case studies from West Africa / edited by Quentin Wodon.
     p. cm. — (World Bank working paper ; no. 79)
  Includes bibliographical references.
  ISBN-13: 978-0-8213-6629-5
  ISBN-10: 0-8213-6629-7
  ISBN-10: 0-8213-6630-0 (electronic)
  1. Poverty—Government policy—Africa, West—Case studies. 2.
Poverty—Africa, West—Case studies. 3.  Africa, West—Economic conditions—Case studies.
4.  Africa, West—Economic policy—Case studies.  I. Wodon, Quentin.
  HC1000.Z9.P613 2007
  339.4'60966—dc22
                    2007000418

# Contents

## LIST OF TABLES

## LIST OF FIGURES

## LIST OF BOXES

# Foreword

Growth is key for the reduction of poverty. Poverty, as traditionally measured, captures the fact that household consumption is not high enough in order to satisfy food and non-food basic needs. In order to reduce monetary poverty, it is necessary therefore either to increase the average level of consumption of households, or to reduce the inequality between households in their levels of consumption. In most countries, and especially in the poorest countries, many of which are located in Sub-Saharan Africa, the long-term gains in terms of poverty reduction that can be obtained from growth are much larger than those that can be achieved through the reduction in inequality. This is why growth is central in the Poverty Reduction Strategies prepared by developing countries.

While the role of growth in poverty reduction is well recognized, good data have been missing in most of West Africa in order to measure the impact of growth on poverty. Until recently, few countries had two or more comparable household surveys over time that could be used to measure poverty trends, and thereby assess the gains from growth for poverty reduction. This is now changing, with a larger number of countries being able to fill these data and knowledge gaps. The objective of this volume is to assess the relationships between growth and poverty reduction on the basis of a number of case studies, all but one of which are based on recent household survey data.

The first part of the volume presents data on Ghana and Senegal, two countries that have benefited from high levels of growth over the last dozen years. The analysis suggests that growth led to substantial reductions in the share of the population in poverty. Yet growth could not be said to be "pro-poor" because the gains in consumption for better off households were proportionately larger than the gains for poorer households. In the second part of the volume, case studies for Burkina Faso and Cape Verde are presented to solve the paradox of high growth without poverty reduction. It was initially believed in both countries that there had been no poverty reduction despite high growth during the 1990s. Yet a closer examination of the data suggests that this paradox was actually due to measurement errors: more careful work confirmed that poverty reduction was substantial. The third and last part of the volume presents case studies for Guinea-Bissau and Nigeria on the impediments to growth, with a focus on the negative impact of conflict and macroeconomic volatility on growth, and thereby on poverty.

Overall, this volume makes a strong case for the positive impact of growth for the reduction in income and consumption poverty in West Africa but it also points to the need to pay close attention to changes in inequality as such changes have limited the gains from growth for the poor in several of the countries considered here.

**Sudhir Shetty**
Sector Director, Poverty Reduction and Economic Management
Africa Region, World Bank

# Abstract

This volume provides a set of six case studies from West Africa in order to contribute to an assessment of the benefits of growth (or the costs of a lack of growth) for poverty reduction in those countries. The first part of the volume describes the experience of two countries (Ghana and Senegal) that achieved high levels of growth in the 1990s, and that also experienced important reductions in poverty, even though growth was not strictly pro-poor. The second part of the volume describes the experience of two other countries (Burkina Faso and Cape Verde) that also achieved high levels of growth in the 1990s, but where due to data and methodological issues, there was an initial perception that growth did not lead to much poverty reduction. The more detailed analysis of poverty presented here suggests however that these two countries did witness a sharp reduction in their population share in poverty, as would have been expected given their growth record. Finally, in the third part of the volume, it is argued that a lack of growth in the 1990s in the last two countries under review (Guinea-Bissau and Nigeria) has been a key reason for their persistently high levels of poverty. Overall, the case studies in this volume make a strong case for the positive impact of growth for the reduction in poverty in West Africa, but they also point to the need to pay close attention to changes in inequality as such changes have limited the gains from growth for the poor in several of the countries considered here.

# Acknowledgments

The papers included in this book were prepared as background work for Poverty Assessments and Risk and Vulnerability Assessments prepared at the World Bank in West Africa over the last few years, specifically for Burkina Faso, Cape Verde, Ghana, Guinea-Bissau, Nigeria, and Senegal. This work is part of a larger effort of the Poverty Reduction and Economic Management Unit for the Sub-Saharan Africa region at the World Bank to analyze household surveys in order to document and explain poverty trends in the Africa region. The papers rely on the nationally representative household surveys implemented in these various countries by National Statistical Institutes.

The authors are especially grateful for the support provided for this work by Paula Donovan and Sudhir Shetty, PREM Directors, as well as Robert Blake, PREM Sector Manager for West Africa. Thomas Pave Sohnesen provided very useful suggestions as peer reviewer for this work. The work benefited from financial support from three trust funds managed by the World Bank: the Trust Fund for Environmentally and Socially Sustainable Development (TFESSD), the Bank Netherlands Partnership Program (BNPP), and the Belgian Poverty Reduction Partnership (BPRP). The views expressed here are those of the authors, and do not necessarily represent those of the World Bank, its executive directors, or the countries they represent.

# CHAPTER 1

# Growth and Poverty Reduction in West Africa— A Brief Overview

*By Quentin Wodon*

*This volume provides a set of six case studies from West Africa in order to contribute to an assessment of the benefits of growth (or the cost of a lack of growth) for poverty reduction in those countries. The first part of the volume describes the experience of two countries (Ghana and Senegal) that achieved high levels of growth in the 1990s, and that also experienced important reductions in poverty, even though growth was not strictly pro-poor. The second part of the volume describes the experience of two other countries (Burkina Faso and Cape Verde) that also achieved high levels of growth in the 1990s, but where due to data and methodological issues, there was an initial perception that growth did not lead to much poverty reduction. The more detailed analysis of poverty presented here suggests however that these two countries did witness a sharp reduction in their population share in poverty, as would have been expected given their growth record. Finally, in the third part of the volume, it is argued that a lack of growth in the 1990s in the last two countries under review (Guinea-Bissau and Nigeria) has been a key reason for their persistently high levels of poverty. Overall, the case studies in this volume make a strong case for the positive impact of growth for the reduction in poverty in West Africa, but they also point to the need to pay close attention to changes in inequality as such changes have limited the gains from growth for the poor in several of the countries considered here.*

Poverty as traditionally defined using household income or consumption data is a function of both the level of mean income or consumption in a population, and the inequality in the distribution of these resources. Hence, both growth (a change in the mean) and changes in inequality can lead to changes in poverty. There is consensus that broad economic growth is important for poverty reduction. Economic growth typically leads to higher household incomes, which in turn enable households to increase their consumption and thereby reduce their probability of being poor. However, there are also concerns that growth often may not be enough, and that policies to reduce inequality also are important for poverty reduction. These concerns were echoed in the latest report of the World Bank's Independent Evaluation Group on development effectiveness.[1] They are also echoed in discussions within Sub-Saharan African countries. For example, several Poverty Reduction Strategies adopted by governments in West Africa have discussed the apparent lack of a strong enough link between economic growth and poverty reduction.

The authors of the papers in this volume are certainly convinced that a reduction in inequality is important for the reduction of monetary poverty, and the work presented in this volume does suggest that inequality is actually worsening in many of the countries considered here. At the same time, the authors also argue that without strong economic growth, it will be difficult to achieve sustainable poverty reduction and reach the Millennium Development Goal target of halving extreme poverty by 2015. Especially for African countries which tend to be poorer, the long-term gains in terms of poverty reduction that can be obtained from growth tend to be larger than those that can be achieved through the reduction in inequality, simply because there is often not that much initially to redistribute. This does not mean that policies towards inequality reduction should not be considered. However, it does imply that growth should remain central in the Poverty Reduction Strategies prepared and implemented by developing countries.

Until recently, good household survey data that were comparable over time were lacking in many African countries, including in West Africa. This made it difficult to properly measure changes in poverty over time, and assess the links between growth, changes in inequality, and changes in poverty. Today however, in part thanks to the monitoring and evaluation components of the countries' poverty reduction strategies, the availability of good survey data is becoming more widespread. In the context of a larger effort at the World Bank to measure changes in poverty over time in Sub-Saharan African countries, the objective of this volume is to document the trends in growth and poverty reduction in six West African countries (Burkina Faso, Cape Verde, Ghana, Guinea-Bissau, Nigeria, and Senegal). In four of the six countries, the focus is on poverty measures obtained by comparing results from two household surveys over time. In the last two countries, because only one household survey was available for the work presented here, the analysis focuses somewhat more on growth itself (or the lack thereof) than on poverty reduction, although poverty measures are estimated and estimations of their trend over time are provided using simple simulation techniques. These somewhat naive simulation techniques certainly have important limits, but they are nevertheless instructive to give a rough idea of the potential impact of a lack of growth on poverty.

The objective of this introductory chapter is to provide a quick overview of the key findings from the six case studies, as well as a brief conclusion on the lessons learned from this work.

## Overview of the Case Studies

The first part of the volume is devoted to Ghana and Senegal, two countries with high rates of economic growth in the 1990s and substantial poverty reduction, even though growth in each of these two countries could not be considered as strictly pro-poor.

---

1. See http://www.worldbank.org/ieg/arde2006?intcmp=5287207.

Chapter 2 documents the record of poverty reduction over the 1990s in Ghana, when macroeconomic performance remained good, although less consistent than in the years directly following the reforms that started in 1983. The analysis is based on comparable household surveys conducted at the beginning and end of the decade. At the national level poverty fell, and the evidence for this seems quite robust. Non-monetary indicators of well-being available from the surveys also show improvements over time, except for use of health care facilities. Yet, poverty reduction was concentrated in specific areas (including Accra and the rural forest region) and particular household activities (notably export oriented sectors and commerce). Households in other localities and working in other activities experienced little poverty reduction, with some evidence of increasing depth or severity of poverty in some locations (especially in the northern savannah). Thus, despite the reduction in the overall poverty measures, this paper highlights the limited benefits accruing to many of the poorest groups in Ghana over the 1990s and the increased differential between localities that emerged over this period. This could be a consequence of the country's less consistent macroeconomic performance over the period as compared to the post-reforms 1980s, but it also raises questions about the overall policy stance and the extent to which it focused enough on poorer, more remote regions and on non-export agriculture.

Chapter 3 on Senegal starts with the fact that the devaluation of the CFA Franc in 1994 generated a public investment boom. The increase in public investment was made possible thanks to an improved budgetary situation related to the reduction in real terms of the public wage bill which had been too large for some time (the wage bill was reduced because nominal wages were not adjusted for the implicit loss in purchasing power that the devaluation entailed). The rise in public investment was subsequently accompanied by a (smaller) increase in private investment due in part to the attractiveness of Senegal as a place to do business within West Africa, at least compared to other West African nations (this attractiveness has recently been further enhanced with the crisis in Côte d'Ivoire). In turn, higher public, and to some extent private, investment led to higher growth rates and substantial poverty reduction, with the share of the population living in poverty declining from 67.9 to 57.1 percent. However, as was the case in Ghana, poverty in urban areas was reduced faster than in rural areas, as most of the investment benefited the manufacturing and services sectors. Also, a few years of poor rainfall in the second half of the 1990s coupled with an initial drop in the real prices of crops in the aftermath of the devaluation affected negatively rural incomes. As a result, while virtually all segments of the population (including the rural poor) benefited from improved standards of living in 2001 as compared to 1994, growth was not strictly speaking "pro-poor" because the growth in consumption per equivalent adult in the upper half of the distribution was larger than that observed among the poor.

The second part of the volume describes the experience of two other countries (Burkina Faso and Cape Verde) that also achieved high levels of growth in the 1990s, but where due to data and methodological issues, there was an initial perception that growth did not lead to much poverty reduction. The more detailed analysis of poverty presented here suggests however that these two countries did witness a sharp reduction in their population share in poverty, as would have been expected given their growth record.

Chapter 4 provides estimates of the trend in poverty and inequality in Burkina Faso. In order to generate information about living standards, poverty, and inequality, the country implemented three Priority Surveys in 1994, 1998 and 2003. Throughout this period, efforts were made to improve the design and implementation of the surveys, from sampling and questionnaire design, to data entry and quality control. As a result, the precision of the latest poverty and inequality estimates was improved, generating more accurate and nuanced information on living standards. The improvements in survey design increased the precision of the newest poverty estimates, but endangered the comparability with the poverty estimates produced by earlier surveys. As a result, the initial official poverty and inequality estimates using the three surveys, which suggested a lack of progress towards poverty reduction, were not based on comparable data sets. The authors in Chapter 4 have defined an alternative and comparable welfare indicator, constructed using the same methodology and based on a subset of consumption items that were identically recorded across the 1998 and 2003 surveys. Based on this welfare aggregate, the poverty head count went down from about 54.6 percent in 1998 to 46.4 percent in 2003. The reduction in poverty was more pronounced in rural than in urban areas. In other words, a closer examination of the data suggests that the paradox of high growth without poverty reduction was actually due in large part to measurement errors.

Chapter 5 is devoted to Cape Verde, a country that shifted from a socialist to a capitalistic model in the late 1980s. This shift enabled the population to benefit from rapid economic growth, but concerns have been expressed about a potential increase in inequality. Two household surveys with consumption data implemented in 1988–89 and 2001–02 provide information that can be used to assess the impact on welfare of this policy shift. Initial estimates based on these two surveys suggested that there had been an increase in poverty over time, but this was mainly due to the adoption of a relative measure of poverty and to comparability issues between the surveys. The task of assessing the trends in poverty and inequality was also made more difficult because the unit level data of the first survey are not available. For the period 1988–89, the only information at our disposal consists of a number of tables on the distribution of income in the original report prepared 15 years ago on that survey. This makes it necessary to estimate poverty and inequality using group data. In Chapter 5, the authors use the Poverty module of SimSIP (a simulation tool from the "Simulations for Social Indicators and Poverty" project) in order to obtain new poverty and inequality trends over time with group data. They find that despite an increase in inequality over time, and thereby an increase in relative measures of poverty, absolute poverty measures have been reduced dramatically thanks to rapid growth.

Finally, in the third part of the volume, it is argued that a lack of growth in the 1990s in the last two countries under review (Guinea-Bissau and Nigeria) has been a key reason for their persistently high levels of poverty. As for the reasons for the lack of growth in each of the two countries, they differ. Conflict was a major factor in Guinea-Bissau, and macroeconomic instability played a key role in Nigeria.

In Chapter 6, it is argued that conflicts and political instability have been serious constrains to growth in Guinea-Bissau. Of special concern was the civil war of 1998, which lasted 11 months and led to substantial loss of life as well as to a massive decrease in GDP per capita. Based on previous work on the economic cost of conflicts in Sub-Saharan Africa and using a technique to identify outliers in time series and correcting the series for such outliers, the authors estimates that GDP per capita today could have been more than 40 percent higher if there had not been a conflict in 1998. In turn, if one is willing to assume that GDP per capita is closely correlated to the level of consumption per capita of households, about one in three persons today in poverty might not have been poor without the negative impact of the conflict. While there are a number of assumptions involved in these estimations, they do clearly suggest that conflicts can have a devastating impact on the well-being and poverty levels of a population.

The last Chapter is devoted to Nigeria. At the time at which the paper was written, the latest nationally representative survey for Nigeria was from 1996, and estimates suggested that two thirds of the population was poor in that year. The authors argue that this high level of poverty was due in large part to macroeconomic volatility that depressed private investment and growth. Using cross-sectional data for 87 countries, they show that real per-capita growth over the period 1980–94 was a function of productivity growth and investment rates, both of which were negatively effected by volatility (in terms of trade, real exchange rate, and public investments). When comparing Nigeria to high growth nations, they find that most of the growth differential can be attributed to Nigeria's higher macroeconomic volatility. In turn, simple simulations linking changes in per capita GDP to the level of consumption per capita of households suggest that if Nigeria had had lower levels of volatility and better macroeconomic policies, poverty would have been much lower than observed.

## Conclusion

In large part due to lack of data, the documentation on trends in poverty in Africa is limited, and West African countries are no exception to this rule. The objective of this volume has been fairly limited: as part of a broader effort at the World Bank to measure trends in well being in Sub-Saharan Africa, the aim has simply been to provide data on trends in poverty, and on the relationships between poverty, growth and inequality, in six West African countries. While it would not be appropriate to make broad generalizations from the experience of those six countries, the results provide some useful insights.

First, the papers in this volume suggest that long periods of high growth (as in Ghana and Senegal) do lead to poverty reduction, and that when this is apparently not the case (as in Burkina Faso and Cape Verde), the apparent lack of impact of growth on poverty may be due to measurement errors or methodological issues. Second, and at the same time, the impact of growth on poverty has often been more limited than one could have hoped, because inequality has increased in several countries or because growth has not been strictly speaking pro-poor (this is the case in Cape Verde, Ghana, and Senegal). Third, the experience of countries such as Guinea-Bissau and Nigeria suggests on the basis of simple simulations that a lack of growth can be very detrimental for the level of poverty observed in a country, and that conflict and macroeconomic volatility are two key factors that have prevented these countries to achieve economic grow in the past.

Overall, the case studies in this volume make a strong case for the positive impact of growth for the reduction in poverty in West Africa, but they also point to the need to pay close attention to changes in inequality as such changes have limited the gains from growth for the poor in several of the countries considered here.

# PART I

Poverty Reduction in
High Growth Countries

# CHAPTER 2

# Growth with Selective Poverty Reduction—Ghana in the 1990s

*By Harold Coulombe and Andrew McKay[2]*

*This paper assesses the record of poverty reduction in Ghana during the 1990s. Poverty fell at the national level as well as in urban and rural areas, and most non-monetary indicators also suggest an improvement in standards of living. However, poverty reduction was not universal: it was concentrated in Accra and the rural forest region, with the largest gains obtained among households engaged in export oriented sectors and commerce. In other words, beyond the overall reduction in poverty measures, this paper highlights the limited benefits that accrued to many of the poorest groups of households in Ghana over the 1990s and the increased differential between localities that emerged over this period, which now represents an important challenge for policymakers.*

Macroeconomic performance in Ghana was less consistent in the 1990s than it had been in the first few years of economic reform following the launch of its Economic Recovery Program in 1983. This raises the important question of the extent to which the overall poverty reduction which had been apparent over the period 1988–92 was maintained. This paper examines this issue, considering the evolution of both poverty and inequality over the 1990s, drawing on two rounds of the Ghana Living Standards Survey (GLSS) conducted towards the beginning and towards the end of the decade.

The evidence for there having been poverty reduction overall at the national level in Ghana over the 1988–92 period is quite strong. The strongest evidence for this came from analysis based on the results of the first three rounds of the GLSS Surveys (Ghana Statisti-

2. Coulombe is a consultant with the World Bank. McKay is Professor of Development Economics at the University of Sussex (UK). The authors are grateful to two anonymous reviewers and to Lionel Demery and Luc Christiansen for helpful comments on earlier drafts of this work. However, we accept responsibility for any remaining errors. The opinions expressed in this paper are those of the authors and should not be attributed to the World Bank or any of its member countries.

cal Service 1995; Coulombe and McKay 1995; Appiah and others 2000). These studies though had to contend with some comparability difficulties due to substantial changes in the survey questionnaire between the second and third rounds. While adjustments were made for the likely effects of this, such an exercise is invariably subjective so that some uncertainty remains. However, the result of improving average living conditions and falling poverty over 1988–92 is supported by other sources, notably the Demographic and Health Surveys conducted in 1988 and 1993, and macroeconomic statistics covering this period.

It is not clear though whether this poverty reduction at the beginning of the decade has been sustained. The results of a participatory poverty assessment conducted in poor communities in 1993 and 1994 (Norton and others 1995) gave a much less positive message about the recent evolution of poverty. Urban communities considered that the initially beneficial effects of economic reform in the 1980s had not been sustained, and in rural communities vulnerability of livelihoods was widely identified as a key issue, with widespread concern expressed that this was increasing. In addition to this, macroeconomic performance deteriorated in 1993, and per capita growth rates were variable over the 1990s.

This study addresses the question of the evolution of living standards over the specific period 1991/92 to 1998/99, using the results of the latest rounds of the Ghana Living Standards Survey. In this case the fourth round is based on a very similar questionnaire to the third round, so that any problems of comparability between these two surveys are much less severe. Results from the two surveys were used in an initial study prepared by the Ghana Statistical Service for the November 1999 Consultative Group meeting (GSS 2000a), as well as for an in-depth analysis of the robustness of observed changes in consumption poverty (Coulombe and McKay 2000), as well as many others. Building on these studies, this paper examines trends in different dimensions of poverty over this period more thoroughly. It characterizes changes in living conditions more fully than these earlier studies, and explores possible explanations and links to the macroeconomic environment over this period.

This paper begins with a review of the macroeconomic context over the 1990s, which serves as a background to the study. The second section presents the analysis of poverty and inequality as revealed by a consumption-based standard of living measure, including an assessment of the apparent robustness of the observed trends. The third section then considers the evolution of other, non-monetary dimensions of living standards based again on available data from the household surveys. The fourth section then makes an assessment of possible factors accounting for observed changes in poverty, focusing on income sources and labor markets, while the final section summarizes conclusions and identifies issues for follow up work.

## Macroeconomic Context

Over the 1990s Ghana's macroeconomic performance was less consistent than that it attained in the first years following the initial launch of the Economic Recovery Program in 1983. This is particularly evident in terms of the variability of GDP growth and inflation. Though external factors played a part in this, the relatively poor performance has been widely attributed to weak fiscal policy and consequent high deficits, and the political factors underlying this (World Bank 1998, 1999; Lawson and Salpietro 2000).

Official figures covering the 1990s indicate that real GDP increased each year (Table 2.1), with the growth rate varying between 3.3 to 5.3 percent per annum. However, taking account of population growth, this translates in an average per capita growth rate of 1.6 percent. A second key characteristic of this period is the high and variable inflation Ghana experienced. According to the consumer price index, inflation was never less than 10 percent over this period, averaging around 35 percent over 1993–97, and reaching a peak of around 60 percent in 1995 (Table 2.1).

There is no question that the 1990s were characterized by high and volatile inflation, and by real GDP growth that was both unstable and relatively low. From the point of view of living standards the evolution of private consumption expenditure is more relevant in the short term. Official figures suggest that real private consumption increased each year except one over this period, sometimes by quite large proportions (21.5 percent in 1997). However, the average magnitude (4.8 percent per annum) is similar to that of real GDP (translating into a similarly modest increase in per capita consumption).

Lawson and Salpietro (2000) report that the fiscal balance (fiscal deficits after taking account of grants) consistently exceeded 5 percent of GDP over the period 1992–99, reaching over 10 percent in 1997. Indeed these consistently high fiscal deficits seem to be the main explanation for the poor macroeconomic performance over the 1990s. Revenue mobilization was weak or stagnant over much of the 1990s, while high levels of public spending were maintained. Fiscal slippages were particularly evident in 1992 and 1996, both of which were election years (the 1990s also saw significant political liberalization in Ghana). In 1992 there was a sharp increase in the fiscal deficit associated with large salary increases in the public sector (not accompanied by significant retrenchment as had been intended) and a reduction in revenue collection efforts prior to the election (World Bank 1998); in 1996 it partly reflected unbudgeted expenditures.

Of particular interest for this paper are patterns of government spending, notably in the areas of health and education. In these sectors the position in terms of government spending deteriorated between 1992 and 1998 (Table 2.1), especially for health. The proportion of recurrent government expenditure devoted to education fell from 23.7 percent in 1992 to 18.2 percent in 1998; for health the corresponding proportion more than halved over the same period. Recurrent government spending increased only slightly as a proportion of GDP over this period, so government health and education spending also fell as a proportion of GDP. Public spending on agriculture, another key area for many of the poor, also fell sharply over this period.

The level of spending in these areas obviously does not measure the extent and quality of delivery of health and education services to households, but is strongly suggestive of likely trends in these areas. The reduced spending on health has occurred over a period where user charges have increasingly being introduced; according to Lawson and Salpietro (2000) these user charges have been very regressive in their impact, partly because systems for exemptions have not worked. Questions also need to be asked about the extent to which services provided in both education and health reach poorer groups, with an earlier study on this (Demery and others 1995) raising questions about how well targeted to the poor this spending was in the early 1990s.

Even if Ghana did achieve growth in per capita GDP on average over the 1990s decade, the extent to which this translates into reductions in poverty will depend on the distribu-

**Table 2.1. Key Macroeconomic and Public Spending Summary Statistics for Ghana, 1991–99**

| | Year | | | | | | | | |
|---|---|---|---|---|---|---|---|---|---|
| | 1991 | 1992 | 1993 | 1994 | 1995 | 1996 | 1997 | 1998 | 1999 |
| **Levels of variables** | | | | | | | | | |
| Nominal GDP (billions of cedis) | 2,428 | 2,803 | 3,872 | 5,205 | 7,752 | 11,339 | 14,113 | 17,296 | 20,042 |
| real GDP: constant 1993 prices (billions of cedis) | | | 3872 | 3999 | 4160 | 4351 | 4534 | 4747 | |
| real GDP: constant 1975 prices (millions of cedis) | 7215 | 7495 | 7867 | | | | | | |
| exchange rate cedis/$ (period average) | 368 | 437 | 649 | 957 | 1200 | 1637 | 1845 | 2321 | 2646 |
| dollar value of nominal GDP (billions) | 6.996 | 6.399 | 5.966 | 5.440 | 6.458 | 6.926 | 7.651 | 7.451 | 7.573 |
| private consumption: nominal (billions of cedis) | 2369 | 2738 | 3078 | 3843 | 5917 | 8443 | 11869 | 13386 | |
| private cons: const. 1993 prices (billions of cedis) | | | 3017 | 2785 | 3010 | 3057 | 3713 | 3904 | |
| private cons: const. 1975 prices (millions of cedis) | 5711 | 5995 | 6224 | | | | | | |
| **Percentage changes:** | | | | | | | | | |
| nominal GDP | 26.4 | 15.4 | 38.1 | 34.4 | 48.9 | 46.3 | 24.5 | 22.6 | 15.9 |
| GDP deflator | 20.0 | 11.1 | 24.9 | 30.1 | 43.2 | 39.8 | 19.5 | 17.1 | |

| | | | | | | | | |
|---|---|---|---|---|---|---|---|---|
| real GDP | 5.3 | 3.9 | 5.0 | 3.3 | 4.0 | 4.6 | 4.2 | 4.7 |
| real GDP per capita | 2.7 | 1.0 | 1.9 | 0.6 | 1.3 | 1.8 | 1.5 | 1.9 |
| nominal consumption | | 15.6 | 12.4 | 24.9 | 54.0 | 42.7 | 40.6 | 12.8 |
| real consumption | 3.6 | 5.0 | 3.8 | -7.7 | 8.1 | 1.6 | 21.5 | 5.1 |
| consumer price index | 18.0 | 10.1 | 25.0 | 24.9 | 59.5 | 46.6 | 27.9 | 19.3 |
| **% of recurrent government expenditure devoted to:** | | | | | | | | |
| Education | 23.2 | 23.7 | 22.0 | 18.0 | 20.1 | 19.9 | 18.0 | 18.2 |
| Health | 8.4 | 7.9 | 7.0 | 5.1 | 5.7 | 5.5 | 4.6 | 3.9 |
| Social security and welfare | 7.0 | 6.9 | 7.1 | 9.7 | 10.8 | 11.9 | 7.2 | 7.5 |
| **Government expenditures as a percentage of GDP:** | | | | | | | | |
| Education | 3.2 | 4.2 | 4.6 | 4.0 | 3.3 | 3.5 | 3.7 | 3.5 |
| Health | 1.2 | 1.4 | 1.5 | 1.2 | 1.0 | 1.0 | 1.0 | 0.8 |
| Social security and welfare | 1.0 | 1.2 | 1.6 | 2.3 | 1.9 | 2.1 | 1.5 | 1.4 |
| Total recurrent expenditure | 14.0 | 17.8 | 22.1 | 23.2 | 16.5 | 17.7 | 20.6 | 19.4 |

*Source: Dollar Source:* Dollar value of nominal GDP from Lawson and Salpietro (2000); all other data from IMF Ghana Statistical Annex, 1998 and 2000.

tional pattern of this growth. One important factor is often the movements in the real exchange rate. In this case though the real exchange rate appears not to have changed significantly over the period, suggesting no strong differences between those working in traded and non-traded activities. Looking at sectoral growth data within traded and non-traded activities suggests that in each case some subsectors have benefited and others not, and this sectoral pattern of growth is likely to be an important factor influencing changes in living conditions.

Because poverty tends to be more prevalent in some sectors than others, the sectoral patterns of growth is clearly of greater importance in the distributional effect of economic growth. However a close look at the quality of macroeconomic sectoral data in Ghana reveals many doubts on their accuracy such that they need to be analyzed with some precaution. Nevertheless the sectoral pattern of growth suggests that one important group that may not have experienced much improvement in their living conditions are food crop farmers, the activity undertaken by the majority of the poor. The aggregate figures suggest that those farming cocoa and engaged in other export oriented activities (mining, timber), as well as those engaged in commerce, are likely to have experienced improvements in their living conditions, because these subsectors have known fast growth over the period. If this is borne out by the micro data (the sectoral aggregates of course do not provide information about distributional patterns within these groups) then this is also likely to suggest important geographic dimensions to changes in living conditions, with potentially little benefit in the north.

Reduced government spending on health strongly suggests likely adverse effects in terms of the use of, or quality of, health facilities, so it will be important to see to what extent individual consultation behaviour has changed over this period. The increased need to spend on healthcare over this period following the introduction of user charges is likely to be an important impoverishing factor over this period for households experiencing frequent ill health.

The remainder of this paper uses micro data to examine changes in living standards between two points in time towards the beginning and end of this decade, including an analysis of whether these patterns correspond to those suggested by the macroeconomic picture over this period.

## Evolution of Consumption-based Measures of Living Standards over the 1990s

As noted above, the main data source for the analysis of poverty and inequality in this paper is the latest two rounds of the Ghana Living Standards Survey (GLSS), a nationally representative household survey which collected information on a wide variety of different household characteristics. The latest two rounds were conducted in 1991/92 and 1998/99, using essentially the same questionnaire.[3] Comparing the results between these two sur-

---

3. The latest two rounds of the GLSS have respectively samples of 4523 and 5998 households which allow statistically valid inference at the seven locality level. A recent poverty map (Coulombe, 2006) combining GLSS4 and Census 2000 data permits to have GLSS4 consistent poverty figures at the level of the 110 districts.

veys enables an assessment of changes in household well being over the 1990s, covering several different dimensions of living standards. This part of the paper focuses on changes in consumption-based standard of living measures, to be complemented in the following part by an examination of trends in other dimensions.

This section of the paper begins by explaining the construction of the standard of living measure, and by summarizing its key characteristics. This leads into the discussions of poverty and of inequality.

## The Consumption-based Standard of Living Measure

As in many other studies, for reasons that are both conceptual and practical, the analysis of the monetary dimension of living standards is considered here using a consumption-based measure. In this approach the standard of living is measured at the household level, based on its level of consumption (a proxy for permanent income), taking account of differences between households in their size and composition and in the prices they face. This will form the basis for the analysis of poverty and inequality later in the following sections. This section briefly explains the construction of the standard of living measure, and summarizes the main characteristics of this measure for Ghana in the periods covered by the two surveys.

For each individual the standard of living is measured as the total consumption expenditure, per adult equivalent,[4] of the household to which they belong, expressed in the constant prices of Accra in January 1999. Total consumption expenditure includes market purchased items and imputations for items consumed from other sources, including own production, payment received in kind, owner occupied dwellings and consumer durable goods owned by the household. GSS (2000a) provides further details on the construction of this measure.

The basic summary statistical properties of the resulting standard of living measure are summarized in Table 2.2, which reports means values by locality (identifying seven main localities) along with robust standard errors. The results show a 18.4 percent increase in the average value of the standard of living measure between 1991/92 and 1998/99. National accounts data (Table 2.1) imply an increase in real consumption per capita of 16.6 percent between 1992 and 1999, so that the estimates are order of magnitude consistent, especially so bearing in mind differences in definitions of concepts, sampling errors affecting the survey data and differences in the precise time periods covered.

According to GLSS data the average value of real household consumption per adult equivalent increases in all localities (except in urban savannah for which the difference is not statistically significant), though the magnitude of the estimates varies. Also the coefficients of variation (not presented here; see Coulombe and McKay, 2003) are large showing a wide distribution about the means.

This provides some preliminary information by way of background to the study of poverty and inequality. The general tendency for the mean standard measure to increase may suggest the likelihood that poverty is likely to have fallen over this period—but in cases

---

4. The use of alternative adult equivalence scales (including per capita), which also try to take account of differences in non-food requirements and which do not make distinction by gender do not change the results presented here significantly (Coulombe and McKay 2000).

Table 2.2. Summary Statistics of the Consumption-based Standard of Living Measure,
by Geographic Locality

| | 1991/92 | 1998/99 | Change (in percentage) |
|---|---|---|---|
| Accra | 2358 (166) | 2793 (107) | 18.4 |
| Urban Coastal | 1813 (96) | 2127 (221) | 17.3 |
| Urban Forest | 1949 (82) | 2618 (249) | 34.3 |
| Urban Savannah | 1722 (99) | 1459 (174) | −15.3 |
| Rural Coastal | 1325 (61) | 1633 (114) | 23.2 |
| Rural Forest | 1197 (49) | 1568 (96) | 31.0 |
| Rural Savannah | 894 (41) | 968 (87) | 8.3 |
| Ghana | 1441 (39) | 1783 (74) | 23.7 |

*Note:* Mean values are expressed in thousands of cedis per year. The robust standard errors are in parentheses.
*Source:* Authors' calculation from the Ghana Living Standards Survey, 1991/92 and 1998/99.

where inequality has increased this will offset the poverty reduction effect of the increased mean value. A specific analysis of poverty is required.

### The Evolution of Consumption Poverty, 1992–98

This section focuses on those whose consumption based standard of living measure (as defined above) falls below a minimum threshold (or poverty line). The poverty line represents that level of the standard of living measure below which it is judged insufficient to satisfy minimum subsistence needs. The first issue is to determine the level of this line. Past studies of poverty in Ghana have set poverty lines as fractions of the mean value in the first round of GLSS (GSS 1995; World Bank 1995; Coulombe and McKay 1995; Appiah and others 2000). Although set at reasonable levels, these poverty lines were not explicitly established based on a concept of minimum consumption requirements. For this study though, as with other studies comparing the latest two GLSS rounds (GSS 2000a), it was regarded as important to establish a Ghana-specific poverty line explicitly based on a minimum consumption concept.

Although the establishment of a poverty line may be guided by minimum consumption requirements, establishing such a line is not a precise scientific exercise. The principles underlying this were discussed at a workshop with policymakers and researchers in Accra in September 1999. The poverty line was set predominantly based on minimum calorie requirements which, based on the same scale used to construct the standard of living measure, are set at 2900 kilocalories per adult equivalent.[5] The basket of food commodities satisfying this minimum is identified based on the average consumption pattern of the bottom 40 percent of the distribution ranked according to the standard of living measure. Valuing the resulting basket at the reference prices gives the food poverty line, as the level of food expenditure that on average will satisfy minimum calorie requirements.

---

5. This may seem high, but it is important to remember that a majority of the poor in Ghana are engaged in physically demanding economic activities, so implying greater energy requirements. Furthermore, that per adult equivalent calorie figure translates into 2250 calories per capita, a level in line with most other poverty studies.

The overall poverty line must also include an allowance for essential non-food requirements, which is more difficult—and subjective—to estimate. Here the overall poverty line is set using the cost of basic needs method suggested by Ravallion and Bidani (1994). Non-food requirements are estimated as the average level of expenditure devoted to non-food consumption by those whose standard of living measure corresponds to the food poverty line, estimated based on a regression relationship. These are items of non-food expenditure that the household judges sufficiently important that it sacrifices meeting its calorie requirements (or consumes a less preferred diet); such expenditure can reasonably be considered as essential. Applying these methods gives a poverty line of, in round figures, 900,000 cedis per adult equivalent per year, again in the constant prices of Accra in January 1999. GSS (2000a) provides more detail on the estimation of the poverty line.[6]

Based on this standard of living measure and poverty line, nationally poverty according to each of the widely used $P_\alpha$ class of poverty indices has fallen between 1991/92 and 1998/99 (Table 2.3). The proportion of individuals in poverty ($P_0$) fell from 51.7 percent to 39.5 percent, a statistically significant change at the 1 percent level. $P_1$ and $P_2$ indices also fell markedly at the national level. However, the average depth of those in poverty ($P_1/P_0$) hardly changed. The national pattern though masks a sharp disparity of performance by geographic region (Table 2.3); poverty reduction was concentrated in Accra and the rural forest, where it fell markedly, while it fell much more modestly or even rose elsewhere. Small increases in poverty are particularly notable in the savannah where the incidence of poverty ($P_0$) rose in urban areas and both $P_1$ and $P_2$ rose in rural areas. The northern savannah, by far the poorest of the ecological zones anyway, has clearly been left behind in the national reduction in poverty. Moreover, the depth of poverty, as well as the incidence of extreme poverty (defined as those with a standard of living below the food poverty line), both rose in the rural savannah. Those relatively few that escaped poverty in the rural savannah appear to have been those that were closer to the poverty line (though this hypothesis cannot be formally verified in the absence of panel data). Finally, the results also suggest the presence of persistent poverty in coastal areas. Although poverty levels here are much lower than in the savannah, coastal areas have experienced only relatively modest reductions in poverty, with a small increase in the $P_1$ and $P_2$ measures in urban areas and the $P_2$ measure in rural areas.[7] Again, this suggests that the poorest may not have escaped poverty.[8]

---

6. The level of the food poverty line can also be used to set an extreme poverty line, as that level of the overall standard of living measure only just adequate to meet food requirements (if nothing was spent on non-food items). In round figures this gives an extreme poverty line of 700,000 cedis per adult equivalent per year. This line was used frequently in the analysis presented by GSS (2000a); the pattern of poverty it gives is broadly similar to that given by the higher line, but with a clearer identification of the most deprived groups.

7. Using lower poverty lines (for example, set at level of the food poverty line, 700,000 cedis per equivalent adult per year) shows even more clearly the disparate experiences of different regions, showing in particular increases in extreme poverty in the rural savannah.

8. A thorough analysis has also been conducted of the impact of using an alternative estimate of inflation in comparing GLSS3 and GLSS4 data, and of making choices from a range of justifiable alternatives about precisely how the consumption standard of living measure is estimated (Coulombe and McKay 2000). Though such factors may affect the precise magnitude of poverty change, the overall direction pattern of poverty change seems to be remarkably robust. No matter what choices are made, the results suggest a reduction in consumption poverty at the national level, with large reductions in Accra and the rural forest. In the remaining localities levels of consumption poverty continue to change only modestly. Similarly, no real seasonality effect has been found.

**Table 2.3.  Indices of Poverty by Location, 1991/92 and 1998/99**
(Poverty Line = 900,000 cedis)

**1991/92**

| | Sample Share | Average Welfare | Poverty indices | | | | Contribution to national poverty | | |
|---|---|---|---|---|---|---|---|---|---|
| | | | $P_0$ | $P_1$ | $P_2$ | $P_1/P_0$ | $C_0$ | $C_1$ | $C_2$ |
| Accra | 8.2 | 1844.8 | 0.231 | 0.051 | 0.017 | 0.219 | 3.7 | 2.2 | 1.6 |
| Urban Coastal | 8.7 | 1433.6 | 0.283 | 0.070 | 0.024 | 0.246 | 4.7 | 3.3 | 2.3 |
| Urban Forest | 11.0 | 1618.9 | 0.258 | 0.064 | 0.022 | 0.249 | 5.5 | 3.8 | 2.8 |
| Urban Savannah | 5.3 | 1321.2 | 0.378 | 0.136 | 0.069 | 0.359 | 3.9 | 3.9 | 4.2 |
| Rural Coastal | 14.2 | 1085.5 | 0.525 | 0.161 | 0.067 | 0.306 | 14.4 | 12.3 | 10.8 |
| Rural Forest | 29.6 | 938.0 | 0.616 | 0.227 | 0.106 | 0.369 | 35.3 | 36.4 | 35.8 |
| Rural Savannah | 23.1 | 762.9 | 0.730 | 0.305 | 0.161 | 0.418 | 32.6 | 38.1 | 42.5 |
| All | 100.0 | 1130.8 | 0.517 | 0.185 | 0.088 | 0.357 | 100.0 | 100.0 | 100.0 |

**1998/99**

| | Sample Share | Average Welfare | Poverty indices | | | | Contribution to national poverty | | |
|---|---|---|---|---|---|---|---|---|---|
| | | | $P_0$ | $P_1$ | $P_2$ | $P_1/P_0$ | $C_0$ | $C_1$ | $C_2$ |
| Accra | 8.8 | 2468.5 | 0.038 | 0.008 | 0.002 | 0.208 | 0.8 | 0.5 | 0.3 |
| Urban Coastal | 7.8 | 1769.9 | 0.242 | 0.070 | 0.028 | 0.288 | 4.8 | 3.9 | 3.4 |
| Urban Forest | 11.8 | 2005.0 | 0.182 | 0.051 | 0.020 | 0.281 | 5.4 | 4.3 | 3.6 |
| Urban Savannah | 4.8 | 1191.6 | 0.430 | 0.114 | 0.042 | 0.265 | 5.2 | 4.0 | 3.1 |
| Rural Coastal | 14.6 | 1248.3 | 0.452 | 0.141 | 0.061 | 0.312 | 16.7 | 14.8 | 13.3 |
| Rural Forest | 31.6 | 1297.9 | 0.380 | 0.107 | 0.044 | 0.283 | 30.4 | 24.4 | 20.8 |
| Rural Savannah | 20.6 | 826.8 | 0.700 | 0.323 | 0.178 | 0.462 | 36.6 | 48.0 | 55.5 |
| All | 100.0 | 1412.1 | 0.395 | 0.139 | 0.066 | 0.352 | 100.0 | 100.0 | 100.0 |

*Notes:* sample share is expressed in percent, and 'average welfare' denotes the mean value of the standard of living measure, expressed in thousands of cedis. $P_0$, $P_1$, $P_2$ denote values of the $P_\alpha$ poverty indices for $\alpha = 0$, 1, 2 respectively; $C_0$, $C_1$, $C_2$ are the percentage contributions of each group to national poverty as defined by $P_0$, $P_1$, $P_2$ respectively; and $P_1/P_0$ is the income gap ratio for the poverty line: the average proportion by which the poor fall below the poverty line.
*Source:* Authors' calculation from the Ghana Living Standards Survey, 1991/92 and 1998/99.

Poverty reduction is clearly related to households' ability to increase their living standards, raising the issue of which types of economic activity have enabled households to escape poverty. A starting point in answering this is to consider the pattern of poverty by the main economic activity of the household (Table 2.4), defined as the economic activity of the main "earner" of the household (note, not necessarily the person identified as the household head). Of course many households are engaged in more than one activity, and this will be considered in further analysis later.[9]

---

9. An alternative criterion would be to take the income source from which the household earns the most, but in practice this definition gives almost exactly the same results as the criterion adopted here.

**Table 2.4.  Trends in Incidence of Poverty by Main Economic Activity, 1991/92 and 1998/99**

| Main economic activity | 1991/92 | | | 1998/99 | | |
|---|---|---|---|---|---|---|
| | Population share | $P_0$ | $C_0$ | Population share | $P_0$ | $C_0$ |
| Public sector empl. | 13.5 | 0.347 | 9.1 | 10.7 | 0.227 | 6.2 |
| Private formal empl. | 3.9 | 0.303 | 2.3 | 4.9 | 0.113 | 1.4 |
| Private informal empl. | 3.1 | 0.386 | 2.3 | 2.9 | 0.252 | 1.9 |
| Export farmers | 6.3 | 0.640 | 7.8 | 7.0 | 0.387 | 6.9 |
| Food crop farmers | 43.6 | 0.681 | 57.3 | 38.6 | 0.594 | 58.1 |
| Non-farm self empl. | 27.6 | 0.384 | 20.5 | 33.8 | 0.286 | 24.5 |
| Non-working | 2.0 | 0.188 | 0.7 | 2.1 | 0.204 | 1.1 |
| All | 100.0 | 0.517 | 100.0 | 100.0 | 0.395 | 100.0 |

*Note:* Notation as defined in Table 2.3.
*Source:* Authors' calculation from the Ghana Living Standards Survey, 1991/92 and 1998/99.

As would be anticipated based on the geographic trends and also from the above discussion of the sectoral patterns of growth, poverty reductions have been particularly large for households engaged primarily in export farming (mainly cocoa producers). There have also been large falls in poverty among wage earners in the formal private sector and the public sector (though there are significantly fewer of the latter in 1998/99 than in 1991/92, presumably reflecting public sector retrenchment, which is likely to have affected lower levels more). Reductions in the incidence of poverty over the period have been more modest for other groups, particularly for food farmers (by far the biggest group), but also for the non-farm self employed and informal sector wage employees. That these groups have experienced lower poverty reductions than others is particularly evident when placing increasing emphasis on the depth of poverty or on the poorest among the poor. Finally, poverty appears to have increased among non-working households, although this is a group for which the sample size is small.

It is valuable also to consider the distribution of poverty according to the industry in which the economic head is worked, using the same sectoral classification as used in the national accounts. Such an analysis (Table 2.5) shows that of the three broadly-defined sectors, poverty is lowest among those working in services, followed by the industrial sector, and so highest in the agricultural sector. Poverty reduction over this period was greatest in the industrial sector, though the incidence of poverty also fell substantially among those working in the agriculture and services sectors.

To the extent that sample size permits, it is important to look at a more detailed sectoral level. This shows important differences between subsectors within each of agriculture, industry and services. A further general phenomenon is that it was in those sectors where the incidence of poverty fell the most that increases in the proportion of households engaged in these activities increased. Examples include mining and quarrying; transport, storage and communication; fishing; and wholesale and retail trade. This relates strongly to the sectoral pattern of growth discussed above. Two other sectors making quite large contributions to the reduction in the incidence of poverty were agriculture and livestock

**Table 2.5. Trends in Incidence of Poverty by Industry of Main Occupation of Household, 1991/92 and 1998/99**

| Industry | 1991/92 | | | 1998/99 | | |
|---|---|---|---|---|---|---|
| | Population share | $P_0$ | $C_0$ | Population share | $P_0$ | $C_0$ |
| Agriculture and livestock | 51.6 | 0.668 | 66.6 | 46.9 | 0.558 | 66.3 |
| Forestry and logging | 0.8 | 0.200 | 0.3 | 0.2 | 0.344 | 0.2 |
| Fishing | 0.9 | 0.486 | 0.8 | 2.2 | 0.336 | 1.8 |
| *Agriculture* | 53.3 | 0.658 | 67.8 | 49.3 | 0.547 | 68.3 |
| Mining and quarrying | 0.8 | 0.292 | 0.5 | 1.2 | 0.071 | 0.2 |
| Manufacturing | 8.7 | 0.426 | 7.2 | 10.5 | 0.288 | 7.6 |
| Electricity, water & gas | 0.2 | 0.130 | 0.1 | 0.3 | 0.237 | 0.2 |
| Construction | 1.6 | 0.450 | 1.4 | 1.9 | 0.318 | 1.6 |
| **Industrial** | 11.4 | 0.414 | 9.1 | 13.9 | 0.272 | 9.6 |
| Wholesale and retail trade | 17.0 | 0.352 | 11.6 | 18.6 | 0.267 | 12.6 |
| Transport, storage & comms | 2.8 | 0.326 | 1.8 | 3.4 | 0.108 | 0.9 |
| Finance, real estate and business services | 0.7 | 0.166 | 0.2 | 1.0 | 0.147 | 0.4 |
| Public admin, defence and other services | 12.8 | 0.348 | 8.6 | 11.9 | 0.236 | 7.1 |
| **Services** | 33.3 | 0.344 | 22.2 | 34.8 | 0.238 | 21.0 |
| **Non-working** | 2.0 | 0.242 | 0.9 | 2.0 | 0.210 | 1.1 |
| All | 100.0 | 0.517 | 100.0 | 100.0 | 0.395 | 100.0 |

*Note:* Notation as defined in Table 2.3.
*Source:* Authors' calculation from the Ghana Living Standards Survey, 1991/92 and 1998/99.

and public administration, but these were both sectors in which smaller proportions of households were engaged by 1998/99.

Much of this is broadly consistent with the aggregate sectoral patterns shown by the national accounts. Combined with the previous evidence about migration being a contributory factor to poverty reduction, this table provides evidence that some households are changing both location and economic activity, moving into developing sectors and expanding sectors. Beaudry and Sowa (1994) identified a similar phenomenon based on 1987/88 data in terms of responses of labor to changing sectoral wages. It seems likely that those that are immobile or otherwise unable to respond to changing opportunities may be disproportionately represented among those that remained poor.

## The Evolution of Inequality

In contrast to poverty, inequality is concerned with the whole distribution. While many different summary inequality measures are available, the analysis here will focus on the class of entropy indices of inequality, which have the advantage of being decomposable by subgroups. As before, attention focuses on changes in inequality between 1991/92 and 1998/99, in aggregate and for different groups.

The generalised entropy class of inequality indices, $E(\phi)$, takes the general form:

$$E(\phi) = \frac{1}{\phi(\phi-1)} \sum_{i=1}^{n} \left[ \left( \frac{y_i}{\mu} \right)^{\phi} - 1 \right], \forall \phi \neq 0,1$$

where: $n$ is the population size, $\mu$ the mean value of $y_i$ (the standard of living measure), and $\phi$ is a parameter. When $\phi = 0$ or 1 the index takes the following forms:

$$E(0) = \frac{1}{n} \sum_{i=1}^{n} \ln \left( \frac{\mu}{y_i} \right)$$

$$E(1) = \frac{1}{n} \sum_{i=1}^{n} \frac{y_i}{\mu} \ln \left( \frac{y_i}{\mu} \right)$$

The value $\phi = 0$ therefore gives the mean log deviation of the distribution (sometimes referred to as the Theil L index), and $\phi = 1$ gives the Theil T index, a commonly used measure of inequality related to the physical concept of entropy (Theil 1967). When $\phi = 2$ the index is one half of the squared coefficient of variation of the distribution. $\phi$ is a parameter the magnitude of which reflects a value judgment, as it indicates the relative weight given to inequality in different parts of the distribution. When $\phi = 0$ the index places more weight on inequality in the lower tail, when $\phi = 2$ or above it gives disproportionate weight to inequality in the upper tail of the distribution, while when $\phi = 1$ it gives equal weight throughout the distribution (Cowell, 1995; Litchfield, 1999). As noted above, in addition to other desirable properties (Cowell, 1995), these indices are decomposable to distinguish intra-group and between group components of inequality.

Inequality as measured by E(0) increased between 1991/92 and 1998/99 (Table 2.6), though for higher values of $\phi$ inequality increased much less ($\phi = 1$) or fell modestly ($\phi = 2$). This difference according to the value of $\phi$ suggests that inequality is increasing at the lower end of the distribution and may be falling slightly in the upper tail. By locality, for all values of $\phi$ inequality fell sharply in Accra and urban savannah (though it should be remembered that the sample sizes here are quite small, especially in the latter case), and for $\phi = 1, 2$ it falls sharply in the rural forest.[10] By contrast, inequality increased substantially in coastal areas and the rural savannah for all values of $\phi$. This is of course reflected in changes in the contributions of these areas to overall inequality as revealed by the decomposition (last three columns). Within a given year, as $\phi$ increases the contribution of the wealthier (chiefly urban) localities to overall inequality increases, and that of poorer (chiefly rural) localities falls, which is to be expected given the definition of the indices. Thus for example, even though inequality in Accra as measured by E(2) has fallen sharply, in 1998/99 Accra still accounts for a substantial proportion of overall inequality according to this measure.

In all cases the contribution of the between group component of inequality is quite large; in 1991–92 between group variation accounts for around 19, 18, and 13 percent of

---

10. The fact that the inequality reductions in the rural forest were more modest when $\phi = 0$ suggests that inequality fell less at the lower tail.

**Table 2.6. Entropy Indices of Inequality for Ghana by Locality, 1991/92 and 1998/99**

**1991/92**

| Locality | Population share | Entropy indices | | | Contribution to overall inequality | | |
|---|---|---|---|---|---|---|---|
| | | $\phi = 0$ | $\phi = 1$ | $\phi = 2$ | $\alpha = 0$ | $\alpha = 1$ | $\alpha = 2$ |
| Accra | 8.2 | 0.215 | 0.234 | 0.326 | 7.6 | 12.6 | 19.9 |
| Urban Coastal | 8.7 | 0.152 | 0.163 | 0.207 | 5.7 | 7.2 | 8.0 |
| Urban Forest | 11.0 | 0.190 | 0.203 | 0.266 | 9.0 | 12.8 | 16.7 |
| Urban Savannah | 5.3 | 0.229 | 0.228 | 0.305 | 5.3 | 5.7 | 6.2 |
| Rural Coastal | 14.2 | 0.170 | 0.184 | 0.242 | 10.4 | 10.0 | 8.8 |
| Rural Forest | 29.6 | 0.191 | 0.220 | 0.348 | 24.5 | 21.7 | 19.8 |
| Rural Savannah | 23.1 | 0.186 | 0.192 | 0.250 | 18.6 | 12.0 | 7.4 |
| (contribution of between group inequality) | | | | | 18.9 | 18.0 | 13.1 |
| Ghana | 100.0 | 0.231 | 0.249 | 0.358 | 100.0 | 100.0 | 100.0 |

**1998/99**

| Locality | Population share | Entropy indices | | | Contribution to overall inequality | | |
|---|---|---|---|---|---|---|---|
| | | $\phi = 0$ | $\phi = 1$ | $\phi = 2$ | $\alpha = 0$ | $\alpha = 1$ | $\alpha = 2$ |
| Accra | 8.8 | 0.133 | 0.144 | 0.211 | 4.6 | 8.6 | 16.0 |
| Urban Coastal | 7.8 | 0.224 | 0.231 | 0.301 | 6.9 | 8.8 | 10.4 |
| Urban Forest | 11.8 | 0.208 | 0.202 | 0.239 | 9.6 | 13.0 | 16.0 |
| Urban Savannah | 4.8 | 0.142 | 0.148 | 0.177 | 2.7 | 2.3 | 1.7 |
| Rural Coastal | 14.6 | 0.211 | 0.237 | 0.404 | 12.0 | 11.8 | 12.9 |
| Rural Forest | 31.6 | 0.178 | 0.187 | 0.240 | 22.0 | 20.9 | 18.0 |
| Rural Savannah | 20.6 | 0.256 | 0.284 | 0.429 | 20.7 | 13.2 | 8.5 |
| (contribution of between group inequality) | | | | | 21.5 | 21.3 | 16.3 |
| Ghana | 100.0 | 0.255 | 0.259 | 0.355 | 100.0 | 100.0 | 100.0 |

*Source:* Authors' calculation from the Ghana Living Standards Survey, 1991/92 and 1998/99.

overall inequality according to $E(0)$, $E(1)$ and $E(2)$ respectively. In other words, this is the proportion of overall inequality due to differences in average living standards between localities. These proportions are quite high for this type of decomposition (partly perhaps because inequality within localities is not very high). The proportions accounted for by between group variation increased by 1998–99, by then accounting for around 21 percent of inequality according to $E(0)$ and $E(1)$. This is presumably partly due to the fact that average living standards have increased a lot in Accra, the richest locality, while those for the poorest groups in the rural savannah have not improved or worsened. Reductions in inequality within some localities account for inequality not increasing more.

The changes in poverty for different groups are directly related to changes in inequality among these groups and in their average standard of living. An informative decomposition of changes in poverty identifies the relative importance of growth and redistribution effects in observed changes in poverty (Datt and Ravallion 1992). Taking 1991/92 as the reference period, applying this decomposition for $\alpha = 0, 1, 2$ (Tables 2.7 and 2.8) shows that the reduction of the incidence of poverty at the national level exclusively reflects the effect of the growth on average living standards. The impact of the redistribution effect on the incidence of poverty $P_0$ is largely negligible, while it increases poverty for $\alpha = 1, 2$. Again this strongly suggests that the poorest among the poor have benefited less from the reduction in poverty. They experienced lower increases in their mean living standards.

**Table 2.7. Changes in Poverty 1991/92–1998/99, Decomposed into Growth and Redistribution Effects, by Geographic Locality**

|  | Total change | Growth effect | Redistribution effect | Residual |
|---|---|---|---|---|
| $P_0$: *Poverty Incidence Index* |  |  |  |  |
| Accra | −19.6 | −11.6 | −11.5 | 3.5 |
| Urban Coastal | −2.8 | −12.4 | 8.8 | 0.8 |
| Urban Forest | −9.0 | −11.2 | −0.3 | 2.6 |
| Urban Savannah | 4.8 | 6.7 | −3.1 | 1.1 |
| Rural Coastal | −7.3 | −10.8 | 2.3 | 1.1 |
| Rural Forest | −25.1 | −22.3 | −2.4 | −0.5 |
| Rural Savannah | −1.9 | −4.5 | 1.4 | 1.3 |
| GHANA | −12.1 | −13.4 | −0.2 | 1.5 |
| $P_1$: *Poverty Gap Index* |  |  |  |  |
| Accra | −4.9 | −3.5 | −3.4 | 2.0 |
| Urban Coastal | 0.4 | −3.8 | 5.3 | −1.0 |
| Urban Forest | −1.1 | −3.8 | 2.4 | 0.4 |
| Urban Savannah | −2.0 | 2.8 | −5.0 | 0.3 |
| Rural Coastal | −1.8 | −4.9 | 3.1 | 0.0 |
| Rural Forest | −11.7 | −11.1 | −1.2 | 0.6 |
| Rural Savannah | 1.9 | −3.1 | 4.8 | 0.2 |
| GHANA | −4.5 | −6.5 | 1.7 | 0.3 |
| $P_2$: *Poverty Severity Index* |  |  |  |  |
| Accra | −1.5 | −1.2 | −1.2 | 0.9 |
| Urban Coastal | 0.5 | −1.5 | 3.0 | −1.0 |
| Urban Forest | 0.2 | −1.5 | 2.0 | −0.3 |
| Urban Savannah | −2.8 | 1.6 | −4.2 | 0.1 |
| Rural Coastal | −0.5 | −2.5 | 2.3 | −0.3 |
| Rural Forest | −6.2 | −6.1 | −0.5 | 0.4 |
| Rural Savannah | 1.7 | −2.1 | 3.9 | −0.2 |
| GHANA | −2.1 | −3.6 | 1.7 | −0.1 |

*Source:* Authors' calculation from the Ghana Living Standards Survey, 1991/92 and 1998/99.

**Table 2.8. Changes in Poverty 1991/92–1998/99, Decomposed into Growth and Redistribution Effects, by Main Economic Activity**

|  | Total change | Growth effect | Redistribution effect | Residual |
|---|---|---|---|---|
| $P_0$: *Poverty Incidence Index* | | | | |
| Public sector empl. | −13.5 | −9.9 | −3.7 | 0.1 |
| Private formal empl. | −17.6 | −16.9 | −2.5 | 1.8 |
| Private informal empl. | −9.7 | −10.0 | −0.3 | 0.6 |
| Export farmers | −28.4 | −25.7 | −0.7 | −2.1 |
| Food crop farmers | −8.1 | −9.1 | −0.2 | 1.2 |
| Non-farm self empl. | −9.8 | −12.2 | 0.7 | 1.7 |
| Non-working | −4.4 | −12.7 | 4.5 | 3.8 |
| GHANA | −12.1 | −13.4 | −0.2 | 1.5 |
| $P_1$: *Poverty Gap Index* | | | | |
| Public sector empl. | −5.3 | −3.9 | −1.8 | 0.4 |
| Private formal empl. | −5.4 | −5.5 | −0.4 | −0.6 |
| Private informal empl. | −2.8 | −4.0 | 1.0 | −0.2 |
| Export farmers | −14.2 | −12.5 | −1.7 | 0.0 |
| Food crop farmers | −2.7 | −5.5 | 2.5 | 0.3 |
| Non-farm self empl. | −2.6 | −4.8 | 2.1 | 0.1 |
| Non-working | 2.3 | −4.0 | 6.4 | 0.0 |
| GHANA | −4.5 | −6.5 | 1.7 | 0.3 |
| $P_2$: *Poverty Severity Index* | | | | |
| Public sector empl. | −2.5 | −1.9 | −0.9 | 0.3 |
| Private formal empl. | −2.1 | −2.2 | 0.0 | 0.1 |
| Private informal empl. | −1.0 | −1.9 | 0.9 | −0.1 |
| Export farmers | −7.9 | −7.0 | −1.3 | 0.4 |
| Food crop farmers | −1.0 | −3.4 | 2.5 | −0.1 |
| Non-farm self empl. | −0.9 | −2.3 | 1.7 | −0.3 |
| Non-working | 2.8 | −1.6 | 5.3 | −1.0 |
| GHANA | −2.1 | −3.6 | 1.7 | −0.1 |

*Source:* Authors' calculation from the Ghana Living Standards Survey, 1991/92 and 1998/99.

The pattern varies by locality (Table 2.7), and at this level redistribution effects become much more important. Growth effects still often predominate in looking at changes in $P_0$, while redistribution effects become relatively more important in many cases looking at $P_1$ or $P_2$. The large reductions in the incidence of poverty in Accra reflect favourable growth and redistribution effects, with the latter making a major contribution. While the reduction in inequality was already evident from the inequality indices presented above, this highlights its importance in contributing to the observed substantial poverty reduction. Nevertheless the magnitude of the reduction in inequality in Accra invites further investigation to provide additional confirmatory evidence and to understand the factors behind it. By contrast in the rural forest very small proportions of the observed reductions in poverty (for whatever value of $\alpha$) are due to the (more modest) reduction in inequality there. Here the poverty reduction almost exclusively reflects higher average living standards.

As seen above, inequality increased in most of the localities that experienced only very small reductions in poverty. In these localities the adverse redistribution effect offset, sometimes almost completely (for example, urban coastal), what in most cases was a favorable (though often modest) growth effect. However, the increase in poverty urban savannah reflected a large adverse growth effect, only very partly offset by the reduction in inequality (even if the latter was substantial).

The directions of the growth and redistribution effects remain the same in looking at higher values of $\alpha$ though their relative magnitudes often differ in many cases. Thus in urban coastal and rural savannah, poverty according to $P_1$ or $P_2$ increases; for these poverty indices the growth effect is now modest, and the adverse redistribution effect outweighs it. In urban savannah, where the incidence of poverty increased due to an adverse growth effect, the values of the $P_1$ and $P_2$ indices fall. In these instances the favourable redistribution effect more than outweighs the adverse growth effect. However, the relative importance of the growth and redistribution effects for Accra in the declines of the $P_1$ and $P_2$ indices are similar to those observed for the $P_0$ index.

Looking at the pattern by main economic activity (Table 2.8), average values of the living standards measures have increased in all groups, so that the growth effects have a downward influence on poverty in all instances. The redistribution effects vary by group and with $\alpha$. When $\alpha = 0$ the redistribution effect reduces poverty modestly in all groups except the non-farm self-employed and the non-working. For higher values of $\alpha$ though the redistribution effect more often contributes to increases in poverty; it only contributes to reductions in poverty as measured by $P_1$ and $P_2$ among the formal (public and private) sector wage employees and the export crop farmers. Given that the former are disproportionately in Accra and the latter disproportionately in the rural forest, this is as would be expected given the pattern by locality, and is of course consistent with the reduction in inequality in these groups.

## The Evolution of Non-Monetary Dimensions of Living Standards

The analysis of living standards presented above only relates to one dimension of living conditions; how did other dimensions of living standards evolve over this period? Do they too show similar variations across groups, say by geographic locality? The evolution of several non-monetary aspects of living standards can also be examined over the same period based on GLSS data, and the analysis here focuses particularly on health and education, access to adequate amenities (drinking water and lighting facilities), and household ownership of assets.

In this analysis the variation of these non-monetary indicators between individuals and households will be also considered across quintile groups of the consumption standard of living measure (referred to as "income groups" for conciseness), to see the degree of association between monetary deprivation and other dimensions of wellbeing.

### Access to Education and Health Facilities

Health and educational status are obviously key dimensions of living standards and have the advantage that they can be measured at the individual level (unlike the consumption-based measure above). Unfortunately though the GLSS surveys do not contain any really satisfactory comparable measures of either. Health status measures are self-reported (on incidence of illness or injury), while an error in the design of the GLSS3 questionnaire meant that literacy and numeracy status could not be measured without bias. In these circumstances it is really only meaningful to focus on the use by different household groups of health and education facilities. In practice though, variations in use of facilities are likely to be important influences of variations in outcomes, and are also likely to show more short-term changes. Moreover, given that most services are publicly provided, they are directly related to policy questions in these areas.

Concerning health a key issue to consider is the use of health facilities by individuals when they are ill or injured (Table 2.9). In interpreting the table, it is important to bear in mind that what being "ill or injured" means is defined by the respondent. This could lead differences between poorer and richer households to be underestimated if poorer

**Table 2.9. Trends in Consultation Practices by Those Who Were Ill or Injured in the Two Weeks Preceding the Survey, 1991/92 and 1998/99**

| | % not consulting anyone | | % that consulted a doctor or pharmacist | | % that consulted in a hospital | |
|---|---|---|---|---|---|---|
| | 1991/92 | 1998/99 | 1991/92 | 1998/99 | 1991/92 | 1998/99 |
| *All households, by locality:* | | | | | | |
| Accra | 44.9 | 35.2 | 50.5 | 58.4 | 22.2 | 16.1 |
| Urban Coastal | 41.7 | 51.0 | 48.9 | 32.9 | 30.2 | 28.0 |
| Urban Forest | 34.4 | 46.3 | 46.9 | 41.3 | 30.5 | 27.5 |
| Urban Savannah | 55.9 | 54.1 | 15.5 | 25.5 | 9.3 | 24.0 |
| Rural Coastal | 47.7 | 53.3 | 30.3 | 20.4 | 19.0 | 12.5 |
| Rural Forest | 52.3 | 62.3 | 24.2 | 16.7 | 18.2 | 12.1 |
| Rural Savannah | 63.4 | 61.4 | 11.2 | 8.2 | 9.8 | 7.3 |
| ALL GHANA | 50.7 | 56.2 | 28.2 | 22.4 | 18.6 | 15.0 |
| *Urban households, by standard of living quintile* | | | | | | |
| Lowest | 37.0 | 56.3 | 50.0 | 25.0 | 17.4 | 20.8 |
| Second | 53.9 | 58.3 | 28.1 | 20.5 | 21.1 | 18.0 |
| Third | 46.4 | 50.5 | 36.1 | 30.5 | 22.1 | 24.2 |
| Fourth | 50.6 | 46.6 | 36.1 | 39.3 | 21.4 | 24.7 |
| Highest | 33.9 | 40.1 | 50.7 | 51.8 | 28.6 | 28.2 |
| ALL URBAN | 42.5 | 46.6 | 42.3 | 39.9 | 24.5 | 25.0 |
| *Rural households, by standard of living quintile* | | | | | | |
| Lowest | 61.0 | 66.5 | 13.5 | 7.5 | 11.4 | 5.2 |
| Second | 58.0 | 61.7 | 18.7 | 12.4 | 14.3 | 8.9 |
| Third | 56.5 | 60.9 | 21.9 | 15.3 | 14.8 | 10.8 |
| Fourth | 50.4 | 59.8 | 26.4 | 16.8 | 19.3 | 12.3 |
| Highest | 44.5 | 48.8 | 29.8 | 27.2 | 20.8 | 19.8 |
| ALL RURAL | 54.7 | 60.2 | 21.6 | 15.1 | 15.8 | 10.9 |

*Source:* Authors' calculation from the Ghana Living Standards Survey, 1991/92 and 1998/99.

households are less likely than richer households in the same circumstances to self-report themselves as ill or injured. However, this ought not to affect comparisons over time, where there is a sharp decline between 1991–92 and 1998–99 in the use of health facilities by individuals when they are ill or injured. Over this period increasing numbers do not consult anyone at all, while fewer consult a doctor or pharmacist, and fewer of those consulting do so in a hospital. The increasing tendency not to consult anyone in the event of illness is apparent in most income groups in urban areas and all in rural areas. Geographically it is most evident in the coastal and forest zones. The reduced likelihood to consult a doctor or a pharmacist, as well as the reduced likelihood to consult in a hospital, are each particularly evident in rural areas, in all income groups. Thus, the difference between urban and rural areas in such consultations, which was already large in 1991–92, had further widened by 1998–99.

The changes in where consultations take place might partly reflect more appropriate behavior (for instance if there is now less consultation in hospitals that could more efficiently have been done in clinics), but this important issue clearly needs to be investigated further (it cannot be properly verified from the relatively limited health information available from the questionnaire). Whatever, the increasing tendency not to consult anyone in the event of illness or injury is a matter of serious concern. Clearly this aspect of living standards has worsened over this period, and this is likely to be a consequence of reduced government spending on health.

Educational attendance is considered here by examining net enrolment rates, which refer to either public or private schools. In so doing it is important to note that there are significant differences in estimated enrolment rates between GLSS, the CWIQ survey conducted in 1997, and the census. Whether this reflects differences in definition or reflects the accuracy with which the information is collected in some cases has not yet been determined, but it is still meaningful to use the GLSS data here to compare trends. At primary level (Table 2.10) net enrolment rates for girls and boys show an increase of around 10 and 8 percentage points respectively between 1991/92 and 1998/99. While that for girls increased slightly more, it was still three percentage points lower in 1998/99. For both girls and boys the increases were much bigger in rural than urban areas, and in the savannah zone than elsewhere, but these were the groups for which enrolment rates were initially lower. And despite this, net enrolment rates in the rural savannah in 1998/99 remain much lower than elsewhere. Quite large increases were also observed for girls in rural coastal, and in the Urban and rural forest zones. The data also suggest that net enrolment rates have increased slightly faster among the first three quintile groups than among the richest two (of course reflecting lower starting points). Also, among the first three quintiles increases are lower in the poorest quintile than in the second and third.

At secondary level (Table 2.10), net enrolment rates for girls have grown more than for boys, so that the differential in net enrolment rates is only 3.4 percentage points in 1998/99, compared to 7.2 in 1991/92. Net enrolment rates for boys have grown only modestly, and have fallen slightly in rural areas and in the urban coastal zone. Overall increases in enrolment are bigger in urban areas than rural areas, and within both enrolment rates are generally higher in richer quintiles compared to poorer ones. The level of net enrolment rates in secondary school is quite low at around 40 percent. And the differential between urban and rural areas increased over this period, although gender differentials fell in both urban and rural areas.

**Table 2.10.   Trends in Net School Enrolment, by Locality, Quintile, Level, and Sex, 1991/92 and 1998/99**

| | Primary level | | | | Secondary level | | | |
| | Girls | | Boys | | Girls | | Boys | |
| | 1991/92 | 1998/99 | 1991/92 | 1998/99 | 1991/92 | 1998/99 | 1991/92 | 1998/99 |
|---|---|---|---|---|---|---|---|---|
| *All households, by locality:* | | | | | | | | |
| Accra | 87.4 | 85.9 | 91.3 | 94.2 | 37.9 | 53.7 | 54.3 | 60.5 |
| Urban Coastal | 82.6 | 87.8 | 85.0 | 87.0 | 43.3 | 47.3 | 54.2 | 53.0 |
| Urban Forest | 82.5 | 88.9 | 90.1 | 94.9 | 39.3 | 43.8 | 47.2 | 49.5 |
| Urban Savannah | 66.7 | 90.1 | 81.1 | 94.9 | 36.0 | 44.4 | 28.1 | 47.8 |
| Rural Coastal | 70.3 | 84.6 | 80.1 | 83.5 | 29.6 | 35.0 | 42.6 | 40.6 |
| Rural Forest | 81.8 | 88.3 | 84.7 | 91.1 | 35.4 | 39.9 | 44.0 | 43.3 |
| Rural Savannah | 45.6 | 61.1 | 51.3 | 66.0 | 22.1 | 21.5 | 25.8 | 24.6 |
| ALL GHANA | 71.5 | 81.9 | 76.5 | 84.9 | 33.7 | 39.0 | 40.9 | 42.4 |
| *Urban households, by standard of living quintile* | | | | | | | | |
| Lowest | 60.5 | 89.1 | 78.9 | 85.1 | 25.0 | 32.6 | 39.6 | 40.7 |
| Second | 72.7 | 87.7 | 80.6 | 92.3 | 26.9 | 46.4 | 41.2 | 50.1 |
| Third | 77.9 | 84.2 | 85.3 | 93.8 | 43.1 | 41.9 | 47.5 | 39.4 |
| Fourth | 86.6 | 87.9 | 86.1 | 91.8 | 40.3 | 50.4 | 50.3 | 56.2 |
| Highest | 88.4 | 90.7 | 95.7 | 96.3 | 44.2 | 50.4 | 49.7 | 64.6 |
| ALL URBAN | 81.6 | 88.1 | 87.4 | 92.9 | 39.6 | 47.2 | 47.3 | 52.9 |
| *Rural households, by standard of living quintile* | | | | | | | | |
| Lowest | 57.9 | 66.9 | 63.6 | 71.3 | 27.4 | 20.7 | 33.8 | 26.3 |
| Second | 67.6 | 78.5 | 71.3 | 83.1 | 28.6 | 35.5 | 36.1 | 41.6 |
| Third | 66.9 | 87.6 | 75.3 | 87.0 | 30.4 | 41.1 | 42.8 | 45.1 |
| Fourth | 74.6 | 87.3 | 77.9 | 88.8 | 32.8 | 39.7 | 38.6 | 39.2 |
| Highest | 81.4 | 81.9 | 87.0 | 90.2 | 33.7 | 34.3 | 46.3 | 40.6 |
| ALL RURAL | 66.5 | 78.9 | 71.7 | 81.4 | 29.8 | 33.8 | 37.7 | 37.0 |

*Source:* Authors' calculation from the Ghana Living Standards Survey, 1991/92 and 1998/99.

Thus the evidence does suggest increased enrolment rates overall at primary and secondary level, though of course this says nothing about quality, which has been a continual concern in Ghana.

## Asset Poverty

Another dimension of changing living conditions of households is their ownership of key assets, notably consumer durable goods. Of course whether or not households own particular durable goods also depends on factors outside their immediate control, such as whether they have access to electricity (to be considered below), but it is still a good indicator of changing living standards.

Information is available from the GLSS surveys on household ownership of a range of durable goods, so that it is possible to examine the changes in the proportion of different categories of households owning these goods. This is an easily observed and measured indicator of wellbeing, even if it does not allow for changes in the quality of these goods. Overall there is a substantial increase in the proportion of households owning most consumer durable goods (if often from a low base in 1991/92, see Table 2.11). For present purposes though, it is more interesting to investigate changes for key assets across different categories of households (for example, by geographic location or by income group). The analysis here focuses on six key assets: land, bicycle, radio, refrigerator, electric iron and television. Land is a key productive asset; bicycles are an important means of transport of value for both production and consumption purposes (especially in the north); a radio is important for access to information; refrigerators and electric irons are valuable for facilitating household activities; while a television is predominantly a consumption good.

For all of these assets except bicycles and land, levels of ownership are much higher in urban areas than rural areas (Table 2.11), this of course partly reflecting differential access to electricity, but also likely to be due to urban-rural differences in living standards and in lifestyles. Within urban and rural areas the proportion of households owning these assets is higher in wealthier localities than poorer ones, so that ownership is lowest in the savannah zone in all cases (similarly ownership increases with the income quintile within each of urban and rural areas). For each of these four assets, the proportion of households that owned one or more increased over this period, this being the case at national level, within each of urban and rural areas, and within most income groups. Nonetheless, the magnitudes of the increases in ownership have been much larger in the richer groups than in poorer ones, and in urban areas than rural ones. These patterns are is consistent with the pattern suggested by the analysis of consumption poverty, that is that the poorest groups have experienced much less improvement in their living conditions despite the aggregate poverty reduction which Ghana experienced over this period.

The pattern for bicycle ownership is somewhat different. The proportion of households owning bicycles is highest by far in the northern savannah (urban and rural), presumably reflecting larger distances and poorer public transport there. Yet, bicycle ownership increased much less than for other assets. This could be seen as another indicator of the relative poverty of this locality, and its lack of development over this period.[11]

## Access to Potable Water and Electricity

As discussed under assets, access to electricity varies substantially across Ghana despite widespread rural electrification measures undertaken in the years between these two surveys. Presumably as a direct result, the number of households in rural areas with access to electricity increased substantially between 1991/92 and 1998/99, though from a very low base (Table 2.12). This improvement has occurred in all rural quintiles, but more so in the higher groups. Access to electricity increases with the standard of living and is much lower in the lower quintile groups than in the higher groups (presumably partly reflecting

---

11. However, nationally the magnitude of bicycle ownership increased modestly in most localities and most income groups between 1991/92 and 1998/99.

**Table 2.11. Trends in Percentage of Households Owning Specific Consumer Durable Goods, 1991/92 and 1998/99**

| | % owning refrigerator | | % owning television | | % owning bicycle | | % owning radio | | % owning iron (electric) | | % owning land/plot | |
|---|---|---|---|---|---|---|---|---|---|---|---|---|
| | 1991/92 | 1998/99 | 1991/92 | 1998/99 | 1991/92 | 1998/99 | 1991/92 | 1998/99 | 1991/92 | 1998/99 | 1991/92 | 1998/99 |
| *All households, by locality:* | | | | | | | | | | | | |
| Accra | 33.1 | 44.1 | 39.0 | 51.8 | 2.4 | 7.2 | 62.1 | 77.0 | 50.5 | 63.5 | 7.2 | 12.9 |
| Urban Coastal | 16.2 | 31.4 | 22.0 | 38.9 | 4.3 | 6.1 | 48.7 | 58.6 | 38.4 | 40.6 | 11.9 | 14.6 |
| Urban Forest | 18.0 | 30.8 | 22.3 | 36.6 | 6.8 | 8.3 | 56.4 | 60.0 | 33.8 | 43.9 | 21.3 | 16.6 |
| Urban Savannah | 5.2 | 14.7 | 7.2 | 25.5 | 38.1 | 43.7 | 43.3 | 64.8 | 14.4 | 22.1 | 19.1 | 23.2 |
| Rural Coastal | 1.5 | 7.8 | 4.3 | 14.1 | 8.4 | 11.0 | 32.2 | 41.2 | 4.5 | 12.5 | 8.5 | 26.4 |
| Rural Forest | 2.8 | 10.5 | 4.1 | 16.5 | 9.1 | 13.1 | 38.9 | 50.6 | 5.8 | 15.3 | 27.5 | 40.2 |
| Rural Savannah | 0.4 | 1.1 | 0.8 | 2.4 | 44.0 | 52.8 | 29.9 | 46.6 | 0.7 | 1.9 | 12.1 | 10.5 |
| ALL GHANA | 8.2 | 16.6 | 10.9 | 22.4 | 15.5 | 19.2 | 41.5 | 53.8 | 15.7 | 23.8 | 17.0 | 24.0 |
| *Urban households, by standard of living quintile* | | | | | | | | | | | | |
| Lowest | 4.2 | 2.2 | 8.3 | 7.6 | 18.8 | 21.1 | 31.3 | 30.0 | 10.4 | 6.3 | 20.8 | 11.2 |
| Second | 4.0 | 7.1 | 8.0 | 19.0 | 10.4 | 20.8 | 36.8 | 49.4 | 17.6 | 16.3 | 14.4 | 17.6 |
| Third | 12.1 | 21.7 | 24.2 | 34.3 | 6.3 | 15.5 | 56.5 | 60.6 | 26.5 | 32.7 | 14.8 | 20.6 |
| Fourth | 19.8 | 31.5 | 24.7 | 42.7 | 9.1 | 12.1 | 53.6 | 67.0 | 36.7 | 43.4 | 13.7 | 15.6 |
| Highest | 26.3 | 44.6 | 29.4 | 48.0 | 8.3 | 7.9 | 58.1 | 72.2 | 45.7 | 61.1 | 14.1 | 14.8 |
| ALL URBAN | 20.3 | 32.8 | 25.2 | 40.1 | 8.7 | 11.8 | 54.3 | 65.2 | 37.6 | 46.1 | 14.3 | 15.9 |
| *Rural households, by standard of living quintile* | | | | | | | | | | | | |
| Lowest | 0.2 | 0.5 | 0.0 | 1.3 | 26.9 | 35.6 | 26.6 | 36.4 | 0.5 | 1.4 | 14.8 | 14.6 |
| Second | 0.2 | 1.8 | 1.2 | 7.0 | 20.5 | 24.9 | 30.8 | 42.8 | 1.3 | 4.2 | 19.5 | 26.9 |
| Third | 1.0 | 6.4 | 1.9 | 10.8 | 19.6 | 21.8 | 34.7 | 49.8 | 4.0 | 8.6 | 19.2 | 33.6 |
| Fourth | 1.3 | 10.1 | 3.5 | 16.0 | 16.4 | 19.9 | 38.8 | 52.5 | 4.2 | 17.2 | 21.4 | 34.4 |
| Highest | 5.9 | 17.7 | 9.0 | 25.4 | 12.5 | 14.8 | 41.9 | 54.7 | 9.5 | 23.8 | 16.9 | 34.3 |
| ALL RURAL | 1.8 | 7.3 | 3.2 | 12.1 | 19.1 | 23.5 | 34.7 | 47.2 | 4.0 | 11.0 | 18.4 | 28.7 |

*Source:* Authors' calculation from the Ghana Living Standards Survey, 1991/92 and 1998/99.

**Table 2.12.  Trends in Access to Potable Water and Electricity, 1991/92 and 1998/99**

| | % with access to potable water | | % with access to electricity | |
|---|---|---|---|---|
| | 1991/92 | 1998/99 | 1991/92 | 1998/99 |
| *All households, by locality:* | | | | |
| Accra | 100.0 | 100.0 | 89.5 | 90.6 |
| Urban Coastal | 92.4 | 95.5 | 60.8 | 72.9 |
| Urban Forest | 84.1 | 91.5 | 70.2 | 83.5 |
| Urban Savannah | 76.3 | 77.9 | 35.1 | 45.8 |
| Rural Coastal | 50.8 | 74.7 | 10.3 | 28.2 |
| Rural Forest | 51.8 | 63.9 | 11.0 | 25.1 |
| Rural Savannah | 50.4 | 56.8 | 3.6 | 3.9 |
| ALL GHANA | 64.8 | 75.1 | 29.8 | 41.4 |
| *Urban households, by standard of living quintile* | | | | |
| Lowest | 76.6 | 77.6 | 40.4 | 30.9 |
| Second | 81.6 | 82.5 | 51.2 | 47.2 |
| Third | 91.0 | 89.0 | 64.3 | 66.8 |
| Fourth | 89.8 | 94.4 | 67.5 | 79.8 |
| Highest | 92.1 | 97.5 | 75.2 | 92.0 |
| ALL URBAN | 90.1 | 93.2 | 68.9 | 78.4 |
| *Rural households, by standard of living quintile* | | | | |
| Lowest | 46.8 | 67.5 | 3.5 | 5.1 |
| Second | 47.2 | 61.1 | 5.6 | 12.4 |
| Third | 50.1 | 60.1 | 8.3 | 17.7 |
| Fourth | 52.5 | 65.4 | 9.8 | 28.5 |
| Highest | 58.7 | 69.1 | 15.9 | 37.0 |
| ALL RURAL | 51.1 | 64.6 | 8.7 | 20.0 |

*Source:* Authors' calculation from the Ghana Living Standards Survey, 1991/92 and 1998/99.

remoteness). In urban areas the percentage having access to electricity also increases with the standard of living. Indeed the extent to which this is true has increased between 1991/92 and 1998/99. More households in the top three quintiles have access to electricity in 1998/99 than in 1991/92, but the proportion of those in the first two quintiles having access to electricity has fallen. These changes in access to electricity are obviously one factor accounting for changes in the proportion of households owning electrically operated durable goods in Table 2.11 above.

A more basic aspect of living conditions though is whether or not households have access to potable water. As the available data makes it difficult to judge the quality of a drinking water source, this is defined for current purposes as not using natural sources for drinking water. In urban areas only small proportions of households are reliant on natural sources for their drinking water (Table 2.12), and these proportions fell modestly over the period (though less so in the two poorest quintiles). Not surprisingly, a much larger proportion of households in rural areas rely on natural sources, but the situation improved markedly over this period. In 1991/92 almost half the households in rural areas used natural sources of drinking water, while by 1998/99 this had declined to just over one third. Moreover, by 1998/99 the proportion of rural households having access to potable water changes little with the standard of living, in contrast to 1991/92 when potable water was more accessible to households in higher quintile groups. Thus not only has access to potable water in rural areas increased substantially between 1991/92 and 1998/99, but this is one change in which the poor have benefited disproportionately.

In summary the pattern of change of non-income indicators does not show the same geographically differentiated pattern of change as consumption poverty. This is not surprising given that these indicators are more or less directly linked to the pattern of growth. Many non-income indicators improved over this period, generally throughout the country, but the apparent sharp deterioration in access to health care services (again apparently throughout the country) is a matter of serious concern, both in its own right and for the impact of health on other key dimensions of poverty.

## Changes in Economic Activities as an Explanation of Changes in Poverty and Inequality

The GLSS survey collects a significant amount of information on the activities in which households and their members are engaged, including on their incomes derived from different sources. This can be used to consider households' livelihoods and their evolution over time as a possible explanation for changing levels and patterns of poverty and inequality. This section of the paper considers information on changes in household livelihoods over this period focusing on an analysis of the composition of household income and of labor market participation and returns.

### Composition of Household Incomes

The GLSS survey results have been used to construct comprehensive estimates of total household income and its components (GSS 2000b). The measures of income are defined broadly to include all relevant "imputed" incomes, in other words valuations for income in kind, most notably valuations of that part of household agricultural production consumed by the household itself. Nevertheless, considerable caution is required in the use and interpretation of this income data. The estimates of total household income are on average significantly less than those of total consumption expenditure, and the evidence strongly suggests that this is due predominantly to underestimation of income (rather than overestimation of consumption expenditure). This tendency to underestimate income is quite common in many household surveys in developing and transition countries (McKay 2000), in part because significant proportions of income are derived from agriculture or non-farm self-employment activities for which formal accounts are generally not available, and because the surveys rarely succeed in identifying the full range of economic activities in which individuals are engaged.

Despite this underestimation problem, income information is potentially very important in understanding what influences living conditions. Income is clearly the main means (and only sustainable means) by which consumption is financed. The GLSS income data already have been used in identifying the main economic activity of the households. Of course, in most countries the majority of households have income from more than one source. They often have more than one member working; individual household members may be engaged in more than one activity at the same time; and many households will have income from rent, transfers and other non-labor sources. This diversification of livelihoods itself may be associated with a household's living conditions, often positively among poorer households at least. As such it is important for the understanding of poverty (a key dimension of which is the household's inadequate income level) to understand the nature of the activities from which different groups derive their livelihoods, and the extent to which these are diversified.

While the level of household income is apparently significantly underestimated, the survey still seems to provide plausible indications of the composition of household income.[12] Even if the different components of income are underestimated to different extents, the surveys still can be used to examine changing patterns of household incomes. This would rely on the assumption that the relative extent of underestimation of the different income components is similar between the two rounds. The fact that the GLSS3 and GLSS4 questionnaires are essentially the same provides some basis for this assumption. Nonetheless considerable care is needed in the use and interpretation of the income data, highlighting the important of corroborating evidence for the income patterns where possible.

In this spirit, GLSS data are used to consider changing sources of household incomes between 1991/92 and 1998/99, focusing exclusively on income composition, reported in terms of six main components. This is computed as follows. If household i has total income $y_i > 0$ and income from source j of $y_{i,j}$ ($j = 1, 2, \ldots 6$), then its share of income from source j is $s_{i,j} = y_{i,j}/y_i$, and the average income composition for source j is computed as the mean value of $s_{i,j}$ across all households under consideration. Note that this average can only be computed meaningfully over strictly positive values of total income $y_i$; this restriction excludes 1.2 percent of households in 1991/92 which reported zero or negative incomes and 2.0 percent in 1998/99.[13]

At a national level in both years the two most important income sources are own account agriculture and non-farm self employment (Table 2.13), followed by income from wage employment and remittances, with the last two sources being relatively small. The average proportions of household income accounted for by each source are plausible in both years. The share of agricultural income is lower in 1998/99 compared to 1991/92, and the share of remittances somewhat higher. The declining share of agriculture at least is probably unsurprising in a growing economy, though this can also be affected by changing prices for outputs. However, the level appears to have marginally increased (or at least not fallen) over this period if it can be assumed that the degree of underestimation of agri-

---

12. Obviously this is a subjective judgment, but which is based on a number of considerations. For instance, information is also available on the time devoted by the different household members to the economic activities in which they are engaged, which appears compatible with the income composition of these households.

13. In 1991/92, 0.8 percent of households reported negative incomes, and the corresponding figure for 1998/99 was 1.7 percent. Negative incomes arise because the two most important components of income (own account agriculture and non-farm self employment) are computed as a difference between revenues and costs.

**Table 2.13. Average Share of Household Income Derived from Different Sources, by Locality and Year**

| Location | Year | Wages | Own account agric. | Non-farm self empl. | Rent (incl. imputed) | Remittances | Other sources | TOTAL |
|---|---|---|---|---|---|---|---|---|
| | | | | Average percentage of household income from: | | | | |
| Accra | 1991/92 | 40.9 | −0.1 | 34.9 | 2.0 | 17.7 | 4.6 | 100.0% |
| | 1998/99 | 31.3 | 5.3 | 39.9 | 5.2 | 16.3 | 2.0 | 100.0% |
| Other urban | 1991/92 | 27.6 | 2.4 | 42.4 | 2.6 | 22.5 | 2.5 | 100.0% |
| | 1998/99 | 23.5 | 9.8 | 35.0 | 5.0 | 23.3 | 3.4 | 100.0% |
| Rural coastal | 1991/92 | 12.7 | 35.3 | 33.3 | .5.0 | 12.3 | 1.5 | 100.0% |
| | 1998/99 | 14.5 | 26.2 | 31.6 | 8.5 | 17.8 | 1.4 | 100.0% |
| Rural forest | 1991/92 | 11.1 | 55.6 | 18.3 | 2.5 | 11.2 | 1.3 | 100.0% |
| | 1998/99 | 12.0 | 35.6 | 22.1 | 3.7 | 24.7 | 2.0 | 100.0% |
| Rural savannah | 1991/92 | 6.5 | 62.5 | 16.4 | 9.4 | 4.8 | 0.5 | 100.0% |
| | 1998/99 | 4.0 | 58.1 | 17.1 | 6.7 | 12.2 | 1.9 | 100.0% |
| ALL | 1991/92 | 17.6 | 34.9 | 28.0 | 4.1 | 13.6 | 1.8 | 100.0% |
| | 1998/99 | 16.0 | 28.1 | 27.9 | 5.5 | 20.2 | 2.3 | 100.0% |

*Note:* Definitions of income sources are reported in GSS (2000b).
*Source:* Authors' calculation from the Ghana Living Standards Survey, 1991/92 and 1998/99.

cultural income was similar in the two rounds of the survey.[14] Coulombe and McKay (2006) provide further analysis of the increase in remittances over this period.

There are significant differences in income composition between localities. In urban areas, the main income sources are non-farm self employment and wage employment (the latter especially in Accra), with remittances also being a substantial source. However, the data suggest important changes between 1991/92 and 1998/99, including an increased share obtained from agricultural activities (even in Accra) and a reduced share from wage employment. In Accra, the substantial fall in the contribution of wage income is accompanied by an increase in the importance of non-farm, self-employment income.

In rural areas own-account agriculture and non-farm self employment are by far the most important income sources, with the relative importance of agriculture as an income source greatest in the northern savannah zone and lowest in the coastal zone (as anticipated). Again, the data suggest important changes in the relative importance of different sources between the two rounds, but particularly in the forest zone, where the vast majority of rural poverty reduction occurred. There was a sharp increase in the importance of remittances in all zones, particularly in the forest zone. In all zones the contribution of agriculture to household income also fell over this period, though this decline was relatively small in the savannah zone. By contrast, the decline in this share in the coastal and forest zone was quite substantial, although in the forest zone the data suggest that the absolute level of income from agriculture did not fall there. Given the observed geographic pattern

---

14. There is no objective way of assessing the validity of this assumption, but the fact that the questionnaire structure in relation to agriculture remained largely unchanged provides some degree of support.

of rural poverty reduction, it is not surprising that the largest changes (and greatest poverty) occurred in the forest zone. This seems to reflect in particular good agricultural performance and increases in remittance income there, both of which were experienced much less in the other two ecological zones.

Considering the composition of household incomes by economic activity categories provides information on how diversified households' income sources are (Table 2.14). In both years those in households whose main economic activity was formal sector (public or private) wage employment obtained around three quarters of their income from wages, with the remainder of their income mainly derived from non-farm, self-employment activities or agriculture. More detailed analysis (not presented here) shows that urban households in these categories obtain an even higher proportion of their income from wages. Those in households whose main activity is informal wage employment obtain lower proportions of their income from wages, presumably reflecting lower average wages and/or greater job insecurity associated with this activity. Remittances make a larger proportionate contribution to income for this group than for those whose principal activity is formal sector employment.

Households whose primary economic activity is export farming obtain a substantial proportion of their income from agriculture, where this agricultural income encompasses food crops, livestock and processing as well as export crops. Those households classified as export farmers in 1998/99 obtained an even higher proportion of their income from agriculture in that year than their counterparts in 1991/92. By contrast, the importance of agricultural income for households whose primary activity was food farming was substantially lower in 1998/99 than 1991/92, such that it represented less than half of their income on average in 1998/99. At the same time there was a large increase in the proportion of their

**Table 2.14. Extent of Diversification of Income Sources, by Main Household Economic Activity and Year**

| Main household economic activity | Year | Population share (%) | Average household share of income from: | | | |
|---|---|---|---|---|---|---|
| | | | Wage | Own account agriculture | Non-farm self employment | Remittances |
| Public sector wage employment | 1991/92 | 13.5 | 75.8 | 8.5 | 8.9 | 3.9 |
| | 1998/99 | 10.7 | 72.6 | 8.9 | 11.0 | 5.2 |
| Private formal sector wage employment | 1991/92 | 3.9 | 72.2 | 5.2 | 10.0 | 6.9 |
| | 1998/99 | 4.9 | 76.9 | 3.7 | 8.0 | 8.7 |
| Private informal sector wage employment | 1991/92 | 3.1 | 61.0 | 10.0 | 14.6 | 11.3 |
| | 1998/99 | 2.9 | 68.9 | 10.0 | 7.5 | 10.4 |
| Export farming | 1991/92 | 6.3 | 1.0 | 70.4 | 10.5 | 12.6 |
| | 1998/99 | 7.0 | 1.4 | 78.9 | 8.7 | 6.0 |
| Food crop farming | 1991/92 | 43.6 | 1.5 | 63.4 | 13.2 | 14.5 |
| | 1998/99 | 38.6 | 1.4 | 46.8 | 13.8 | 27.2 |
| Non-farm self employment | 1991/92 | 27.6 | 4.1 | 10.7 | 70.5 | 11.3 |
| | 1998/99 | 33.8 | 3.5 | 13.4 | 60.8 | 15.7 |

*Note:* Definitions of income sources are reported in GSS (2000b).
*Source:* Authors' calculation from the Ghana Living Standards Survey, 1991/92 and 1998/99.

income received as remittances—indeed this is the group of households that experienced by far the largest part of the national level increase in the income from remittances. This may suggest an increasing problem of vulnerability associated with this group, although on the other hand they do at least have relations with other households that can send transfers to them.

A similar analysis disaggregated by geographic location shows that the biggest changes in income composition occurred in the locations experiencing the greatest poverty reduction: Accra and rural forest. In Accra in 1998/99 there were many more households in the non-farm, self-employment category compared to 1991/92, and substantially fewer public sector workers (reflecting public sector retrenchment). In the rural forest region the share of income export farmers obtain from agriculture increases over this period, but for food farmers the share of agricultural income falls substantially, compensated by a large increase in the share of income from remittances. This suggests that for some of these households their food farming activities may not be particularly remunerative; it raises questions about the sustainability of this poverty reduction. In other locations the changes in income sources are much smaller over this period, and in particular the impact of remittances on poverty reduction is much less in other rural areas.

## Economic Activities Undertaken by Individuals

The labor market behaviour of individuals is a key determinant of both the level and composition of household income. Important issues will be the extent of labor supply by individual household members, and the activities in which they are engaged. Often different household members will work in different sectors, and individuals may work also in more than one activity by having multiple occupations.

Labor market activity is considered for the first instance here for individual household members aged between 15 and 64 years, and is based on their economic activity profile in the twelve months prior to the survey interview, covering their main and secondary occupations. In this respect it would be of particular interest to examine changes in the average number of hours worked, but unfortunately this cannot be computed based on the GLSS4 questionnaire. Instead therefore, it is necessary to focus on the proportion of individuals working. The proportion of those aged 15–64 years (whether in full time education or not) that were engaged in any economic activity in the previous twelve months fell from 81.5 percent in 1991/92 to 73.8 percent in 1998/99, with declines observed for both men and women and in most localities. However, the corresponding calculations for those aged 25–64 years shows that this was almost entirely due to increased educational participation in that participation rates for both men and women in this age range (around 92–93 percent) scarcely changed in aggregate and within most groups (Coulombe and McKay 2003). The proportions engaged in a second occupation in this same time horizon changed very little over the 1990s. In both years just fewer than 20 percent of men and just over 21 percent of women were also engaged in a second occupation, the rates being higher in rural areas.[15]

---

15. Note that given the reference period used in the questionnaire, these activities were not necessarily held simultaneously with the primary occupation.

Defining economic occupation categories for individuals in an analogous way to that used for households shows the same patterns of change at the individual level (Table 2.15). For both men and women the numbers engaged in own account agriculture have fallen substantially, while the proportions engaged in non-farm self-employment activities have risen. The proportion of those working that are engaged in own account agriculture is 4.6 percentage points lower in 1998/99 than 1991/92, and in non-farm self employment is 6.6 percentage points higher. The numbers working in the public sector have also fallen (reflecting retrenchment), while the numbers working in the (small) formal private sector have risen by a smaller amount. These changes are similar for both men and women, even if overall women are much more highly represented in non-farm self employment and less in wage employment compared to men. By industrial sector, larger proportions of men that are working are active in the manufacturing; trading and construction in 1998/99 compared to 1991/92; for women the proportions working in manufacturing also increases. Further analysis (not presented here) shows that for both women and men most secondary occupations are in agriculture, manufacturing and trading, and are almost exclusively undertaken as self-employment activities.

To what extent can the information on individuals' labor market activities explain the large poverty reduction in Accra, a phenomenon which is not easily explained by the analy-

**Table 2.15. Sectoral Distribution of Main Economic Activity Undertaken by Individuals that Worked, by Gender and Year**
(in percent)

| Main economic activity | 1991/92 | | | 1998/99 | | |
|---|---|---|---|---|---|---|
| | Female | Male | All | Female | Male | All |
| *By employment status* | | | | | | |
| Public sector empl. | 4.6 | 13.6 | 8.7 | 3.4 | 10.7 | 6.6 |
| Private formal empl. | 1.2 | 6.2 | 3.6 | 1.4 | 7.5 | 4.2 |
| Private informal empl. | 2.3 | 4.8 | 3.4 | 1.3 | 4.7 | 2.8 |
| Own account agric, | 57.7 | 62.1 | 59.6 | 53.5 | 57.2 | 55.0 |
| Non-farm self empl. | 34.1 | 13.3 | 24.7 | 40.4 | 19.9 | 31.3 |
| *By industry* | | | | | | |
| Agriculture | 58.7 | 67.1 | 62.5 | 53.9 | 62.2 | 57.6 |
| Mining/quarrying | 0.1 | 1.0 | 0.5 | 0.1 | 1.3 | 0.6 |
| Manufacturing | 9.3 | 6.5 | 8.0 | 13.1 | 8.0 | 10.8 |
| Utilities | 0.1 | 0.2 | 0.1 | 0.1 | 0.4 | 0.2 |
| Construction | 0.1 | 2.4 | 1.1 | 0.1 | 3.2 | 1.5 |
| Trading | 25.3 | 4.7 | 15.9 | 26.2 | 6.3 | 17.4 |
| Transport/communicat. | 0.2 | 4.3 | 2.1 | 0.1 | 4.6 | 2.1 |
| Financial services | 0.2 | 0.9 | 0.5 | 0.1 | 1.5 | 0.8 |
| Other services | 6.0 | 13.0 | 9.2 | 6.3 | 12.4 | 9.0 |
| ALL | 100.0 | 100.0 | 100.0 | 100.0 | 100.0 | 100.0 |

*Note:* this table is based on those aged 15 years and above.
*Source:* Authors' calculation from the Ghana Living Standards Survey, 1991/92 and 1998/99.

sis to date? It certainly is likely to be important that Accra is the only locality where the proportion of the population working did not fall, although the relative importance of labor supply and demand factors in accounting for this is not clear from the available information. To what extent did the changing composition of income identified in the previous subsection account for this? This can be considered more clearly by looking at the changing sectoral pattern of employment in Accra, and maybe from available information from incomes from different activities.

By employment status, the major change in Accra over this period has been the sharp reduction in the numbers working in the public sector (reflecting the effects of retrenchment) and the increase in the numbers working in non-farm self-employment activities. This is true for both men and women and the changes in percentage points are similar in each case. The proportions working as employees in the private sector have fallen modestly over the period (although with a modest increase in the proportion of men working as informal sector employees). It is clear from this table that the retrenched from the public sector have predominantly moved into non-farm self-employment activities, with few of them finding wage jobs in the private sector.

By industry, the proportions of both men and women working in trading activities increased substantially between 1991/92 and 1998/99, and the proportions in the other services sector fell substantially (Table 2.16). The latter includes public services and so again

**Table 2.16. Distribution of Main Economic Activity, by Gender and Year, Accra Only**
**(in percent)**

| Main economic activity | 1991/92 | | | 1998/99 | | |
|---|---|---|---|---|---|---|
| | Female | Male | All | Female | Male | All |
| *By employment status:* | | | | | | |
| Public sector empl. | 18.1 | 30.8 | 23.4 | 7.4 | 20.2 | 13.2 |
| Private formal empl. | 8.7 | 24.8 | 15.6 | 6.3 | 22.1 | 13.5 |
| Private informal empl. | 5.8 | 13.8 | 9.1 | 4.0 | 16.4 | 9.7 |
| Own account agric, | 0.0 | 1.2 | 0.5 | 0.2 | 0.3 | 0.3 |
| Non-farm self empl. | 67.1 | 29.6 | 51.4 | 82.1 | 41.2 | 63.2 |
| | | | | | | |
| *By industry:* | | | | | | |
| Agriculture | 0.3 | 3.2 | 1.5 | 1.2 | 4.1 | 2.5 |
| Mining/quarrying | 0.0 | 0.8 | 0.3 | 0.0 | 0.0 | 0.0 |
| Manufacturing | 28.3 | 19.4 | 24.6 | 19.1 | 20.2 | 19.6 |
| Utilities | 0.9 | 1.2 | 1.0 | 0.0 | 0.8 | 0.5 |
| Construction | 0.3 | 6.5 | 2.9 | 0.0 | 6.5 | 3.0 |
| Trading | 46.4 | 11.3 | 31.7 | 63.5 | 18.0 | 42.5 |
| Transport/communicat. | 1.2 | 12.1 | 5.8 | 0.5 | 14.2 | 6.8 |
| Financial services | 1.7 | 7.3 | 4.1 | 0.7 | 8.4 | 4.3 |
| Other services | 21.0 | 38.1 | 28.1 | 14.9 | 27.8 | 20.8 |
| ALL | 100.0 | 100.0 | 100.0 | 100.0 | 100.0 | 100.0 |

*Note:* this table is based on those aged 15–64 years.
*Source:* Authors' calculation from the Ghana Living Standards Survey, 1991/92 and 1998/99.

**Table 2.17. Distribution of Estimated Average Annual Real Wages in Accra, by Gender and Year**

(thousands of cedis, constant January 1999 Accra prices)

|  | 1991/92 | | | 1998/99 | | |
|---|---|---|---|---|---|---|
|  | Female | Male | All | Female | Male | All |
| *By activity category:* | | | | | | |
| Public sector empl. | 2460.7 | 3472.5 | 3017.9 | 2334.3 | 3427.6 | 3097.5 |
| Private formal empl. | 1794.4 | 1878.9 | 1850.4 | 2326.9 | 2922.4 | 2773.5 |
| Private informal empl. | 635.4 | 1450.8 | 1148.8 | 853.2 | 1799.0 | 1590.2 |
| Non-farm self empl. | 1669.4 | 2557.2 | 1883.3 | 2386.2 | 3670.5 | 2771.0 |
| *By industrial sector:* | | | | | | |
| Manufacturing | 1822.0 | 2662.8 | 2100.4 | 2142.3 | 2749.3 | 2430.3 |
| Construction | 2606.8 | 1766.6 | 1816.0 | . . . | 3004.9 | 3004.9 |
| Trading | 1405.0 | 2271.6 | 1534.8 | 2330.1 | 3349.7 | 2528.6 |
| Transport/communicat. | 1541.2 | 2363.1 | 2266.4 | 3440.5 | 3401.6 | 3403.1 |
| Financial services | 3066.4 | 3928.4 | 3712.9 | 4164.4 | 4536.6 | 4503.8 |
| Other services | 2346.0 | 2552.2 | 2462.8 | 2440.0 | 2880.5 | 2710.7 |
| ALL | 1763.4 | 2491.3 | 2068.2 | 2317.3 | 3141.1 | 2696.6 |

*Note:* only the larger categories are reported here. This table is based on those aged 15–64 years.
*Source:* Authors' calculation from the Ghana Living Standards Survey, 1991/92 and 1998/99.

in large measure reflects public sector retrenchment. Other smaller changes are the increased proportion of men working in transport and communications, and the reduced proportion of women engaged in manufacturing activities or financial services (the latter sector employing few women anyway). This represents a substantial change in employment patterns in Accra, one which is not observed in the remaining urban locations where for example the proportions working in the trading sector change very little and fall in some instances (figures not presented here).

It is important to consider this changing sectoral structure in Accra along with estimates of changes to the returns of different occupations. Notwithstanding the limitations of the income data, this can be considered by looking at the changes in the relative incomes across sectors. The GLSS data allow annual wage and self-employment income to be estimated computed at the individual level. This enables comparison of individual's average nominal incomes in 1991/92 and 1998/99 according to economic activity type (Table 2.17). In one sense this is inevitably an approximate exercise because it does not control for changes in the characteristics of the individuals involved (age, education, and so forth),[16] but this is less important for present purposes where the focus is on identifying the groups and sectors where income levels are increasing faster for whatever reason.

It is clear from Table 2.17 that even though public sector activities continue to give higher average income levels in 1998/99 than was the case in 1991/92, the differential between the incomes from working in the public sector and non-farm self employment narrowed sharply

16. In any case the sample size within Accra is insufficient to control adequately for these factors.

over this period. But disaggregating by gender shows much more clearly what really happened. For both men and women in Accra, the average income from self-employment activities is higher than for public sector employment, in sharp contrast to 1991/92 when income from self employment was substantially lower. Assuming the data underlying this comparison are sufficiently reliable, they strongly suggests that self-employment activities now have the highest return in Accra. The reason the aggregate data hide this is that (as seen above) women are much more represented in non-farm self employment and less in public sector employment, and women are receiving significantly lower incomes in both.

Considering the equivalent information by industry (Table 2.17), the biggest increase by far in the average income earned in Accra (and substantially in excess of inflation) is in the trading sector. Again this magnitude of increase in incomes from this sector is generally not observed in the other urban areas. The sharp poverty reduction in Accra (which was identified based on consumption data, not the income data used here) is consistent with these findings. Although the relatively well-paid public sector did contract over this period, the poverty reduction appears to have been mainly due to a substantial increase in both the size and profitability of the trading sector, a sector in which most households are self-employed. However, it is questionable whether the apparently rapidly increasing profitability of this sector can be sustained.

A similar analysis in the rural forest zone (Tables 2.18 and 2.19) shows a rather different pattern. Here individuals mostly work on their own account, and among these there

**Table 2.18. Distribution of Main Economic Activity in the Rural Forest, by Gender and Year (in percent)**

|  | 1991/92 | | | 1998/99 | | |
|---|---|---|---|---|---|---|
| Main economic activity | Female | Male | All | Female | Male | All |
| *By employment status:* | | | | | | |
| Public sector empl. | 2.7 | 10.4 | 6.2 | 2.6 | 7.3 | 4.7 |
| Private formal empl. | 0.7 | 3.2 | 1.9 | 0.5 | 4.8 | 2.4 |
| Private informal empl. | 1.2 | 2.8 | 2.0 | 0.9 | 3.0 | 1.8 |
| Own account agric, | 77.1 | 74.4 | 75.9 | 69.7 | 72.0 | 70.6 |
| Non-farm self empl. | 18.4 | 9.1 | 14.1 | 26.5 | 13.0 | 20.3 |
| *By industry:* | | | | | | |
| Agriculture | 77.9 | 79.4 | 78.6 | 69.9 | 75.4 | 72.4 |
| Mining/quarrying | 0.1 | 1.6 | 0.8 | 0.1 | 1.7 | 0.8 |
| Manufacturing | 6.3 | 4.8 | 5.6 | 8.5 | 6.0 | 7.4 |
| Utilities | 0.0 | 0.1 | 0.0 | 0.0 | 0.2 | 0.1 |
| Construction | 0.1 | 1.5 | 0.7 | 0.0 | 2.7 | 1.2 |
| Trading | 12.1 | 2.2 | 7.5 | 16.1 | 4.6 | 10.9 |
| Transport/communicat. | 0.0 | 1.6 | 0.7 | 0.1 | 1.5 | 0.7 |
| Financial services | 0.0 | 0.3 | 0.2 | 0.0 | 0.4 | 0.2 |
| Other services | 3.6 | 8.4 | 5.8 | 5.3 | 7.5 | 6.3 |
| ALL | 100.0 | | | | 100.0 | 100.0 |

*Source:* Authors' calculation from the Ghana Living Standards Survey, 1991/92 and 1998/99.

**Table 2.19. Distribution of Estimated Average Annual Real Wages in Rural Forest, by Gender and Year**
(thousands of cedis, constant January 1999 Accra prices)

| | 1991/92 | | | 1998/99 | | |
|---|---|---|---|---|---|---|
| | Female | Male | All | Female | Male | All |
| *By activity category:* | | | | | | |
| Public sector empl. | 1326.5 | 1817.8 | 1704.2 | 1935.6 | 2620.7 | 2415.6 |
| Private formal empl. | *339.2 | 1546.2 | 1315.2 | *1344.4 | 2391.1 | 2287.7 |
| Private informal empl. | *307.8 | 1013.7 | 807.0 | *475.5 | 989.9 | 863.4 |
| Agric self empl | 183.6 | 586.8 | 367.0 | 285.1 | 761.9 | 503.5 |
| Non-farm self empl. | 1244.0 | 1594.1 | 1349.7 | 1044.5 | 1838.2 | 1271.7 |
| *By industrial sector:* | | | | | | |
| Agriculture | 185.9 | 641.8 | 399.5 | 285.1 | 783.6 | 519.2 |
| Manufacturing | 908.8 | 1102.4 | 986.0 | 741.5 | 1530.3 | 1030.1 |
| Construction | *500.3 | *1828.5 | *1758.6 | . . | 1438.7 | 1438.7 |
| Trading | 1390.8 | *1947.8 | 1466.3 | 1232.6 | 2400.1 | 1453.3 |
| Other services | 1146.4 | 1761.0 | 1558.9 | 1350.8 | 2351.7 | 1886.8 |
| ALL | 412.5 | 850.0 | 615.5 | 534.4 | 1122.7 | 799.5 |

*Note:* only the larger categories are reported here. This table is based on those aged 15–64 years and * denotes less than 30 observations.
*Source:* Authors' calculation from the Ghana Living Standards Survey, 1991/92 and 1998/99.

has been a shift over this period of about 5 percent of the working population from agricultural to non-agricultural self-employment activities (this applying to women in particular). However, the income data suggests that over this period real incomes for those working in agriculture have increased while those in non-farm self employment have fallen (even if the latter still remain substantially higher). Unfortunately it is not possible based on this individual level data to distinguish agricultural income from producing export crops from that derived from food crops, especially as most households engaged in export farming produce significant quantities of food crops as well. Household level data though suggests that agricultural incomes appear to have increased for both export farming households and food farming households, though much more for the former group.

This suggests that increasing returns to agriculture, as well as remittances, are likely to have been an important factor behind poverty reduction (and growth) in the rural forest. Both women and men have experienced quite large proportionate increases in their incomes from agriculture, though the levels remain substantially lower for females compared to males. The other industrial sector where incomes have increased somewhat has been the other services sector, with much of this being to increased earnings among public sector employees (among whom there has also been some reduction in their numbers).

In summary, some specific factors appear to have accounted for the poverty reduction that occurred in Accra and the rural forest, and that occurred to a much lesser extent elsewhere (where poverty did not fall, or fell much less). In particular in Accra this has been associated with increasing numbers working into own account, notably in commerce/trading activities, the return to which appears to have increased somewhat over this period. In the rural forest the increasing importance of non-farm self-employment activities has also played a part, but much more important factors appear to have been the increasing returns to cocoa cultivation and a large inflow of remittances. Fast growth in these sectors is consistent with national accounts data. Other areas of the country benefited much less, if at all, from these generally favorable effects. This is partly because of the concentration of many export activities in the rural forest zone, and due to the importance of increasing incomes in Accra and increasing imports over this period (imported in the south of the country) in contributing to the growth in trading and transport activities.

## Conclusions

The period between 1991/92 and 1998/99 in Ghana was characterized by less consistent growth in per capita incomes than in the previous decade, as well as high and volatile inflation. Notwithstanding this, there is quite robust evidence for a reduction in monetary measures of poverty at the national level over this period, as well as improvements in most non-monetary dimensions of wellbeing.

A careful analysis though shows that the significant improvements have been largely been confined to only a few groups. Poverty reduction is particularly apparent over this period in Accra and the rural forest where average income levels have increased and inequality has fallen. By contrast in the rest of Ghana poverty and average incomes have changed little, and inequality has tended to increase. These geographic differences tend to cut across economic activity categories. Thus, the poorest group, food farmers, experienced little change in their living conditions in the coastal and savannah zones, but quite large reductions in poverty in the rural forest zone. Those engaged in non-farm self employment experienced large improvements in their living conditions in Accra, but not in some other regions.

This pattern of poverty change is entirely consistent with macroeconomic performance over this period, and in particular the sectoral pattern of growth. In the localities where poverty has fallen several different economic activities appear to have gained notably cocoa; fishing; forestry and logging; transport storage and communication; and wholesale and retail trade. Others, including the non-export agricultural sector where large numbers of the poor are concentrated, grew slowly or not at all. In Accra poverty reduction was associated primarily with increased income from non-farm self-employment activities, notably trading, and with increased numbers of households working in these activities. In the rural forest poverty reduction has been associated with increased income from cocoa (reflecting partly past planting decisions and favourable prices), but also increased receipts of remittance income, including from Accra. The latter has been an important factor behind the poverty reduction among food farming households in the rural forest. By contrast food farming households in the rural coastal and Savannah have benefited received much smaller inflows of remittances, and this is one important factor accounting for the differential poverty reduction experiences.

The pattern that emerges over this period is one of an increasing concentration of monetary poverty in initially poorer or less well endowed regions of Ghana, in particular in the three northern regions of the savannah zone.[17] This region has clearly benefited much less from what growth there was. Indeed some groups in the north appear to have

---

17. The southern parts of the savannah zone, more accurately the transition zone, did experience some poverty reduction over this period.

lost in absolute terms. The coastal zone has also experienced economic stagnation over this period, notwithstanding its greater proximity to Accra. This all strongly suggests that large numbers of households in the rural coastal and savannah zone are in a situation of chronic or persistent poverty, even if this cannot be proved formally here in the absence of panel data. Such households have failed to benefit from a pattern of (modest) growth associated particularly with the cocoa sector and trading activities in Accra, and the associated flow of remittances, and this is reflected in the overall increase in inequality over this period. Additional or different policies are likely to be required to lead to poverty reduction in these persistently poor regions, because the spillover effects of growth in richer regions to poorer regions seem to be small, as do those between rich and poor within regions.

Offsetting this though, the pattern in non-income indicators has not been spatially differentiated in the same way, and sometimes poorer regions have seen faster improvements (if from a lower initial base). This may have potential benefits for future growth. However, the general deterioration of health indicators over this period (partly reflecting a reduction of public spending and the introduction of charging) is a matter of considerable concern, in and of itself and for its implications for vulnerability and future growth.

Furthermore, there must be some concern about the sustainability of the poverty reduction that has occurred over this period, given what appear to be the important driving factors, many of which appear sensitive to the macroeconomic environment (which has a history of instability in Ghana), or to international conditions. Cocoa farmers in the forest zone have benefited from increased investment due to new planting, but remain vulnerable to fluctuations in the world price and to inelastic world demand. Households that have received significant inflows of remittances are obviously very dependent on the income levels of the remitting household. In Accra trading has been a major source of increased income, but such households are rather dependent on levels of demand. Over this period there has not been very much evidence of increased agricultural production (except perhaps cocoa) or the emergence of a significant private sector in urban areas. This raises concerns both about long term growth prospects and about how broadly based future growth is likely to be in Ghana.

## References

Appiah, K., S. G. Laryea-Adjei, and L. Demery. 2000. "Poverty in a Changing Environment." In E. Aryeetey, J. Harrigan, and M. Nissanke (eds), *Economic Reforms in Ghana: The Miracle and the Mirage.* Oxford: James Currey.

Beaudry, P., and N. K. Sowa. 1994. "Ghana." In S. Horton, R. Kanbur, and D. Mazumdar (eds), *Labour Markets in an Era of Adjustment Vol. 2: Case Studies.* Washington D.C.: World Bank.

Coulombe, H., and A. McKay. 1995. "An Assessment of Trends in Poverty in Ghana, 1988–92." PSP Discussion Paper No. 81, Poverty and Social Policy Department, The World Bank, Washington D.C.

———. 2000. "Assessing the Robustness of Changes in Poverty in Ghana over the 1990s." World Bank and UK Department for International Development. Processed.

———. 2003. "Selective Poverty Reduction in a Slow Growth Environment: Ghana in the 1990s." Paper prepared for the World Bank Human Development Network and presented at ISSER-Cornell International Conference on Ghana at the Half Century, Accra, July 2004.

―――. 2006. "With a Little Help from My Friends . . . The Role of Remittances in Poverty Reduction in Ghana." In Q. Wodon, editor, *Migration, Remittances, and Poverty: Case Studies for Sub-Saharan Africa.* Washington, D.C.: The World Bank.

Coulombe, H. Forthcoming. "Ghana Census-based Poverty Map: District and Sub-District level Results." In Ernest Aryeetey and Ravi kanbur (eds.), Ghana at the Half Century. Oxford: James Currey.

Cowell, F. A. 1995. *Measuring Inequality.* Second ed. Hemel Hempstead: Prentice Hall/Harvester Wheatsheaf.

Datt, G., and M. Ravallion. 1992. "Growth and redistribution components of changes in poverty measures: A decomposition with applications to Brazil and India in the 1980s." *Journal of Development Economics* 38(2):275–295.

Demery, L., S. Chao, R. Bernier, and K. Mehra. 1995. "The Incidence of Social Spending in Ghana." Poverty and Social Policy Working Paper No. 82, The World Bank, Washington, D.C.

Ghana Statistical Service. 1995. *The Pattern of Poverty in Ghana, 1988–1992.* Accra, Ghana.

―――. 2000a. *Poverty Trends in Ghana in the 1990s.* Accra, Ghana.

―――. 2000b. "The Estimation of Components of Household Incomes and Expenditures: A Methodological Guide Based on the Ghana Living Standards Survey, 1991/92 and 1998/99." Accra, Ghana.

Lawson, A., and G. Salpietro. 2000. Government Revenue, User Charges and their Incidence in Ghana. Report to Danish Ministry of Foreign Affairs and Development Cooperation, Oxford Policy Management, Oxford, UK.

Litchfield, J. A. 1999. "Inequality: Methods and Tools." Available at: http://www.world-bank.org/poverty/inequal/index.htm

McKay, A. 2000. "Should the Survey Aim to Measure Total Household Income?" In M. Grosh and P. Glewwe, eds., *Designing Household Survey Questionnaires for Developing Countries: Lessons from Fifteen Years of LSMS Experience.* The World Bank and Oxford University Press.

Norton, A., E. Bortei-Doku Aryeetey, D. Korboe, and D. K. T. Dogbe. 1995. "Poverty Assessment in Ghana using Qualitative and Participatory Research Methods." PSP Discussion Paper No. 83, The World Bank, Washington, D.C.

Ravallion, M., and B. Bidani. 1994. "How Robust is a Poverty Profile?" *World Bank Economic Review* 8(1):75–102.

Theil, H. 1967. *Economics and Information Theory.* Amsterdam: North Holland.

World Bank. 1995. "Ghana: Poverty Past, Present and Future." Report No. 14504-GH, The World Bank, Washington D.C.

―――. 1998. "Report and Recommendation of the President of the International Development Association to the Executive Directors on a Proposed Economic Reform Support Operation Credit of SDR 37.1 Million to the Republic of Ghana." Report No. P-7247 GH, The World Bank, Washington, D.C.

―――. 1999. "Report and Recommendation of the President of the International Development Association to the Executive Directors on a Proposed Second Economic Reform Support Operation Credit of SDR 132.7 Million (US$ 180 Million Equivalent) to the Republic of Ghana." Report No. P-7311 GH, The World Bank, Washington, D.C.

# CHAPTER 3

# Has Growth in Senegal After the 1994 Devaluation Been Pro-Poor?*

By Jean-Paul Azam, Magueye Dia, Clarence Tsimpo, and Quentin Wodon

*The devaluation of the CFA Franc in 1994 generated a public investment boom in Senegal. The increase in public investment was made possible thanks to an improved budgetary situation related to the reduction in real terms of the public wage bill which had been too large for some time. The rise in public investment was subsequently accompanied by a (smaller) increase in private investment due in part to the attractiveness of Senegal as a place to do business within West Africa, at least compared to other West African nations. In turn, higher public, and to some extent private, investment led to higher growth rates and substantial poverty reduction, with the share of the population living in poverty declining from 67.9 to 57.1 percent. Poverty in urban areas was reduced faster than in rural areas, as most of the investment benefited the manufacturing and services sectors. Also, a few years of poor rainfall in the second half of the 1990s coupled with an initial drop in the real prices of crops in the aftermath of the devaluation affected negatively rural incomes. As a result, while virtually all segments of the population (including the rural poor) benefited from improved standards of living in 2001 as compared to 1994, growth was not strictly speaking "pro-poor" because the growth in consumption per equivalent adult in the upper half of the distribution was larger than that observed among the poor.*

Senegal has witnessed a fairly high level of growth over the last decade, which has led to a substantial reduction in poverty (Siaens, Sylla, Toure, and Wodon 2005). This paper analyzes Senegal's growth experience, with a focus on its impact on the poor. Beside some special features of the country by African standards (including a higher level of

*This paper was prepared as part of a global study on pro-poor growth managed by Louise Cord at the World Bank. The authors gratefully acknowledge support from AFD (Agence Française de Développement), as well as comments from Jacques Morisset. The views expressed here are those of the authors and need not reflect those of the World Bank, its Executive Directors or the countries they represent.

urbanization and a lower share of agriculture in GDP), Senegal's economic features reflect largely those of the other countries belonging to the West African Economic and Monetary Union (UEMOA in French). The major macroeconomic event that took place in the UEMOA countries was the 1994 devaluation of the CFA Franc, their common currency unit. In many respects, this event draws a clear dividing line between a "before" and an "after" for the affected countries, two periods characterized by a very different macro-economic adjustment strategy. Nationally representative household survey data available for 1994/95 and 2001 enable us to assess whether the growth performance observed after the devaluation has been pro-poor or not.

Senegal's economy shares some of the features of the Sahelian countries, like its agriculture dominated by groundnut exports, and frequent droughts. However, its coastal position gives it a definite advantage for industrial development. It is the closest Sub-Saharan African economy to the main European markets by sea. This has also given rise to a long tradition of out-migration, with a resulting large inflow of remittances (Manchuelle 1997). Hence, many non agricultural sources of income have allowed this country to be one of the most urbanized one in Africa, with almost 50 percent of its population living in the urban sector. Its capital city, Dakar, was the capital city of the French AOF (Afrique Occidentale Française) in the colonial days, and still plays a prominent role in the UEMOA. It hosts in particular the headquarters of the BCEAO (Central Bank of West African States).

Being a medium-sized country by the standards of West Africa, Senegal reflects the evolutions of the UEMOA economies, as far as its macroeconomic experience is concerned, without affecting them much in return. At the same time, its relatively high level of industrial development and of urbanization give this country some relevant idiosyncratic features. In particular, in contrast to many neighboring countries, agriculture plays here a secondary role in determining growth, while manufacturing and services are playing a central part.

Another characteristic of Senegal is the fact that it is the most democratic country of the region, with competitive elections taking place on schedule with very limited violence (Ka and Van de Walle 1994; Azam, Dia, and N'Guessan 2002). The first two presidents after independence, Leopold Senghor and Abdou Diouf were members of the socialist party. However, the latter was a more technocratic "modernizer" than the poet-president Senghor, whose development strategy was more focused on cementing national unity than on the development of an efficient economy. Until 1993, the ballot was not really secret, and a lot of social pressure were exerted on the voters, especially in the groundnut basin (Schaffer 1998). There, the Mouride brotherhood was controlling the votes, and benefited from a long-lasting relationship with the government (Boone 2003). The re-introduction of the secret ballot in 1993 improved the working of the democratic institutions. The last presidential elections saw the replacement of the socialist Abdou Diouf by the liberal Abdoulaye Wade, who took over in April 2000.

The only serious stain on the democratic reputation of the Senegalese government since independence has been the problem of lower Casamance (Boone 2003). This region is predominantly peopled by an ethnic minority, the Diola, whose social system is very different from the hierarchical Sahelian social organization characteristic of the other ethnic groups. The latter is based on a typical caste system, with a well-defined ruling elite. The numerically dominant Wolof group is already marginally different from the typical Sahelian type. Their religious leaders have overthrown the traditional aristocracy in the course of the

18th century, giving rise to the current domination by the Sufi brotherhoods. Yet the Diola, like the smaller groups also present in the area, are radically different. They have no traditional hierarchy, and are resisting any type of authority. The Muslim brotherhoods, which play a crucial role in the political control of the rest of the country, are powerless in this region. There is thus no basis on which the typical African system of political management, relying on the co-optation of the traditional elite into the government-sponsored system, can be grafted onto such an ethnic group (Boone 2003). The attempts made by the different governments in Dakar to control administratively this area, with an increasing military presence, ended up in a low-intensity civil war. Many civilians were killed by both sides in the 1980s and 1990s. Hence, this potentially rich region, fit for export agriculture as well as for tourism and fishery, has remained relatively under-developed. A peace agreement has however been signed in March 2001, but lower Casamance is the region of Senegal with the highest incidence of poverty (République du Sénégal 2004).

Figure 3.1 depicts the growth experience of Senegal over the last three decades or so. Three phases can clearly be identified: (i) the instability phase, until 1984, (ii) the "real-side" structural adjustment phase, 1985–93, and (iii) the post-devaluation boom. The devaluation was a clear success from a macroeconomic viewpoint, as it entailed a significant turnaround from low and unstable growth to a sustained boom. The instability phase that preceded the devaluation was by contrast marked by a series of external shocks, including the groundnuts and phosphates boom, in the wake of the 1974 oil shock (Azam and Chambas 1999). The subsequent downturn was punctuated by two severe drought periods, in 1978 and in 1983–84, as well as by the world recession of 1980–81. Although Senegal implemented a first stabilization plan as early as 1979, with some support from the Bretton Woods institutions, it is not until 1985 that the government got seriously involved in the adjustment effort (Rouis 1994; Ka and Van de Walle 1994). Moreover, a serious banking crisis occurred all across the UEMOA in 1987 and 1988, which seems to have given a "wake-up call" to the political elite of the Zone, entailing the emergence of a genuine

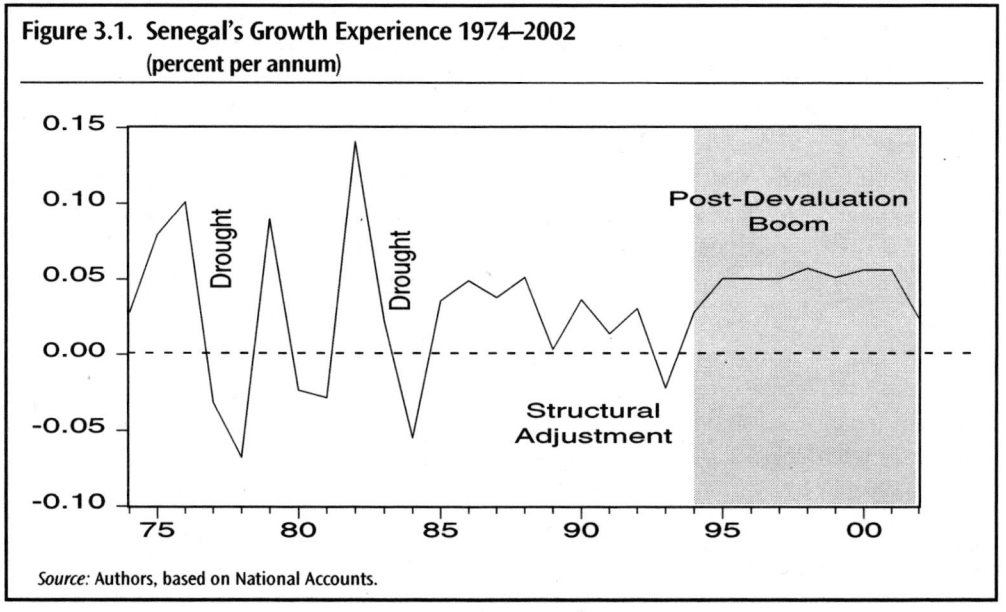

**Figure 3.1. Senegal's Growth Experience 1974–2002**
(percent per annum)

*Source:* Authors, based on National Accounts.

"ownership of reforms" in some of these countries (Azam, Biais, and Dia 2004). As a result, structural adjustment really got started in Senegal in the late 1980s, and included among other reforms the privatization of several parastatals (Azam, Dia, and N'Guessan 2002).

In most countries of the CFA Zone, before the 1994 devaluation, the main problem of the "real-side" adjustment policy (i.e. without changing the exchange rate) was the inability of the governments to cut significantly their wage bills. The wages and salaries of the civil servants and the public sector employees have been cut only in some countries, during that period, and only by a marginal percentage. The high level of these wages was correctly perceived as the main adjustment problem by many analysts (for example, van de Walle 1991; Azam 1995; Rama 2000). This problem had two important dimensions. One was that the government wage bill was then consuming an excessive share of fiscal resources, while these wages were also exerting a strong influence on those of the formal sector. For example, the wage rates in the civil service and the public sector may play a leading role in the determination of the cost of labor for the whole formal sector, thus affecting significantly its competitiveness.

Unfortunately, while reforms were seriously starting in some of the countries of the Zone, the terms of trade of the most important CFA economies deteriorated markedly, and for several years from 1987 onward (Azam 1997). In particular, the terms of trade of Côte d'Ivoire deteriorated severely, with a depressing influence on the whole UEMOA area (then UMOA). The early 1990s thus witnessed a relatively disappointing growth experience, which ended up in a serious recession in 1993, affecting more or less the whole UEMOA zone. Together with some uninspired policy decisions, which are spelt out in Azam (1997), this made the 1994 devaluation unavoidable. The latter had been postponed for a long period, and was largely anticipated by the relevant agents in the area.

As shown econometrically by Azam and Wane (1999), the devaluation had little impact on relative consumer prices. Figure 3.2 depicts the real prices of food, clothing and transport and other services in Dakar, in logarithm. Taken together, these prices account for 79.8 percent of the basket of goods included in the CPI. This graph provides a mixed picture of the effects of the devaluation on relative prices. There is some evidence of real depreciation, if one regards clothing as a non traded good. Then, we observe an increase in the real price of food, a tradable good, by a few percentage points. There is a more sizable fall in the real prices of transport, more or less representative of the non tradable service sector, by about 10 percent. A similar fall had taken place just before the devaluation. However, the real price of clothing goes even further down, by more than 10 percent, while it is hard to believe that this is really a non traded good.[18] Moreover, the transport index is in fact mainly comprised of public transports, which account for 40 percent of this item. The data show that this is the price that mainly lagged behind inflation, because it was fully controlled. Lastly, one observes a convergence of the food and transportation indexes at the end of the period, suggesting that the change in relative consumer prices was over at the end of the fourth year after the devaluation. Hence, the examination of these real prices suggests that too much confidence on a growth story emphasizing real exchange rate adjustment would be unwarranted. Moreover, because the relative consumer price changes are at best of short duration, they cannot explain the longer stretch of growth during the post-devaluation boom.

---

18. May be the trading margins are the dominant component of the price of clothing, explaining this real fall. However, the clothes "made in Sandaga," the Dakar clothes-producing informal sector, can be found all over West Africa.

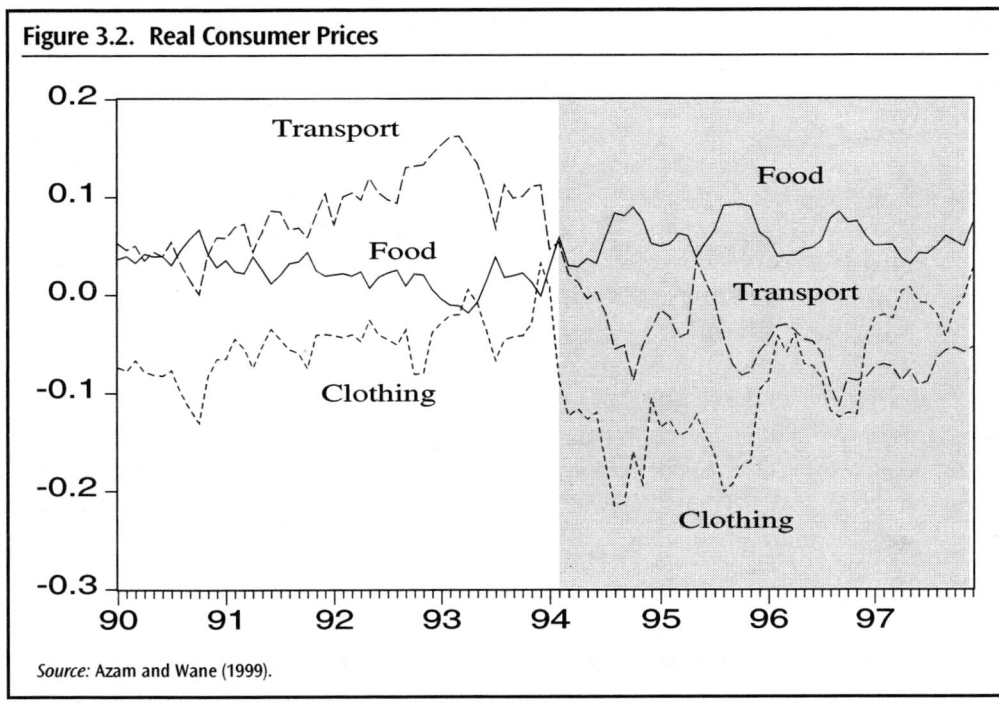

**Figure 3.2. Real Consumer Prices**

*Source:* Azam and Wane (1999).

Much more significant is the change in real wages and salaries in the formal sector. The main effect of the devaluation was indeed a highly significant cut in the real wage rates in the formal sector. The formal-sector wage cut may have led to a deterioration in the poverty situation of urban areas (Azam 2004; Azam, Dia, Tsimpo, and Wodon 2005), as has been the case in Côte d'Ivoire and Niger. However, the survey data for Senegal used in this paper do not allow a thorough analysis of the dynamics of poverty before and after the devaluation at the national level, because the two high-quality surveys available were both implemented after the devaluation, in 1994/95 (ESAM 1) and in 2001 (ESAM 2).

Still, we can analyze the impact on poverty of the growth spur that took place after the devaluation, and analyze whether this post-devaluation boom was pro-poor or not. As shown in Figure 3.1, the post-devaluation boom was remarkably long lasting. In particular, together with Benin, another democratic regime among the UEMOA countries, Senegal did not experience the recession of the year 2000 that plagued the economies of the zone.

In the next section, we provide general background on Senegal's growth experience after the devaluation, suggesting that a public investment boom, made possible by the improved budgetary situation entailed by the devaluation, played a crucial part in boosting growth and keeping it going after 1997. It is only after this additional and lasting impulse was given by the government that private investment picked up (in absolute terms rather than as a share of GDP), turning the post-devaluation boom into a lasting growth episode. Hence, the expected competitive effect of the devaluation did not materialize entirely, as export agriculture did not respond as expected, and its share in GDP shrunk. In the meantime, its fiscal effect played the central part, through the fall in the real value of the government wage bill (nominal wages were not adjusted to reflect the reduction in the value of public servants' pay after the devaluation), which in turn freed the resources that financed the increased public investment. In other words, the devaluation of the CFA Franc in 1994 generated a public investment boom, and this rise in public investment was subsequently accompanied by an increase in private investment (in absolute terms, rather than a share of GDP) due in part to the attractiveness of Senegal as a place to do business within West Africa.

In turn, higher public, and to some extent private, investment led to higher growth rates and substantial poverty reduction, with the share of the population living in poverty declining from 67.9 percent to 57.1 percent. However, as shown in the second section, poverty in urban areas was reduced faster than in rural areas, as most of the investment benefited the manufacturing and services sectors. Also, a few years of poor rainfall in the second half of the 1990s coupled with an initial drop in the real prices of crops in the aftermath of the devaluation probably affected negatively rural incomes. As a result, while virtually all segments of the population (including the rural poor) benefited from improved standards of living in 2001 as compared to 1994, growth was not strictly speaking "pro-poor" because the growth in consumption per equivalent adult in the upper half of the distribution was larger than that observed among the poor. This was observed at the national level as well as within urban areas.

## Patterns of Growth in Senegal After the Devaluation

This section aims at identifying the main determinants of the overall growth observed in Senegal after the devaluation, and the resulting fall in poverty between 1994 and 2001. The analysis starts with a simple sectoral decomposition of GDP growth, which brings out some significant structural change. Berthélemy and others (1996) have shown that the change in the allocation of labor among the different production sectors was the key determinant of aggregate growth in Senegal. The following analysis provides some support to this view.

### Production Sector Effects

As will be discussed in the next section, a particularly good performance towards poverty reduction has been observed in urban areas after the devaluation. In rural areas by contrast, poverty reduction has been reduced to a lower extent, in part because of a fairly irregular growth path of the agricultural and livestock sector. The latter experienced a serious depression in 1997 and 1998, followed by a brisk recovery in 2000 and 2001.

Figure 3.3 shows a decomposition of GDP (at constant 1987 prices, in log) over the 1991–2001 decade. It shows that the tertiary sector, which comprises mainly transportation, commerce and other services, experienced a pretty fast growth since the devaluation. In real terms, several of its component sectors experienced some very fast growth episodes during this period, like transportation for example, which grew by 8.1 percent per annum on average over 1997–2001. This tertiary sector claims more than half of total GDP in this country (nearly 60 percent in fact). It includes also the telecommunication sector, which was profoundly reformed during that period in Senegal, and grew quite fast subsequently (Azam, Dia, and N'Guessan 2002).

Similarly, the secondary sector experienced a fast growth of output after the devaluation. The chart shows that this sector, which comprises mainly industry and construction and public works (in addition to the relatively negligible mining and oil milling sectors),

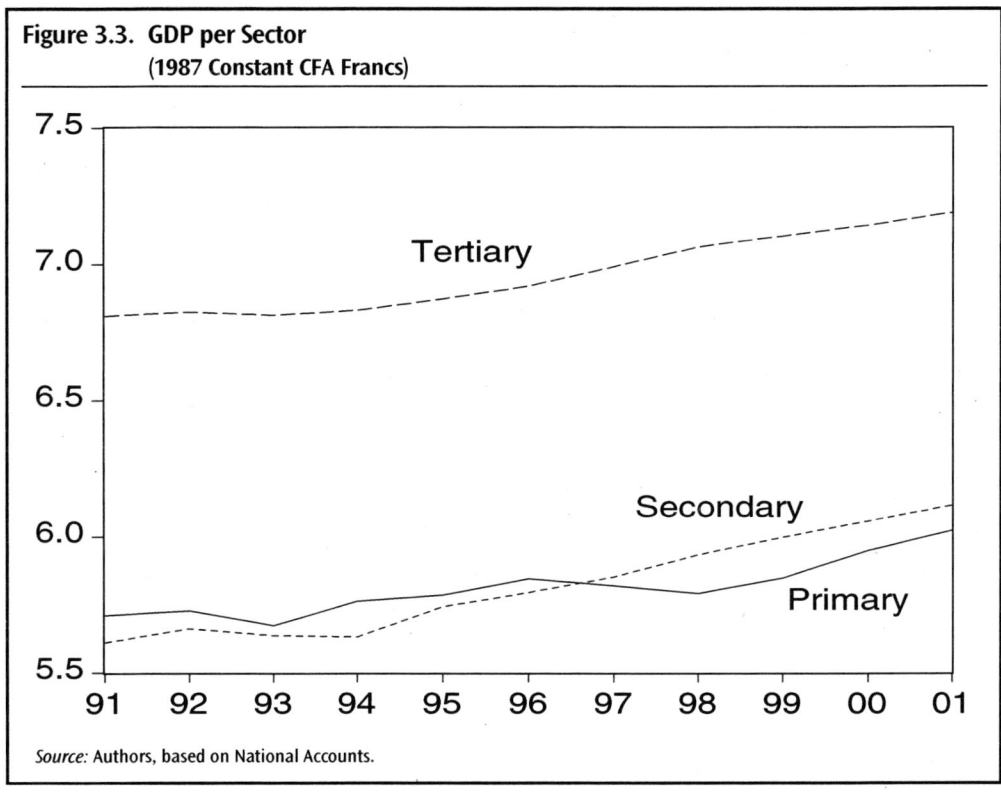

Figure 3.3. **GDP per Sector**
(1987 Constant CFA Francs)

*Source:* Authors, based on National Accounts.

benefited markedly from the devaluation. It experienced two years of negative growth in 1993 and 1994, during and just after the recession that affected the whole UEMOA area, and recovered briskly after that. In fact, its growth was uninterrupted until 2001.

By contrast, the primary sector, mainly agriculture and livestock, experienced a slower growth, and its relative share went down. Its growth rate was negative in 1997 and 1998 (−10.6 percent and −7.4 percent, respectively), while it had a very fast recovery in 2000 and 2001, with two digit growth rates (21.3 percent and 13.8 percent, respectively). These wide fluctuations are largely due to the vagaries of the Sahelian climate, while price effects do not seem to have been very significant determinants of the supply response. This comes out pretty clearly from the following two charts.

Figure 3.4 represents the level of rainfall on three of the main production areas of the groundnut basin. This chart shows clearly that 1992–93 and 1997–98 were pretty dry years, while 2000–01 were exceptionally good years. By contrast, Figure 3.5 shows that producer prices were recovering from the real shock induced by the devaluation during the period 1997–98. This confirms the well-known result in agricultural economics that price effects on agricultural productions are drawn out, while climatic shocks have immediate effects. On the other hand, the income effects of these real price changes are felt immediately by the farmers.[19] Figure 3.5 also shows that the real price of millet, which is not exported on the

19. It is likely that the fall in the real prices of the crops that occurred in 1994 resulted in an increase in poverty in rural areas, and an analysis of the household survey data for 1991 and 1994/95 suggests so. However, the poor quality of the 1991 household survey makes it difficult to have full confidence in the results.

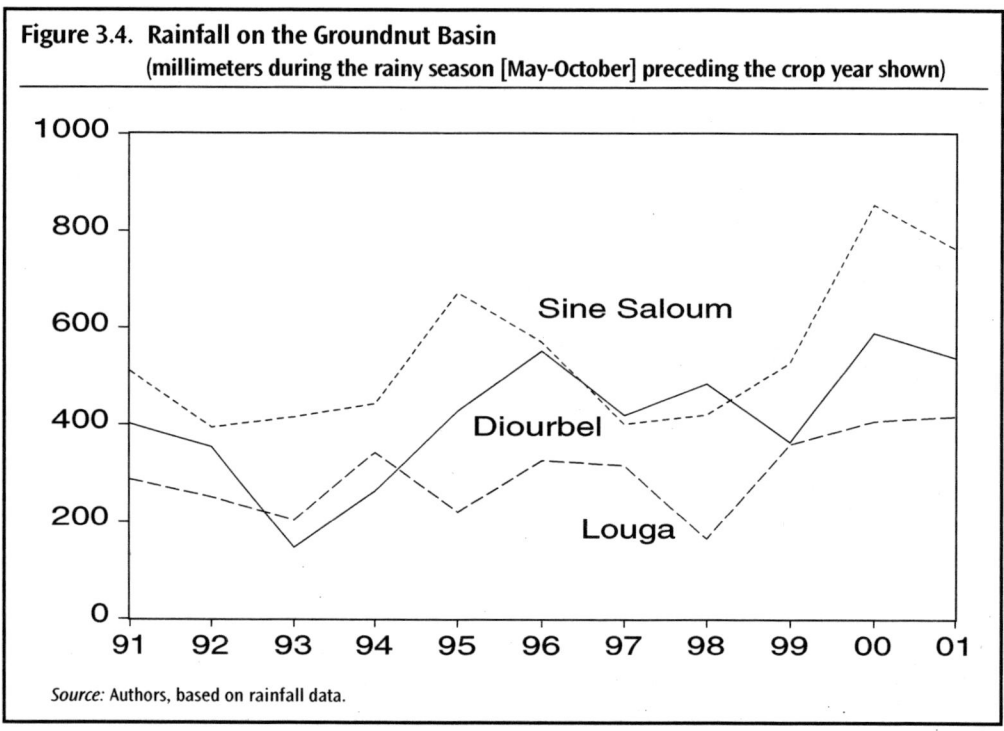

**Figure 3.4. Rainfall on the Groundnut Basin**
(millimeters during the rainy season [May-October] preceding the crop year shown)

*Source:* Authors, based on rainfall data.

international market, except by cross-border trade, fell in 1993, reflecting the recession observed that year for the whole UEMOA. The fall in the real price of the two export crops at the time of the devaluation suggests that the pass-through rate was pretty low, so that the marketing sector benefited most from this policy move, rather than the farmers. In other words, the tertiary sector benefited from an implicit subsidy from the farmers, in the wake of the devaluation. This probably explains to some extent the fast growth of the tertiary sector observed above (see Figure 3.3). Then, real producer prices picked up somewhat, but hardly recovered their pre-devaluation levels. It is only during the drought years that the real price of groundnut went above its pre-1994 level.

To conclude, two factors would suggest that the pace in the reduction in poverty in the rural sector is likely to have been lower than in urban areas after the devaluation. First, the growth rate in the agriculture and livestock sector was lower than in the secondary and tertiary sectors, in part due to bad weather in selected years in the second half of the 1990s. Second, farmers suffered from a drop in real value for their crops after the devaluation. However, the difficulties in rural areas in the few years after of the devaluation did not prevent the country as a whole to experience a high level of growth. It is among others likely that there was a demand-driven migration into the urban areas, where industry and services were thriving, and this could have helped to reduce rural poverty as well. The drought that took place at the end of the century, which revived certainly the memories of the 1970s and 1980s, also provided some incentive for labor to migrate to the more progressive sectors.

These insights are consistent with those of Berthélemy and others (1996) showing that over the period 1961–90, the increase in total factor productivity, which can be estimated using an aggregate production function, is in fact entirely due to the reallocation of labor from the low productivity primary sector to the higher productivity secondary and tertiary sectors. Poverty thus probably fell in the rural sector because the least productive farmers

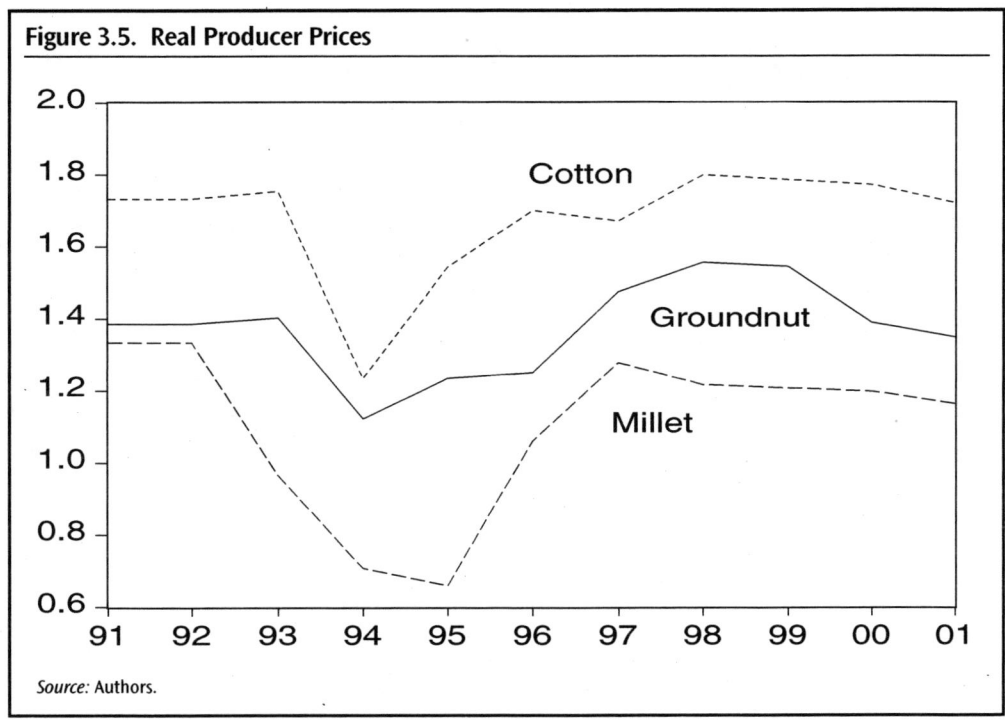

**Figure 3.5. Real Producer Prices**

Source: Authors.

migrated to the cities, where they found higher productivity jobs. Hence, in the case of Senegal, it seems that the rural sector can be viewed as a fairly stagnant reserve of labor, somehow in the spirit of the seminal Lewis model (Lewis 1954). The difference with the latter is that such a diagnosis is true despite the fact that the primary sector is not just a "subsistence sector", but is also exporting a large share of its output. Azam (1993) presents an extension of the Lewis model, motivated by an analysis of Côte d'Ivoire, which brings out the importance for growth of the taxation of the high wages, assumed to accrue to skilled labor, and the productive use of the resulting tax proceeds by the government. The analysis in the next section suggests that the experience of Senegal provides some support to this view, interpreting the outcome of the devaluation as a massive increase in the taxation of the high wages, which was used to boost public investment, with some spillover effects on private investments and a gain in overall growth.

### The Investment Boom

Figure 3.6 shows that the post-devaluation recovery was boosted by a major effort concerning public investment. As a percentage of GDP, it went up from an average share of 4.6 percent of GDP in 1991–93 to an average share of 6.8 percent of GDP over 1996–2001. The resumption of private investment is also quite remarkable, although its time profile is less smooth. It increased from below 10 percent of GDP in 1991–93, to above 10 percent in 1996–2001. It is highly probable that the former played a part in creating the appropriate climate for the latter. The time profile of the private investment share suggests that the devaluation took some time before it elicited a positive response from private investors. This is clearly one of the predictions of the theoretical framework sketched in Azam

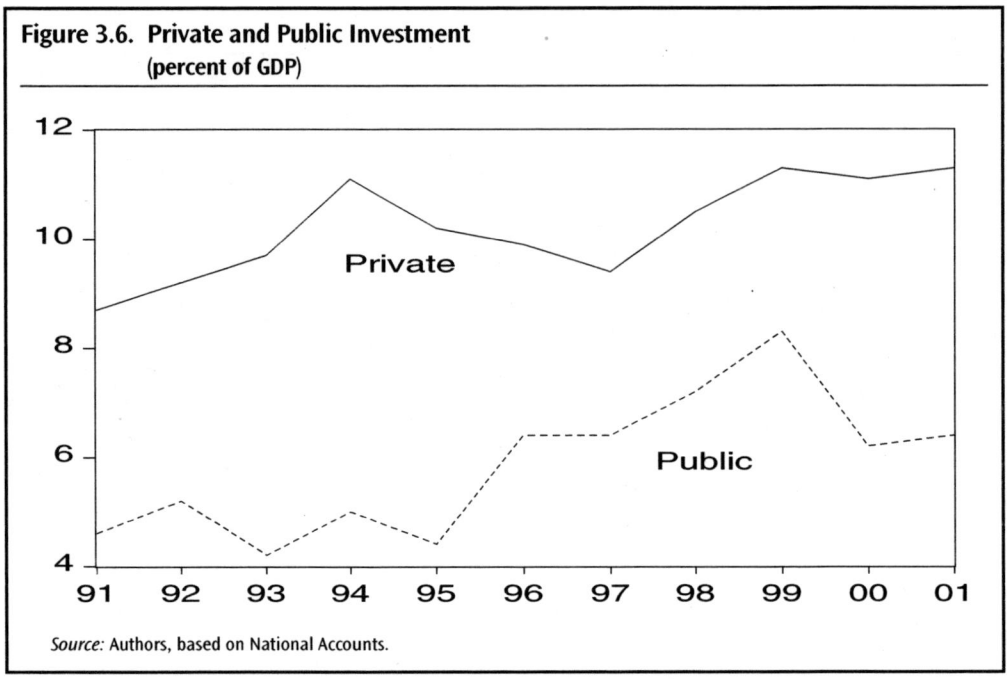

**Figure 3.6. Private and Public Investment**
(percent of GDP)

Source: Authors, based on National Accounts.

(2004). Private saving declines in the wake of the devaluation, and because of the low level of intermediation, this affects private investment simultaneously.

However, other mechanisms have also probably been at work. The pre-devaluation slow growth and recession had probably left quite a lot of productive capacity idle, so that firms had to cut significantly in the latter before the creation of new capital stock became a priority. Moreover, the private sector was also waiting for more information to come about the effects of the devaluation, and about the true intentions of the government regarding the management of the post-devaluation boom. The option value of waiting was then probably enhanced by the unprecedented violence taking place in lower Casamance in 1995. This is epitomized by the disappearance of four French tourists between Ziguinchor and Cap Skirring, widely interpreted as a kidnapping by the Casamance rebellion. The military response to this event triggered a lot of violence all over Casamance, with both civilian and military casualties, followed by a relatively calm period until June 1997.

It seems quite likely that the significant increase in public investment, which occurred from 1996 onward, was the main driver of growth, but it also triggered a private investment recovery. In a financially open economy like Senegal, with a fixed exchange rate, there is no crowding-out effect to be feared, while the demand-boosting and productivity-enhancing effects of public investments are dominant. This central role of public investment, marking the end of a period of falling private investment, does not mean that the devaluation had no useful effect. It means instead that the positive impact took a more roundabout channel than usually expected.

The improved situation of the government budget, and in particular the fall in the real wages of the civil servants and other government employees, triggered by the devaluation, freed some fiscal resources that the government was able to use for investing. This is the main cause of the investment boom described above. The real wage effect was reinforced by a slight fall in the number of civil servants, which fell from 66,696 in 1994 to 65,259 in 2001, so that the civil service wage bill fell from 7.4 percent of GDP in 1994 to 5.2 percent in 2001. However, other policy measures have been adopted by the Senegalese government to create an investor-friendly environment. In particular, the tax burden on firms is lighter than elsewhere in comparable countries.

Although it had a self-proclaimed socialist government ever since independence, until the March 2000 election, Senegal has adopted an investor-friendly policy during the course of the reform period, particularly from the end of the 1980s onward. A wave of privatization took place, mainly in the utilities sector, and sent a good signal to investors (Azam, Dia, and N'Guessan 2002). The main incentive comes from the fiscal burden, which is low by African standards. Table 3.1 represents the scores given to various countries in the UEMOA and its neighborhood by the experts of the Heritage Foundation. This is a composite index that takes into account the highest rate of income tax, as well as the average one, and the most relevant marginal income tax rate for the average tax payer. Additionally, as a check on the credibility of these tax rates, the share of public expenditures in GDP is also taken into account.

Table 3.1 shows that in general, the UEMOA countries have a slightly more favorable score than the comparison countries, which are taken both from North Africa and from non-UEMOA West Africa. Out of these 15 countries, Senegal has by far the best perfor-

**Table 3.1. Fiscal Burden Scores and Maximum Corporate Tax Rate, 2003**

| UEMOA Members | Fiscal Burden Score | Other African Countries | Fiscal Burden Score |
|---|---|---|---|
| Senegal | 2.5 | Gambia | 3 |
| Mali | 3 | Ghana | 3.5 |
| Niger | 3 | Guinea | 3 |
| Togo | 3 | Nigeria | 3.5 |
| Benin | 3.5 | Algeria | 3.5 |
| Burkina Faso | 3.5 | Morocco | 4 |
| Côte d'Ivoire | 3.5 | Tunisia | 4 |
| Guinea-Bissau | 4 | | |

| UEMOA Members | Maximum Corporate Tax Rate (%) | Other African Countries | Maximum Corporate Tax Rate (%) |
|---|---|---|---|
| Senegal | 35 | Gambia | 35 |
| Mali | 35 | Ghana | 32.5 |
| Niger | 42.5 | Guinea | 35 |
| Togo | 40 | Nigeria | 30 |
| Benin | 35 | Algeria | 30 |
| Burkina Faso | 35 | Morocco | 35 (39.6 for banks and insurance) |
| Côte d'Ivoire | 35 | Tunisia | 35 |
| Guinea-Bissau | 35 (50 for oil) | | |

*Note:* The fiscal burden index is coded from 1 (low taxation of profits and incomes) to 5 (high taxation).
*Source:* Heritage Foundation (http://www.heritage.org/research/features/index/), with tax data originally from Ernst & Young 2002 Worldwide Corporate Tax Guide.

mance, even among the UEMOA countries. Hence, the boosting effect of the public investment boom described above was supported by a highly favorable tax framework. As a result
of the investor-friendly climate that the Senegalese government has created over the last
few years of the century, its rating has improved significantly. Since 2001, Senegal is rated
B+ by Standard & Poors, a score that only South Africa and Botswana are also getting in
Sub-Saharan Africa.

Table 3.1 also shows the maximum corporate tax rate among the same group of countries. Most of them have a maximum rate of 35 percent, with the exception of Niger and
Togo, within the UEMOA, which have a slightly higher rate, and the oil producing Algeria
and Nigeria, which have a lower rate aimed at compensating for the "Dutch Disease"
effect due to oil exports, as well as Ghana. The latter is also a coastal country with a potential comparative advantage in non traditional exports, like Senegal, which pursues quite
an aggressive policy aimed at attracting foreign investors.

A further relevant piece of information regarding the investment incentive structure is
provided by Figure 3.7. It shows the ratio of public debt to GDP, which is a major indicator
of macroeconomic stability in the CFA Zone (Azam, 1997). This ratio can be viewed by
investors as a threat of future tax increases, according to the mechanisms described in Cohen
(1993) and Eaton (1993). The intuition for this effect is that a high public debt ratio now
may be regarded by potential investors as entailing a future increase in taxation, for financing the corresponding debt service. This chart clearly shows that the Senegalese government
made a sustained effort for reducing that threat, the so-called "debt overhang" effect, as the
ratio fell from 86.2 in 1994 to 65.8 in 2001. A major dent in this series shows up in 1998,
when Senegal reached a Paris Club agreement worth about CFAF 23 billion. Moreover,

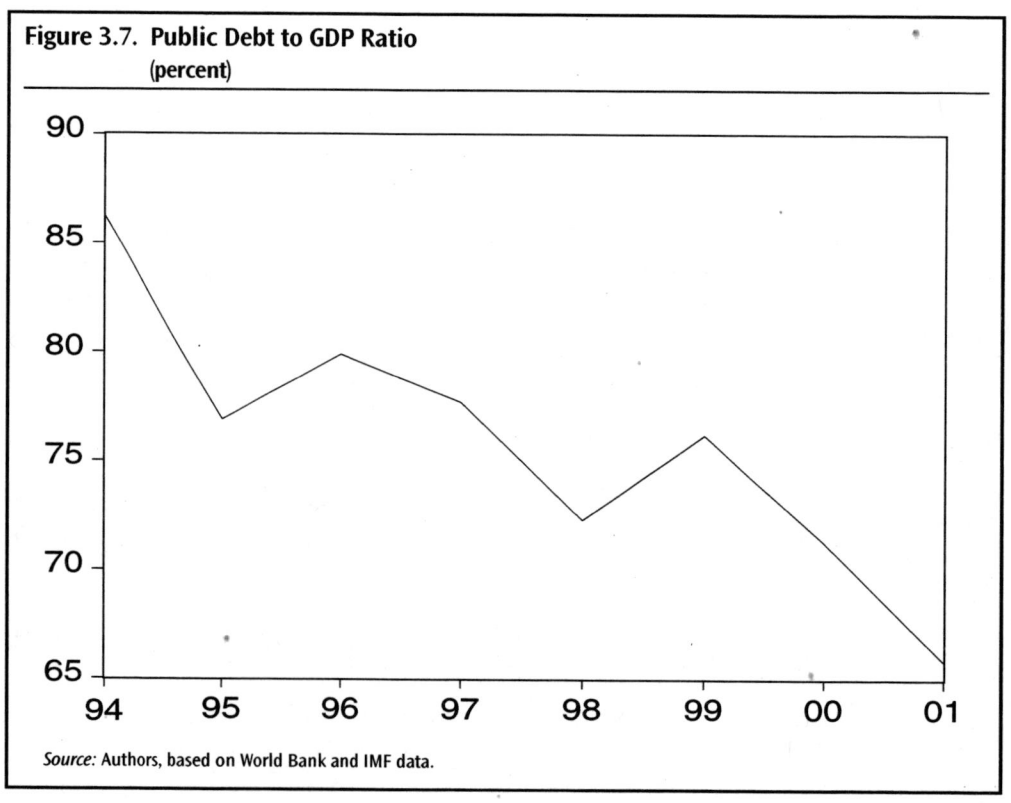

**Figure 3.7. Public Debt to GDP Ratio**
         **(percent)**

*Source:* Authors, based on World Bank and IMF data.

Senegal will benefit from some debt reduction within the HIPC initiative, as decided in June 2000. The latter will be effective only outside the period under analysis, but has probably a positive effect on expectations. All these developments are taking place against a background of sustained reduction of the debt-to-GDP ratio.

Senegal thus comes out as a particularly attractive investment destination among the countries from North and West Africa. It does not seem that the few breaches of privatization contracts have much damaged this country's good reputation. An example is provided by the re-negotiation of the licenses for the mobile telephone operators Alizée and Sentel (see Azam, Dia, and N'Guessan 2002), which ended up in a surcharge being imposed on them. Its attractiveness is also supported unwittingly by Côte d'Ivoire, whose political instability (the 1999 coup d'état, the 2000 uprising, and the civil war as of 2002) has destroyed its own attractiveness. In many ways, Senegal is left as the unique investment opportunity among Francophone countries.

It is also important to note that the sustained growth of the post-devaluation boom was not hampered by a shortage of human capital. Berthélemy and others (1996) have a fairly negative diagnosis about the education policy pursued by Senegal between independence and the early 1990s. Yet, they acknowledge that the enrollment rate has increased massively. Between 1960 and 1990, it went from 22 percent to 57 percent in 1990, as far as primary education is concerned, from 2 percent to 16 percent, in secondary education. They estimate, however, that the quality of education is poor and deteriorating, and not fitted for sustaining economic development. They criticize in particular the Senegalese education policy for putting too much emphasis on classical education. By contrast, Diagne and others (2002) estimate that human capital was not a brake on the resumption of growth after the devaluation. They find a positive and nearly significant impact of enrolment in primary education on growth, with a nine-year lag. This effort has not been reduced during the post-devaluation boom, and the gross rate of enrolment went from 54.3 percent in 1993 to 69 percent in 2000 (Loum 2001).

## Poverty Reduction Between 1994 and 2001

The discussion of the previous section suggests that poverty reduction is likely to have been larger in Senegal's urban areas after the devaluation. This section tests this hypothesis by providing measures of poverty for Senegal for the survey years 1994/95 and 2001. The overall poverty measures and the measurement methodology follow the work by Siaens and others. (2005), which was used in a recent report prepared jointly by the Republic of Senegal and the World Bank (2005). In addition, we provide poverty measures for various groups of households. Then, in the second subsection below, we analyze whether Senegal's growth experience has been pro-poor. Not surprisingly, we find that growth was not strictly speaking pro-poor, even though the poor did benefit a lot from growth. Finally, we briefly comment on the perceptions of poverty of the population, again drawing on work by Siaens and others (2005).

### Poverty Trend

We restrict here our attention to the family of decomposable poverty measures, which allow the partitioning of the population according to various criteria, while providing a consistent set of poverty measures for each group in such partitions. This approach provides some deeper insights into the changes in poverty, by bringing out the change in poverty occurring within some selected groups, deemed relevant because of the criteria used for partitioning (socio-economic categories, gender, and so forth).

Two main classes of decomposable poverty measures have emerged from the literature. The most widely used is the so-called FGT measure, due to Foster and others (1984). Denote by $y_i$ the consumption level per equivalent adult of household i, and assume that the individuals are ordered by increasing income, and denote by z the poverty line. Household i's consumption gap may be defined as the percentage shortfall of consumption level below the poverty line: $G_i = (z - y_i)/z$. More generally, the FGT measures are given by:

$$P_\alpha = \left(\frac{1}{n}\right)\sum_{i=1}^{q}\left(\frac{z-y_i}{z}\right)^\alpha \tag{1},$$

where n is the size of the population, q the index identifying the individual whose consumption level lies just on the poverty line, and $\alpha$ is a parameter capturing the analyst's concern for the depth of poverty. If $\alpha = 0$ is chosen, then this index is just the head-count index $H = q / n$. If $\alpha = 1$ is chosen instead, the poverty measure that we get is the product of the head-count index by the average consumption gap among the poor $H\bar{G}$, where $\bar{G} = \sum_{i=1}^{q} G_i/q$. This index thus takes into account not only the incidence of poverty, but its average depth also. More emphasis can be put on the depth of poverty by weighing each individual's consumption shortfall by itself, that is, by choosing $\alpha = 2$. These three measures are computed for Senegal in Table 3.3 for 1994 and 2001, and are respectively presented under the headings FGT0 (head-count), FGT1 (consumption gap) and FGT2 (distribution sensitive).

Another decomposable poverty measure has been re-discovered recently, originally created by Watts (1968). This Watts measure is:

$$W = \left(\frac{1}{n}\right)\sum_{i=1}^{q}\log\left(\frac{z}{c_i}\right) \tag{2}.$$

By using a Taylor expansion of $\log c_i$ about z, up to the third order, one can show that $W \cong FGT1 + (1/2)FGT2 + (1/6)FGT3$, suggesting that the Watts measure is in fact highly sensitive to the distribution of income among the poor.

Table 3.2 presents the results of the computations of these different poverty measures for Senegal in 1994 and in 2001. As mentioned earlier, the poverty lines used are the "official" ones computed for the Direction de la Prévision et de la Statistique and the World Bank by Siaens and others (2005). They are defined according to the "cost of basic needs" approach (using a fixed basket of goods, the same one in 1994 and 2001). Three different poverty lines have been defined in order to take account of the differential cost of living in Dakar, the other urban areas, and the rural sector, respectively. In all the decompositions presented in Table 3.3, each household's consumption shortfall has been computed using the relevant poverty line, depending on the household's location.

Table 3.3 shows that the growth observed after the devaluation had a dramatic impact towards the reduction of poverty. At the national level, the head-count index decreased from 67.8 percent in 1994/95 to 57.1 percent in 2001, which represents a reduction in the

**Table 3.2. Mean Consumption, Poverty, and Inequality Measures, Senegal 1994/95 and 2001**

| | 1994/95 | | | |
| --- | --- | --- | --- | --- |
| | **Dakar** | **Urban** | **Rural** | **National** |
| Sample size (number of households) | 1,098 | 865 | 1,313 | 3,276 |
| Mean consumption per person | 1,177.3 | 697.4 | 387.4 | 632.4 |
| Mean consumption per equivalent adult | 1,416.2 | 857.3 | 495.7 | 781.3 |
| Head-count index | 56.4% | 70.7% | 70.9% | 67.8% |
| Poverty gap | 17.7% | 24.4% | 25.3% | 23.5% |
| Squared poverty gap | 7.4% | 10.8% | 11.7% | 10.6% |
| Watts poverty index | 23.5% | 33.0% | 35.1% | 32.3% |
| Gini index of inequality | 0.3663 | 0.3403 | 0.2934 | 0.3258 |
| | 2001 | | | |
| | **Dakar** | **Urban** | **Rural** | **National** |
| Sample size (number of households) | 1,977 | 1,397 | 3,191 | 6,565 |
| Mean consumption per person | 1,334.0 | 778.2 | 391.1 | 710.3 |
| Mean consumption per equivalent adult | 1,638.8 | 1,034.4 | 538.9 | 919.8 |
| Head-count index | 42.0% | 50.1% | 65.2% | 57.1% |
| Poverty gap | 12.0% | 16.1% | 21.4% | 18.3% |
| Squared poverty gap | 4.7% | 6.9% | 9.4% | 7.9% |
| Watts poverty index | 15.6% | 21.7% | 29.0% | 24.6% |
| Gini index of inequality | 0.3728 | 0.3523 | 0.3011 | 0.3417 |

*Source:* Authors' estimation, following methodology in Siaens and others (2005).

proportion of the population in poverty of 10.8 percentage points (the share of households in poverty decreased similarly, from 61.4 percent to 48.5 percent.) The estimates suggest that poverty measures are much higher in rural areas than in urban areas as expected, and lower in Dakar than in other urban areas. Importantly, poverty decreased more in urban areas than in rural areas, as expected given the discussion in the previous section. The trend for the poverty gap, the squared poverty gap, and the Watts measures are similar to those observed for the head count. Inequality has apparently increased slightly, not only at the national level (again as expected given the more rapid growth in urban centres), but also within urban and rural areas.

In Table 3.3, several partitions of the population are presented, defining the relevant groups according to their sector of activity, their socioeconomic category (type of occupation), location, gender of the household head, and literacy level. It is remarkable, but not surprising given the overall high level of growth in the country, that poverty has fallen in all the groupings so defined over this period. In most cases, the fall in poverty is large, but there are exceptions. First, the reduction in poverty observed for Government employees has been lower than for other groups, probably because Government employees suffered the most from the devaluation (while immediately after the devaluation, corresponding to the period of the first survey in 1994/95, these employees may have been able to maintain high levels of consumption thanks to savings, this ability to cope with

**Table 3.3. Head-count Index of Poverty by Subgroup, Senegal 1994/95 and 2001**

| | WATTS | | FGT 0 | | FGT 1 | | FGT 2 | |
|---|---|---|---|---|---|---|---|---|
| | 1994 | 2001 | 1994 | 2001 | 1994 | 2001 | 1994 | 2001 |
| **Sectir of activity** | | | | | | | | |
| Government | 12.16 | 8.31 | 31.30 | 28.09 | 9.49 | 6.82 | 3.69 | 2.14 |
| Parastatal or Private Company | 33.27 | 16.99 | 70.48 | 43.45 | 24.34 | 12.80 | 10.92 | 5.24 |
| Self-employee or Family Helper | 51.04 | 26.94 | 88.18 | 61.53 | 36.23 | 19.94 | 18.03 | 8.68 |
| Others | 34.23 | 24.20 | 68.18 | 55.96 | 24.42 | 18.14 | 11.48 | 7.72 |
| Unknown | 26.51 | 23.12 | 64.80 | 51.43 | 20.05 | 17.68 | 8.23 | 7.30 |
| **Socio-economic category** | | | | | | | | |
| Self-employed Non-Farming | 29.51 | 24.31 | 69.29 | 56.22 | 22.26 | 18.19 | 9.35 | 7.74 |
| Self-employed Farming | 36.94 | 30.31 | 73.98 | 69.03 | 26.62 | 22.48 | 12.34 | 9.76 |
| Management | 5.71 | 5.19 | 21.06 | 19.24 | 4.78 | 4.27 | 1.39 | 1.31 |
| Intermediary Professions | 10.38 | 6.91 | 32.76 | 19.10 | 8.37 | 5.12 | 2.87 | 2.22 |
| Workers | 36.24 | 23.77 | 74.90 | 56.91 | 26.61 | 17.61 | 12.05 | 7.58 |
| Employees | 9.07 | 7.57 | 27.48 | 23.00 | 7.40 | 6.16 | 2.44 | 2.05 |
| Others | 34.10 | 23.65 | 68.73 | 54.67 | 24.38 | 17.58 | 11.39 | 7.58 |
| **Region** | | | | | | | | |
| Dakar | 23.50 | 15.65 | 56.39 | 41.98 | 17.74 | 12.04 | 7.44 | 4.72 |
| Others Cities | 33.01 | 21.71 | 70.71 | 50.09 | 24.40 | 16.10 | 10.79 | 6.92 |
| All Urban Areas | 27.88 | 18.44 | 62.98 | 45.72 | 20.81 | 13.91 | 8.98 | 5.74 |
| Rural | 35.12 | 28.95 | 70.94 | 65.16 | 25.27 | 21.44 | 11.69 | 9.36 |
| **Gender** | | | | | | | | |
| Male HH | 32.89 | 26.02 | 68.70 | 59.54 | 23.94 | 19.36 | 10.84 | 8.34 |
| Female HH | 28.98 | 17.40 | 63.04 | 44.79 | 21.26 | 13.07 | 9.49 | 5.39 |
| **Literacy** | | | | | | | | |
| Literate | 25.12 | 20.05 | 58.41 | 48.68 | 18.91 | 15.07 | 7.96 | 6.29 |
| Non-Literate | 36.75 | 27.38 | 73.40 | 62.27 | 26.41 | 20.31 | 12.29 | 8.81 |
| Unknown | 19.33 | 23.17 | 61.58 | 47.41 | 14.49 | 17.77 | 5.92 | 7.44 |
| Senegal | 32.30 | 24.60 | 67.83 | 57.10 | 23.53 | 18.32 | 10.63 | 7.86 |

*Source:* Authors' estimation, following methodology in Siaens and others (2005).

the loss in real wages must have faded overtime, leading to higher poverty in this group for a while before it started to benefit as did other groups from the growth observed after the devaluation). The reduction in poverty among households self-employed in farming activities was also limited, probably for the reasons mentioned above, including the impact of poor weather in selected years, the fact that growth was somewhat lower in agriculture than in other sectors, and the fact that it took some time for nominal crop prices to adjust to the devaluation.

Table 3.4 provides decompositions of the changes in poverty due to growth in consumption per equivalent adult and changes in inequality (see Datt and Ravallion 1992 on

**Table 3.4. Growth-Inequality Decomposition of Changes in Poverty, Senegal 1994/95 and 2001**

| | 1994 | 2001 | Change | Growth Component | Redistribution Component | Residual |
|---|---|---|---|---|---|---|
| **Head-count Index of Poverty** | | | | | | |
| National | | | | | | |
| Base year 1994 | | | | −13.15 | 2.03 | 0.39 |
| Base year 2001 | 67.84 | 57.11 | −10.73 | −12.76 | 2.43 | −0.39 |
| Average effect | | | | −12.96 | 2.23 | 0.00 |
| Urban | | | | | | |
| Base year 1994 | | | | −15.45 | −1.25 | −0.56 |
| Base year 2001 | 62.98 | 45.72 | −17.26 | −16.02 | −1.81 | 0.56 |
| Average effect | | | | −15.74 | −1.53 | 0.00 |
| Rural | | | | | | |
| Base year 1994 | | | | −7.59 | 1.41 | 0.4 |
| Base year 2001 | 70.94 | 65.16 | −5.78 | −7.19 | 1.81 | −0.4 |
| Average effect | | | | −7.39 | 1.61 | 0 |
| **Poverty Gap** | | | | | | |
| National | | | | | | |
| Base year 1994 | | | | −7.40 | 2.24 | −0.05 |
| Base year 2001 | 23.53 | 18.32 | −5.21 | −7.45 | 2.19 | 0.05 |
| Average effect | | | | −7.43 | 2.22 | 0.00 |
| Urban | | | | | | |
| Base year 1994 | | | | −7.68 | 0.39 | 0.39 |
| Base year 2001 | 20.81 | 13.91 | −6.90 | −7.29 | 0.78 | −0.39 |
| Average effect | | | | −7.48 | 0.58 | 0.00 |
| Rural | | | | | | |
| Base year 1994 | | | | −4.51 | 0.75 | −0.064 |
| Base year 2001 | 25.27 | 21.44 | −3.83 | −4.58 | 0.68 | 0.064 |
| Average effect | | | | −4.54 | 0.71 | 0 |
| **Squared Poverty Gap** | | | | | | |
| National | | | | | | |
| Base year 1994 | | | | −4.01 | 1.53 | −0.30 |
| Base year 2001 | 10.63 | 7.86 | −2.78 | −4.31 | 1.23 | 0.30 |
| Average effect | | | | −4.16 | 1.38 | 0.00 |
| Urban | | | | | | |
| Base year 1994 | | | | −4.01 | 0.69 | 0.08 |
| Base year 2001 | 8.98 | 5.74 | −3.25 | −3.93 | 0.76 | −0.08 |
| Average effect | | | | −3.97 | 0.72 | 0.00 |
| Rural | | | | | | |
| Base year 1994 | | | | −2.56 | 0.32 | −0.09 |
| Base year 2001 | 11.69 | 9.36 | −2.33 | −2.65 | 0.23 | 0.09 |
| Average effect | | | | −2.61 | 0.27 | 0 |

*Source:* Authors' estimation, following methodology in Siaens and others (2005).

the methodology). As expected, the fact that there was an increase in inequality limited to some extent the reduction in poverty that was obtained through growth. At the national level for example, an additional reduction in the head-count index of poverty of about 2 percentage points would have been obtained if inequality had not increased.

The fact that inequality increased tends to suggest that growth in consumption was higher in the upper part of the distribution. Table 3.5 and Figures 3.8, 3.9 and 3.10 provide an analysis of the extent to which growth did benefit the poor, as summarized by computing the pro-poor growth rate over the post-devaluation period, and presenting the Growth incidence curve (Ravallion and Chen 2003) at the national level and for urban and rural areas. The pro-poor growth rate is computed as the mean growth rate for the poor, or the percentage change in the Watts index of poverty. It can be clearly seen that the rate of growth in the consumption per equivalent adult at the bottom of the distribution has been below that observed for the population as a whole, suggesting that growth has not been strictly speaking pro-poor. This is confirmed by Figures 3.8, 3.9 and 3.10 that provide the growth incidence curves at the national, urban and rural levels. The growth rates in consumption are much lower at the bottom of the distribution than in the upper half of the distribution, confirming that growth has been stronger among better off households (in rural areas, this is not the case for the poorest, but this may be a data issue, and for the poor as a whole, the conclusion remains valid). Of course, the fact that growth was not "pro-poor" does not mean that poverty was not reduced, even among the poor. Rather, the conclusion is simply that proportional gains in consumption after the devaluation were higher for the non-poor than for the poor.

## The Persistence of Perceived Poverty

Despite the remarkable fall in poverty documented above, based on the change in consumption experienced by Senegalese households over 1994–2001, perceived poverty has increased significantly in this country. This result comes out of the EPPS 2001 survey (Enquête sur la

| Table 3.5. Rate of Pro-poor Growth, Senegal 1994/95 and 2001 | | | |
|---|---|---|---|
| | **National** | **Urban areas** | **Rural areas** |
| Growth rate in the mean | 2,59 | 2,90 | 1,46 |
| Growth rate at median | 1,99 | 2,89 | 1,22 |
| Mean percentile growth rate | 2,16 | 2,71 | 1,38 |
| **Head-count index** | **Rate of pro-poor growth** | | |
| 10 | 1,88 | 1,38 | 2,21 |
| 15 | 1,61 | 1,77 | 1,88 |
| 20 | 1,50 | 2,00 | 1,66 |
| 25 | 1,46 | 2,15 | 1,50 |
| 30 | 1,46 | 2,27 | 1,42 |
| 40 | 1,53 | 2,48 | 1,32 |
| 50 | 1,61 | 2,59 | 1,32 |
| 100 | 2,12 | 2,67 | 1,36 |

*Source:* Authors' estimation, following methodology in Siaens and others (2005).

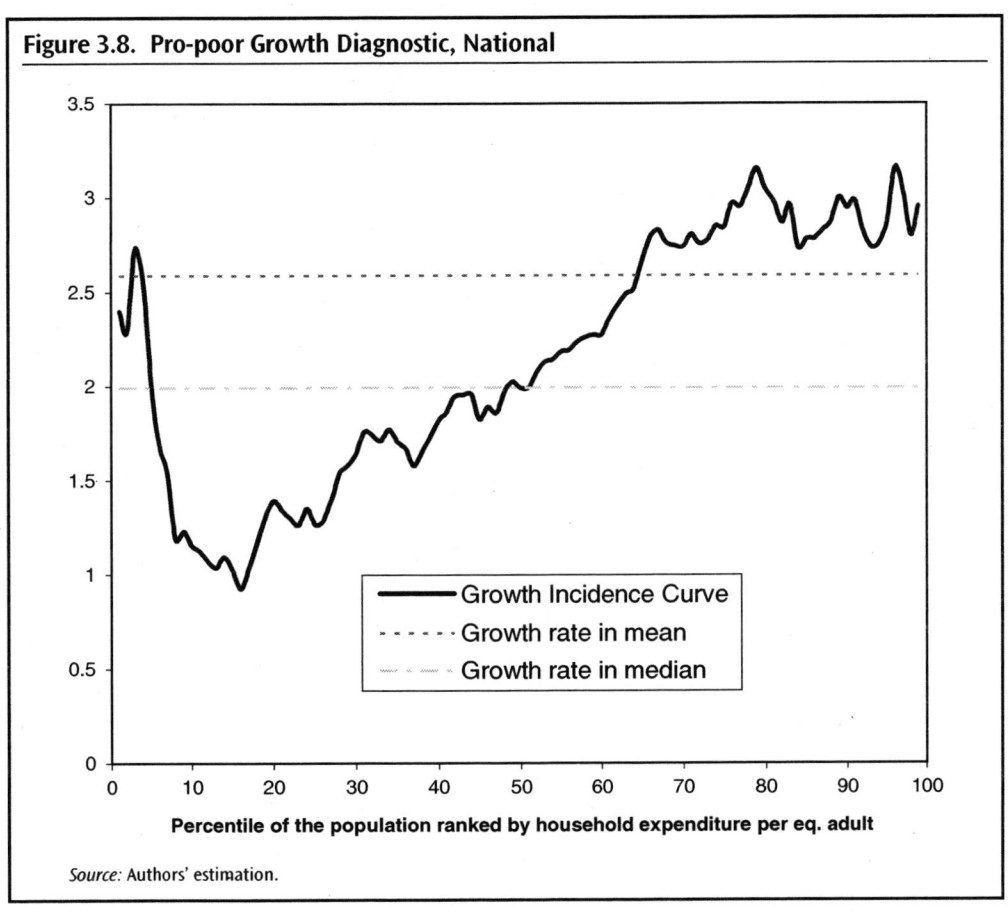

**Figure 3.8. Pro-poor Growth Diagnostic, National**

Percentile of the population ranked by household expenditure per eq. adult

— Growth Incidence Curve
- - - - Growth rate in mean
- - - - Growth rate in median

*Source:* Authors' estimation.

perception de la pauvreté au Sénégal). This is a survey on subjective perceptions of poverty by Senegalese households, which used the same sample as ESAM 2.

Siaens and Wodon (2005) show that a vast majority of the household surveyed did not perceive any improvement in the poverty situation. Indeed more than 85 percent of them estimate that poverty remained stable or deteriorated during the five years preceding the survey. This is particularly noticeable among the "objective" poor or among those who perceive themselves as poor. Almost two thirds of the sample households perceive themselves as poor, which is a proportion of the same order of magnitude as the objective (consumption-based) estimates of poverty. However, the survey shows that these two groups of households are somewhat different, as the overlap between the two categories is imperfect, and a significant share of the objectively poor did not perceive themselves as poor. Note that this imperfect overlap between subjective and objective poverty is not based on a conceptually different view about poverty. Indeed, more than 50 percent of the respondents to the survey consider "the inability to feed one's family" as the main correlate of poverty, which broadly consistent with the consumption-based approach for measuring poverty adjusted by the number of adult equivalent household members used to measure objective poverty.

The data from the EPPS 2001 survey suggests that there is a strong persistence in the perception of poverty. This disconnection between the subjective and the objective changes in poverty has been observed in other West African countries, and it raises a political problem. In a democratic country like Senegal, this disconnection may reduce the incentive faced

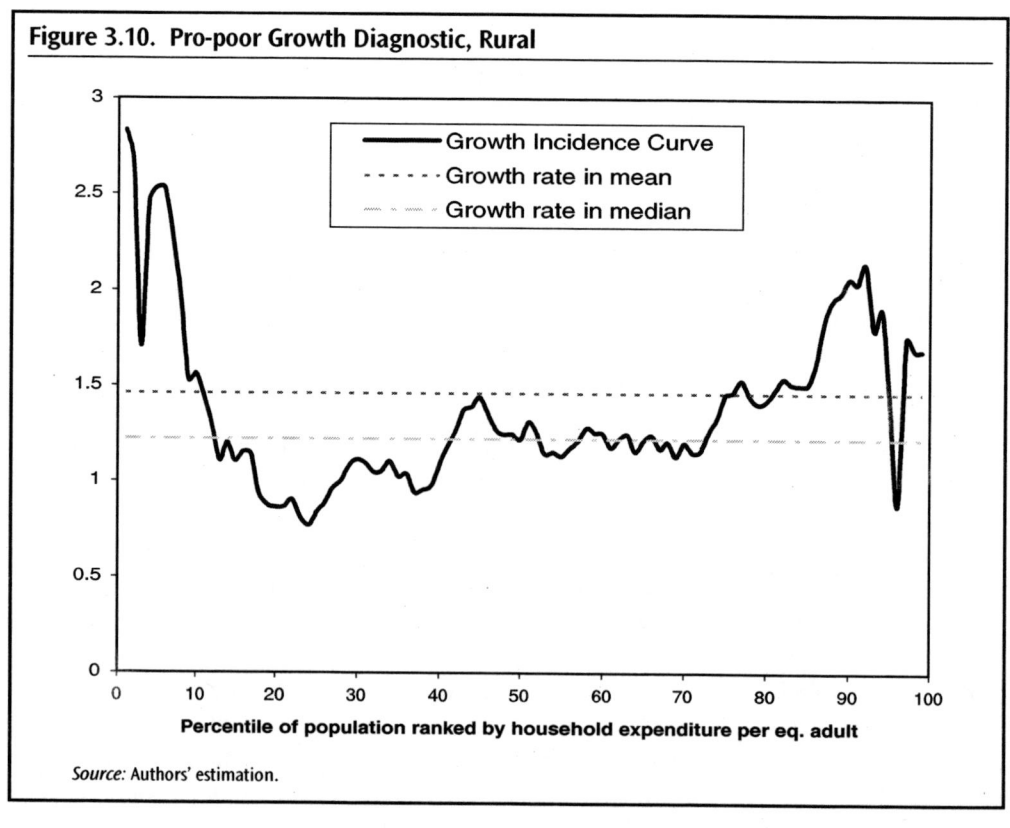

**Figure 3.9. Pro-poor Growth Diagnostic, Urban**

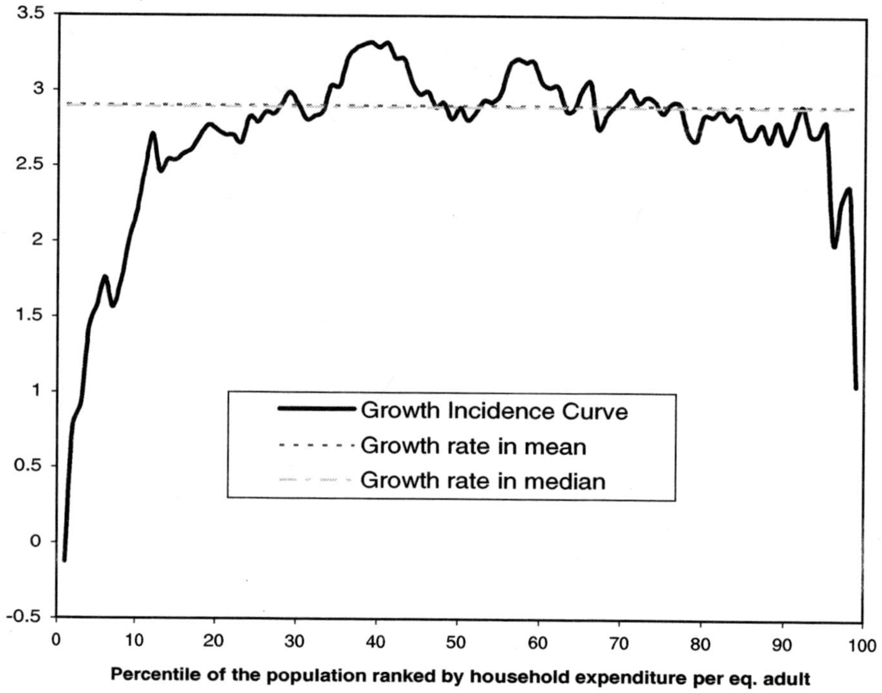

3.5
3
2.5
2
1.5
1
0.5
0
-0.5
0
10
20
30
40
50
60
70
80
90
100
Growth Incidence Curve
Growth rate in mean
Growth rate in median
Percentile of the population ranked by household expenditure per eq. adult

*Source:* Authors' estimation.

**Figure 3.10. Pro-poor Growth Diagnostic, Rural**

3
2.5
2
1.5
1
0.5
0
0
10
20
30
40
50
60
70
80
90
100
Growth Incidence Curve
Growth rate in mean
Growth rate in median
Percentile of population ranked by household expenditure per eq. adult

*Source:* Authors' estimation.

by the government to actively fight poverty, as the resulting improvement may not be correctly perceived as such by the voters. President Diouf, who presided over the implementation of the growth-boosting policy in the late 1990s, was beaten at the March 2000 elections, while a sense of "crisis" was widespread in the electorate. However, nothing proves that the perception by the voters of the absence of a positive change in poverty played any part in determining this outcome.

## Conclusion

In 1994, the devaluation of the CFA Franc in Senegal as in other UEMOA countries led to a drop in the real wages of formal, and especially public sector workers. During the three years following the devaluation, despite the fast recovery of GDP growth, and the fall in the real wage rates in the urban sector, private investment did not pick up. It is only after 1996, when the government used the fiscal resources freed by the reduction in the real value of its wage bill for financing a major increase in public investment that the former picked up. The resulting investment boom stretched out the post-devaluation boom in time, and managed to tide the Senegalese economy over the regional recession of the year 2000. It is during this phase, from 1996 to 2001, that the poverty effect of the accelerated growth must have been the largest, although we cannot check this empirically since we have data only for 1994 and 2001.

The road which led from a cut in the incomes of the rich to an increase in the incomes of the population as a whole was complex. This is probably true also in most countries of the world. The direct impact, which was dominant in the short run but not observed as such in this paper, because we did not have nationally representative survey data prior to the devaluation, entailed a fall in the incomes, especially among formal sector workers, including workers from the public sector. However, the indirect subsequent effect through public and private investment did reduce poverty in the long run. The latter effect is by no means mechanical, and many other governments could have wasted the fiscal windfall created by the devaluation. The bottom line is that poverty reducing growth occurred at the end of the century because the government engineered a sustainable change in the functional distribution of income, from wages to profits. This change was obtained by an increase in public investment and the creation of an "investor-friendly" environment, based on low corporate taxation and low public debt. While the growth observed after the devaluation was not "pro-poor" strictly speaking, all segments of the population benefited from higher standards of living in 2001, as compared to those that prevailed in 1994.

This core lesson of Senegal's growth and poverty reduction experience is simply that investment, both public and private, is the engine of sustained growth, and that profitability and growth themselves boost investment levels. This simple message has been emphasized time and again in the literature (for example, Malinvaud 1980). As the former chancellor of West Germany Helmut Schmit used to say: "The profits of today are the investments of tomorrow and the investments of tomorrow make the employment of the day after tomorrow" (cited in Malinvaud 1980). As poverty reduction may lag by some time behind improvements in profitability and growth, it thus takes a sustained effort in favor of profitability to pull a significant number of people out of poverty. The Senegalese experience shows that devaluation was one of the possible means that could be used for that purpose, acting like a tax on formal sector wages, which had been too high for some time. Senegal's experience also suggests that efficient public investment was quite important, as it was important to cut the public debt overhang and improve the business environment.

These are probably not the only ways that profitability can be supported, and other means to the same end should be sought in different institutional and political settings. The unprecedented stretch of fast economic growth that resulted from this strategy managed to pull a large share of the Senegalese population out of poverty. Unfortunately, from the point of view of the incumbent government, the objective reduction in poverty was not correctly perceived by the voters. This was shown by the survey performed in 2001 on the subjective perception of poverty. Maybe, in a democratic polity like Senegal, one of the political challenges faced by administrations is to find a strategy for reducing the subjective as well as objective perceptions of poverty. More generally, subjective perceptions may matter as much as objectively measured trends in standards of living in order to achieve genuine "ownership" of long-term poverty reduction policies in democratic countries.

## References

Azam, Jean-Paul. 1993. "The 'Côte d'Ivoire' Model of Economic Growth." *European Economic Review* 37:566–76.

———. 1995. "L'Etat auto-géré en Afrique." *Revue d'économie du développement* 1995/4:1–19.

———. 1997. "Public Debt and the Exchange rate in the CFA Franc Zone." *Journal of African Economies* 6(1):54–84.

———. 2004. "Poverty and Growth in the WAEMU after the 1994 Devaluation." *Journal of African Economies* (forthcoming).

Azam, Jean-Paul, Bruno Biais, and Magueye Dia. 2004. "Privatization versus Regulation in Developing Economies: The Case of West African Banks." *Journal of African Economies* 13(3):361–94.

Azam, Jean-Paul, and Gérard Chambas. 1999. "The Groundnuts and Phosphates Boom in Sénégal (1974–1977)." In Paul Collier and Jan Willem Gunning, eds. *Temporary Trade Shocks in Developing Countries, Vol. 1.* Oxford: Oxford University Press.

Azam, Jean-Paul, Magueye Dia, and Tchétché N'Guessan. 2002. "Telecom Sector Reform in Senegal." World Bank Working Paper, WPS 2894 , Washington, D.C. (http://www.worldbank.org/html/dec/Publications/Workpapers/home.html) (Reproduced in: International Training Program on Utility Regulation and Strategy, CD-ROM, Public Utility Research Center, University of Florida, 2003).

Azam, Jean-Paul, Magueye Dia, Clarence Tsimpo, and Quentin Wodon. 2005. "Poverty Reduction Without Net Growth: The Impact of Senegal's 1994 Devaluation on Urban Poverty." World Bank, Washington, D.C. Processed.

Azam, Jean-Paul, and Waly Wane. 1999. "The Impact of the Devaluation of the CFA Franc on Poverty in the WAEMU." World Bank, Washington, D.C. Processed.

Berthélemy, Jean-Claude, Abdoulaye Seck, and Ann Vourc'h. 1996. *La croissance au Sénégal: un pari perdu?* Etudes du centre de développement de l'OCDE. Paris: OCDE.

Boone, Catherine. 2003. *Political Topographies of the African State.* Cambridge: Cambridge University Press.

Cohen, Daniel. 1993. "Low Investment and Large LDC Debt in the 1980s." *American Economic Review* 83:437–49.

Datt, G., and M. Ravallion. 1992. "Growth and Redistribution Components of Changes in Poverty Measures: A Decomposition with Applications to Brazil and India in the 1980's." *Journal of Development Economics* 38:275–95.

Diagne, Abdoulaye, and Gaye Daffé, eds. 2002. *Le Sénégal en quête d'une croissance durable.* Paris: CREA–Karthala.

Eaton, Jonathan. 1993. "Sovereign Debt: A Primer." *World Bank Economic Review* 7:137–172.

Foster, James, Joel Greer, and Erik Thorbecke. 1984. "A Class of Decomposable Poverty Measures." *Econometrica* 52:761–66.

Ka, Samba, and Nicolas Van de Walle. 1994. "Senegal: Stalled Reform in a Dominant Party System." In Stephan Haggard and Steven B. Webb, eds., *Voting for Reform: Democracy, Political Liberalization, and Economic Adjustment.* Oxford: Oxford University Press.

Lewis, W. Arthur. 1954. "Economic Development with Unlimited Supplies of Labour." *Manchester School* 22:139–191.

Loum, Mamadou Lamine. 2001. *La Sénégal au 1er avril 2000.* Dakar: EXCAF Editions.

Malinvaud, Edmond. 1980. *Profitability and Unemployment.* Cambridge: Cambridge University Press.

Manchuelle, François. 1997. *Willing Migrants: Soninke Labor Diasporas, 1848–1960.* Athens, Ohio: Ohio University Press.

Rama, Martin. 2000. "Wage Misalignment in CFA Countries: Were Labour Market Policies to Blame?" *Journal of African Economies* 9(4):475–511.

Ravallion, Martin, and Shaohua Chen. 2003. "Measuring Pro-Poor Growth." *Economics Letters* 78:93–99.

République du Sénégal. 2004. "La pauvreté au Sénégal: de la dévaluation de 1994 à 2001–2002." Ministère de l'économie et des finances, Direction de la prévision et de la statistique, version préliminaire, Dakar, janvier.

Rouis, Mustapha. 1994. "Senegal: Stabilization, Partial Adjustment, and Stagnation." In Ishrat Husain and Rashid Faruqee, eds., *Adjustment in Africa: Lessons from case Studies.* Washington, D.C.: The World Bank.

Schaffer, Frederic C. 1998. *Democracy in Translation.* Ithaca, N.Y.: Cornell University Press.

Siaens, Corinne, Mohamed Sylla, Adama Toure, and Quentin Wodon. 2005. "Poverty trends and determinants in Senegal: 1994–2001." World Bank, Washington, D.C. Processed.

Siaens, Corinne, and Quentin Wodon. 2005. "Perceptions of Poverty in Senegal." World Bank, Washington, D.C. Processed.

Van de Walle, Nicolas. 1991. "The Decline of the Franc Zone: Monetary Politics in Francophone Africa." *African Affairs* 90:383–405.

Watts, H. W. 1968. "An Economic Definition of Poverty." In D. P. Moynihan, ed., *On Understanding Poverty.* New York, Basic Books.

World Bank. 2005. "Senegal: Poverty and Human Development." Report No. 26189-SN, The World Bank, Washington D.C.

# PART II

## Growth Without Poverty Reduction?

# CHAPTER 4

# Burkina Faso

## *Quo Vadis Poverty?*[20]

*By Emil Daniel Tesliuc and Michel Kone*

*This paper provides estimates of the trend in poverty and inequality in Burkina Faso. In order to generate information about living standards, poverty, and inequality, the country implemented three Priority Surveys in 1994, 1998, and 2003. Throughout this period, efforts were made to improve the design and implementation of the surveys, from sampling and questionnaire design, to data entry and quality control. As a result, the precision of the latest poverty and inequality estimates was improved, generating more accurate and nuanced information on living standards. The improvements in survey design increased the precision of the newest poverty estimates, but endangered the comparability with the poverty estimates produced by earlier surveys. As a result, the initial official poverty and inequality estimates using the three surveys, which suggested a lack of progress towards poverty reduction, were not based on comparable data sets. The authors in Chapter 4 have defined an alternative and comparable welfare indicator, constructed using the same methodology and based on a subset of consumption items that were identically recorded across the 1998 and 2003 surveys. Based on this welfare aggregate, the poverty head count went down from about 54.6 percent in 1998 to 46.4 percent in 2003. The reduction in poverty was more pronounced in rural than in urban areas. In other words, a closer examination of the data suggests that the paradox of high growth without poverty reduction was actually due in large part to measurement errors.*

---

20. This paper was prepared as a contribution to the Burkina Faso Poverty Assessment prepared by the World Bank at the request of the Government of Burkina Faso. It is the result of a collaborative effort between INSD and the World Bank staff aimed at constructing a comparable welfare indicator used to monitor changes in poverty and inequality between 1998 and 2003. The views expressed here are those of the authors, and they do not necessarily represent those of the World Bank, its Executive Directors, or the countries they represent, nor those of the management of the INSD. We want to thank Margaret Grosh, Valerie Kozel, Kalanidhi Subbarao, Jan Walliser and Quentin Wodon for guidance provided on an earlier version of the paper. Any remaining errors are our own.

To generate information about the distribution of living standards, including poverty and inequality, the *Institut National de la Statistique et de la Démographie* (INSD) implemented three priority surveys (PSs) in 1994, 1998, and 2003. Throughout this period, the institution devoted substantial and continuous efforts to improve the design and implementation of the PSs. Such improvements encompass all dimensions of survey implementation, from sampling and questionnaire design, to data entry and quality control (see Box 4.1). As a result of these efforts, the institution improved the precision of the latest poverty and inequality estimates, generating more precise and nuanced information on living standards.

---

**Box 4.1. Improvements in the Design of the Priority Surveys Implemented in Burkina Faso**

From 1994 to 2003, the *Institut National de la Statistique et de la Démographie* of Ouagadougou improved substantially the design and implementation of the three Priority Surveys. These improvements range from sampling and questionnaire design, to data entry and quality control:

♦ By adapting the sampling frame to the new administrative organization of the country, the regional representativity of the survey went up from 8 strata in 1994, to 10 regions in 1998 and 13 in 2003.

♦ The collection of regional price statistics was continuously improved, to generate more detailed price deflators needed to correct for the large differences in purchasing power which exist across regions and areas of residence in Burkina Faso.

♦ The design of questionnaire was continuously improved, by increasing the detail with which consumption and income components were recorded, or by adjusting the recall period with the frequency of certain purchases.

♦ The quality of the data entry process was considerably improved in 2003, with the adoption of the CWIQ technology based on pre-coded questionnaires read by scanners, substantially reducing data entry errors.

---

The original objective of the PSs has been relatively modest: to present a picture of monetary and non-monetary poverty at a moment in time, using a shorter and less expensive questionnaire than, for example, the Living Standard Measurement Surveys (LSMS). The improvements in survey design increased the precision of the newest poverty estimates (generated from the last survey), but endangered the comparability with the poverty estimates produced by earlier surveys. However, the simple fact that these surveys used a number of common features and were publicly available invited many researchers to use them for what they were not initially intended: to investigate the trends in monetary poverty, and the factors associated with, or conducive to these changes.

Ignoring this important caveat, the dynamics of growth, poverty and inequality in Burkina Faso illustrated by official figures remain a puzzle (Table 4.1). During 1994 to 2003, the growth rate in output outpaced population growth by 3 percentage points per annum, a good performance compared to other Sub-Saharan countries. Per capita GDP was 14 percent higher in 1998 than in 1994, and 13 percent higher in 2003 than in

Table 4.1. Burkina Faso Puzzle: Rising Poverty with Lower Inequality
and Substantial Growth

|  | 1994 | 1998 | 2003 |
|---|---|---|---|
| Priority Survey based Statistics | | | |
| **Poverty** | | | |
| - Headcount (P0) | 44.5% | 45.3% | 46.4% |
| **Inequality** (Gini Index of PC Consumption) | | | |
| - Population weights | 0.464 | 0.462 | 0.459 |
| - Household weights | 0.534 | 0.530 | 0.503 |
| **Welfare Index (1994∇1)** | | | |
| - Real Consumption Per Capita | 1.000 | 1.411 | 1.272 |
| National Accounts Indicators | | | |
| **Growth** (Per Capita Output Index, 1994=1) | | | |
| - GDP | 1.000 | 1.139 | 1.289 |
| - Consumption of the HH Sector | 1.000 | 1.199 | 1.143 |

*Source:*
- Country Monitoring System and World Development Indicators (2003) for GDP and private consumption growth.
- INSD (1998, 2000, 2004) for poverty and inequality.

1998.[21] Inequality was stable from 1994 to 1998 and fell from 1998 to 2003, as revealed by two Priority Surveys implemented during these years. The combination of robust growth and unchanged or declining inequality should have made a significant dent in poverty. However, this optimistic macro picture is challenged by poverty estimates from household survey data. Official statistics report a slight increase in poverty from 1994 to 1998, and from 1998 to 2003.

The disconnect between the trends in monetary poverty and the national accounts figures is not singular. There is a similar disconnect between worsening poverty trends and improvements in non-monetary welfare indicators derived from the same survey data. Most survey-based non-monetary welfare indicators suggest a continuous improvement in household education and health (Table 4.2).

In this paper, the authors take a closer look at the microeconomic evidence, and find that much of this puzzle can be traced down to comparison of non equivalent welfare measures and poverty lines. Due to substantial changes in the questionnaire design and in the

---

21. According to the SNA statistics, private (household) consumption was 20 percent higher in 1998 compared to 1994, but 5 percent lower in 2003 than 1998. The discrepancy between the growth in per capita GDP (+13%) and the fall in household consumption per capita (−5%) reflects a change in the structure of the national output. As a result of the influx of HIPC resources and tighter control over the trade deficit, the share of investment and net exports in GDP increased substantially from 1998 to 2003, by 68 and 50 percent respectively. Public investment alone went up by 100 percent. See Table A4.1 annexed for details.

Similar trends are found in survey data, although the variance is higher. The survey-based welfare index went up 41 percent during 1994–98, but was 10 percent lower in 2003 compared to 1998.

| Table 4.2. Trends in Non-monetary Welfare Indicators | | | |
|---|---|---|---|
| Survey Year | 1994 | 1998 | 2003 |
| **Education** | | | |
| Literacy rate, % adults | 18.9 | 18.4 | 21.8 |
| Gross enrollment rate: | | | |
|    Primary cycle (grade 1–6) | 35.2 | 40.9 | 44.1 |
|    Secondary cycle (grade 7–13) | 11.2 | 13.0 | 16.0 |
|    Tertiary cycle | 1.4 | 1.3 | 2.1 |
| **Health** | | | |
| Morbidity rate (last 15 days), % | n.a. | 7.1 | 5.8 |
| Use of modern health facilities, % | n.a. | 2.9 | 4.2 |

*Note:* Based on three waves of the Priority Survey.
*Source:* INSD (1998, 2000, 2003).

methodology used to construct the welfare aggregate and the poverty line, the official poverty and inequality estimates produced and reported by INSD are not comparable across surveys. The paper presents an alternative comparable welfare indicator, constructed using the same methodology and based on a subset of consumption items that were identically recorded across surveys.

Applying the same methodology for the construction of the welfare aggregate from successive surveys generates comparable indicators only if the survey design is reasonably similar. In the case of the three PSs, this largely holds for the 1998–2003 comparison, but not for 1994 survey. The comparison of the 1994 survey with the subsequent rounds is risky at best, as this survey was fielded in a different season than the others, and information on food consumption was collected using a longer recall period. One can only sign the bias induced by seasonality and different recall period on reported consumption in 1994 compared to the other surveys. Furthermore, the differences in consumption schedules used in the three surveys are the largest from 1994 to 1998. While the subset of identically recorded consumption items in 1998 and 2003 represents about 88 percent of the total consumption in 2003, the intersection between 1994 and the subsequent survey rounds is only about a third. Thus, attempts to extend the comparison from 1998–2003 to 1994 is not only risky, but will also result in a more imprecise welfare aggregate.

Given these constraints, the authors present a set of alternative poverty and inequality estimates for 1998 and 2003 using a restricted, but comparable, welfare aggregate. Based on this welfare aggregate, poverty head count went down from about 54.6 percent in 1998 to 46.4 percent in 2003. The reduction in poverty was more pronounced in rural than in urban areas.

The case of the poverty statistics in Burkina Faso is not singular, and seems to be more the rule than the exception. Almost all countries have improved their surveys over time, and placed most efforts in generating an improved poverty profile based on the most recent and reliable information. There was considerably less effort directed toward ensuring the comparability of those estimates with those derived from earlier surveys. Awareness of the fragility of poverty statistics derived from non comparable surveys is on the rise, as a number of recent studies have shown (see Box 4.2).

---

**Box 4.2. Revising Poverty Aggregates: Lessons from Other Countries**

---

A number of countries revised their poverty statistics with the view of producing statistics that are comparable over time. Madagascar, Senegal and Cape Verde provide recent examples from Sub-Saharan Africa, while Kyrgyz Republic, India and Russia illustrate that such revisions are not occurring only in the sub-continent. The case of Madagascar is similar to the one in Burkina Faso (Paternostro and others 2001). To ensure comparability of the poverty estimates produced from three non-comparable surveys from 1993, 1997 and 1999, a joint team of specialists from INSTAT, World Bank and Cornell University produced a partial but comparable consumption indicator, using only a subset of commodities recorded similarly in the three surveys. In the case of Senegal, Cape Verde and Kyrgyz Republic, such revision was triggered by the inconsistency between a growing GDP, unchanged inequality and raising poverty, similar to the situation in Burkina Faso. In the case of Kyrgyz Republic, the inconsistent poverty statistics were produced from a series of LSMSs whose reported consumption was severely affected by seasonality (surveys implemented in different months), the 1999 Russian crisis, and the selective attrition of the well-off households. A joint team of experts from the Statistical Office and the World Bank used the panel element of the Household Budget Survey to estimate comparable, annual poverty rates. The use of a comparable welfare aggregate has produced poverty statistics consistent with the dynamics of GDP and inequality.

Finally, two highly publicized statistical experiments in India and Ecuador have illustrated how fragile reported consumption is to changes in recall period, or in the level of detail with which consumption is recorded. In India, shortening the recall period from 30 to 7 days increased reported food consumption by 30 percent, as reported in Deaton (2003). Lanjouw and Lanjouw (2000) report another experiment in Ecuador, where a shorter (24 items) and a longer (97 items) consumption schedule was administered to two non-overlapping random samples. The consumption reported by the household from the poorest decile was 25 percent higher in the sample with the longer consumption schedule. The three PSs are plagued by similarly problems.

## Main Features of the Priority Surveys

The Priority Surveys collect information on household consumption and incomes—including consumption out of own production, or *autoconsommation*—for poverty and inequality measurement, and information about non-monetary dimensions of well-being, such as malnutrition, employment, attainment and access to education, health and basic services, housing conditions and endowment with durables, land or livestock. In addition, the Priority Surveys gather detailed information on household demographics.

The primary purpose of the PSs was to provide: (i) a description of the standard of living of the population; (ii) an analysis of poverty and inequality and the factors associated with it; and (iii) an examination of the non-monetary aspects of well-being. The survey was designed to be representative for the main socio-economic groups, areas of residence and regions. However, changes in the administrative structure of the country between each survey wave, from seven regions and 8 strata in 1994 to 10 strata in 1998 and 13 in 2003, complicated the comparisons at the regional level.

Many survey design parameters are similar in the three surveys, from sample size to the implementation of a two-stage stratified sampling, with selection of areas in stage 1 and random selection of 20 dwellings from those areas in stage 2 (Table 4.3). Stratification improved over time, while clustering was alike across surveys.

Some other changes were more subtle but very important, making comparability of the 1994 survey with the successive ones extremely difficult, such as the implementation

| Priority Survey | PS I | PS II | PS III |
|---|---|---|---|
| **Table 4.3. Survey Design Parameters for the Priority Surveys** | | | |
| Year | 1994 | 1998 | 2003 |
| Period | Oct-94–Jan-95 | May–Aug | Apr–Jul |
| Sample Size | | | |
| - Households | 8628 | 8478 | 8500 |
| - Individuals | 65014 | 63509 | 54034 |
| # Strata | 8 | 10 | 13 |
| # Clusters | 436 | 425 | 425 |
| Households/Cluster | 20 | 20 | 20 |

*Source:* INSD (1996, 2000, 2003).

of the surveys in pre- and post-harvest period, and use of a different recall period for some commodity groups. We can only determine the direction of the bias induced by seasonality and different recall period on reported consumption in 1994 compared to the other surveys.

## Seasonality

The timing of the surveys was substantially different between the first and subsequent rounds. The PS-I was fielded in the post-harvest period, from October 1994 to January 95, while the PS-II and PS-III were implemented during the pre-harvest period, from May to August 1998 and April to July 2003. The pre-harvest period is called by the rural Burkinabes *"période de soudure,"* or hardship/lean period. It is very likely that seasonality influenced the level of reported consumption in Burkina Faso in 1994 compared to 1998 or 2003 in opposite dimensions, thus widening the gap between the true poverty and the one derived from the surveys. As argued in World Bank (2003), there is a potentially large seasonal effect, whose magnitude is impossible to measure accurately.

Other studies from Sub-Saharan Africa reported large differences in household consumption over the seasons of the year. Dercon and Krishnan (2000) follow a panel of 1450 rural households from Ethiopia during 1994 and 1995, before and after the harvest. They found that food consumption was 10 percent higher during the post-harvest period than in the lean period. Such difference in consumption across seasons within the year is very large compared to average GDP growth in the sub-continent. For Burkina Faso, with a per capita GDP growth of 3 percent per annum, this difference is equivalent to three years of average growth.

Dercon and Krishnan (2000) found that the higher consumption during the post-harvest period is explained in part by the seasonal response to labor demand (consumption rises when labor demand, hence effort, increases) and to the price level (consumption falls in the pre-harvest season when prices are high). Shocks are also playing an important role. The study reports a lower incidence of shocks during the post-harvest period, which is likely due to an improvement in the household livelihoods that allows them to manage better the risks they face. The same factors are likely to influence the consumption behavior of the household in rural areas of Burkina Faso, hindering the comparison of the 1994 consumption aggregate with the ones reported in subsequent rounds.

## Recall Period

The three PSs had the same recall period for all consumption items, except for food. Information on food consumption was collected in 1994 using a 30-day recall period, and in 1998 and 2003 for a 15-day recall period. This apparently innocuous change in survey design probably had a large impact on reported consumption.

---

**Box 4.3.  Different Recall Periods Have a Large Impact on the Level
of Reported Consumption**

---

The Case of Indian National Sample Survey (NSS)

"Survey questionnaires differ in the length of the recall period over which respondents are asked to report their consumption. The choice of recall period is often thought to involve a tradeoff between accuracy of memory, which calls for a short period, and the match between consumption and purchases, which is more accurate when averaged over a long period. But there is little understanding of the effects of different recall periods, particularly in poor, agricultural societies. In India between 1989 and 1998, the NSS experimented with different recall periods, replacing the traditional 30-day recall period for all goods with a 7-day recall period for food and tobacco, and with a 365 day period for durable goods and some other infrequently purchased items. The sample was randomly divided, and half were given the old questionnaire, and half the new, so that it is possible to make a clean evaluation of the effects of the change. The shorter reporting period increased reported expenditures on food by around 30 percent, and total consumption by about 17 percent, very much in the right direction to help resolve the discrepancy with the NAS. Because there are many Indians close to the poverty line, the 17 percent increase was enough to reduce the measured head-count ratio by a half, removing almost 200 million people from poverty. What might seem to be an obscure technical issue of survey design can have a major effect on the measurement of poverty, not only in India, but in the world. It should be noted, however, that the higher consumption totals associated with the shorter recall period, although closer to the NAS estimates, are not necessarily more accurate. Indeed, the NSS has carried out a series of controlled experiments with a plausible gold standard in which, for many foods, the 30-day reference period appears to be more accurate than the 7-day period, see NSSO Expert Group on Sampling Errors (2003)."

From: Deaton, A. 2003. *Measuring Poverty in a Growing World (or "Measuring Growth in a Poor World")*. NBER Working Paper 9822; RPDS Working Paper 222, Princeton University.

---

Deaton and Grosh (2000) explain the impact of recall period on consumption as follows:

> . . . people generally forget more events the further such events slip into the past. Purchases of consumer goods are no exceptions to these rules; there is a large body of evidence in industrial countries on "recall bias" or increasing underestimation as the recall period is increased.

Similar findings are found in developing countries. Experiments using households from the Ghanaian LSMS run by Scott and Amenuvegbe found that for 13 high-frequency purchases, reported expenditures fell at an average of 2.9 percent for each day added to the recall period. Similar findings are reported by Mahalanobis and Sen for India in 1954. Deaton (2003) describes a nationally-representative experiment with different recall in India, where shortening the recall period from 30 to 15 days resulted in 30 percent higher annualized consumption (Box 4.3).

The same phenomenon was likely happening in Burkina Faso: shortening the recall period for food items in 1998 and 2003 reduced the amount of "recall bias," and resulted in more food purchases and *autoconsommation* being remembered and reported. In the case of Burkina Faso, there is no statistical experiment (as in India) to estimate the impact of a shorter recall period on reported food consumption. Again, the same phenomenon is likely to influence the consumption behavior of the households in Burkina Faso, hindering the comparison of the 1994 consumption aggregate with the ones reported in subsequent rounds.

### Other Computational Differences

Apart from differences in seasonality and recall period between 1994 and 1998/2003, there are four other differences in the way poverty estimates have been computed which, although potentially important for the comparability of these estimates, can be fixed by adhering to a uniform methodology:

    (i) changes in the questionnaire design;
    (ii) changes in the methodology used to construct the welfare aggregate;
    (iii) changes in the methodology used to construct the poverty line; and
    (iv) changes in the circumstances under which each survey was fielded.

From one survey to the next, INSD implemented a number of *changes in the design of the questionnaire* which may have affected the comparability of the consumption aggregate, such as:

■ Some components of household consumption were collected only in the later surveys. For instance, (i) food consumption received as gift was recorded only in the 1998 and 2003 surveys, (ii) "other non-food purchases" were recorded only in 1998 and 2003; and (iii) the purchases of "school uniforms" were collected only in 2003.

■ More recent surveys collected the same information as the previous ones, but using a more disaggregated schedule. Such changes were substantial in 1998 compared to 1994 surveys, when the number of items used to construct the consumption aggregate went up from 55 to 74. The 1998 and 2003 questionnaires had comparatively few such changes (the corresponding number of items went up from 74 to 89, see Table 4.4).

To ensure that the resulting poverty statistics will be comparable across the 1998 and 2003 surveys, the consumption aggregate used in this paper will include only those items recorded in the same way in the two surveys.

| Table 4.4. Number of Products Used to Construct the Consumption Aggregate | | | | | |
|---|---|---|---|---|---|
| | **Non-Food and Food** | **Services** | **Health** | **Education** | **Total** |
| EP I—1994 | 23 | 22 | 5 | 5 | 55 |
| EP II—1998 | 33 | 31 | 5 | 5 | 74 |
| EP III—2003 | 39 | 39 | 5 | 6 | 89 |

Over time, the *methodology for the construction of the consumption aggregate also changed.* In all three survey years the welfare aggregate was constructed using the same components, such as the sum of the annual consumption of food, schooling, health, rent and other non-food expenditures (including here household investments and durables).

These expenditures were adjusted for regional price differences. However, the way these components have been aggregated, annualized and deflated was different:

- *Durables:* In 1994, household investments and purchases of durables were not annualized (if somebody bought a TV during the last month, this expenditure was not multiplied by 12 to arrive at an annual figure). In 1998 and 2003, these expenditures were annualized. This change will reduce poverty in 1998 and 2003, and increase inequality.
- *Rent:* The surveys collect information on actual rent paid by tenants, and on estimated "rental values" of the dwelling from owners. However, a considerable fraction of the households do not report the "rental value" of their house (24 percent in 1994, 14 percent in 1998 and 6 percent in 2003). In 1994, households who neither reported rents nor estimated their rental incomes were imputed a rental value using a hedonic regression of rent on dwelling characteristics and location dummies. In 1998 and 2003, the households who did not report nor estimate rents have been assigned zero consumption of housing services. Such omission increased both poverty and inequality, ceteris paribus, compared to the 1994 methodology.
- *Adjustments for the cost of living:* Only in 1994 the consumption aggregate was expressed in constant purchasing power using the Ouagadougou CPI to correct for month-to-month inflation, and a regional price deflator to correct for regional price differences. Different CPIs were used for food, non-food, education, schooling and rent. In 1998 and 2003, per capita consumption was adjusted only for regional price differences, although the month-to-month price differences were larger than in 1994.
- *Seasonal adjustments:* To correct for the fact that the 1998 data have been collected in the *"periode de soudure,"* per capita consumption of all households was increased by 12.5 percent. The reason behind such adjustment is to get at an "annual consumption" figure closer to the one derived in the system of national accounts. However, no similar adjustment was made for 2003, when the survey was implemented during the same *"periode de soudure."* The introduction of this adjustment has the largest impact on the resulting poverty trends.
- The impact of different recall period for food in 1994 compared to 1998–2003, or of disaggregating some items over time, was not analyzed or taken into account.

To ensure that the resulting consumption aggregate will be comparable across the 1998 and 2003 surveys, it will be constructed using the same methodology: (i) durables and other household investments will not be included in the aggregate; (ii) rental payments would be imputed to households which do not report or estimate their rental incomes, following the procedure used in 1994 by INSD; (iii) both temporal and regional price indices will be used to correct for differences in the cost of living, following the procedure used in 1994 by INSD; and (iv) no seasonal adjustment factor will be applied in 1998 or 2003.

The *methodology used to construct the poverty line suffered subtle changes* from one survey round to the next:

- The structure of consumption basket used to construct the food component of the poverty line changed over time, thus it is inconsistent (Table 4.5).
- The food basket used for the estimation of the food poverty line represents only a small portion of the total food consumption of the poor, and includes only four basic staples (maize, millet, rice and sorghum). The constraint that generates such choices is substantial: the availability of reliable price information. However, this food

poverty line is not representative of the consumption of the poor, and will understate food poverty as it uses only cheaper sources of calories, compared to other food items consumed by the poorest 40 percent of the population. Ceteris paribus, this choice results in a lower poverty line—this is why poverty in Burkina is lower than in some other neighboring countries with similar per capita GDP.

■ The high seasonality of prices of the main staples, especially during the *"periode de soudure,"* contributes to the fluctuation of the nominal poverty line, and generates dramatic swings in the share of food in total household consumption from one survey to the other (Table 4.5).

---

**Table 4.5. Composition of the Food Poverty Line in 1998 and 2003**

|  | Shorgum | Millet | Maize | Rice |
|---|---|---|---|---|
| **Shares of the staples:** | | | | |
| - in 1998 | 61% | 34% | 4% | 1% |
| - in 2003 | 35% | 37% | 19% | 10% |
| **Average price of the staples, in CFA Francs Ouagadougou prices:** | | | | |
| - in 1998 | 165 | 208 | 163 | 285 |
| - in 2003 | 140 | 145 | 125 | 250 |
| **Food Poverty Line** | | | | |
| - in 1998 | 52295 | | | |
| - in 2003 | 41153 | | | |
| **Ratio non-food/food consumption** | | | | |
| - in 1998 | 1.009 | | | |
| - in 2003 | 0.390 | | | |

---

**Box 4.4. How is the Official Poverty Line Computed?**

INSD constructs a poverty line using the "cost of basic needs" approach, in three steps:

♦ First, the food component of the poverty line is estimated by valuing a consumption vector providing the recommended intake of 2283 calories per capita per day at the prices prevailing during the survey. The vector used by INSD consists of four staples most consumed by the households in Burkina Faso, namely sorghum, millet, maize and rice. A standard conversion table is used to determine the caloric content of each Kg of product. The composition of this food basket reflects the share of these four staples in the consumption of the households for each survey, and thus changes from survey to survey. The basket is evaluated at the prices of the four staples prevailing in Ouagadougou markets at the time of the survey. This is the food component of the poverty line.

♦ Second, the non-food component is equal to the non-food expenditures observed for the households whose food consumption is close to the food poverty line estimated above. The ratio of non-food to food consumption is estimated for each household. Then, the share of non-food consumption in the total poverty line is taken as the share reported by those households whose food consumption is close to the value of the food poverty line (for instance, ±1%). The ratio obtained thus far is multiplied by the food poverty line to get the non-food component of the poverty line.

♦ The official poverty line is the sum of the food and non-food components.

Finally, one should acknowledge that *the circumstances when surveys were fielded were different across the three rounds,* and may have impacted on the comparability (representativity) of this "snapshot" consumption aggregate with an ideal annual aggregate, such as those reported in the System of National Accounts. The priority surveys give only the "snapshot poverty," not "annual poverty" rates. These surveys differ from the practice of the LSMSs, which collect information on consumption during a typical month (average consumption over the year). Shocks and other circumstances may lead to substantial differences between monthly welfare (captured by PSs) and annual welfare (reflected in SNA). In the case of Burkina Faso, the following circumstances are important:

- In 1994, the survey was implemented during the period when the CFA Franc devaluation was still propagating through the economy;
- In 1998, the survey was implemented after one of the most devastating droughts; and
- In 2003, the survey was implemented during the peak period of the crisis induced by the civil war in the neighboring Cote d'Ivoire.

Table 4.6 summarizes the likely impact of these factors on poverty.

**Table 4.6.  Impact of Changes in the Survey Design and Methodology on Official Poverty Statistics**

|  | Year | Impact on Reported Poverty |
|---|---|---|
| **Changes in Questionnaire Design** | | |
| Data collected during the pre-harvest | period1998/2003 | Increases poverty |
| Shortening the recall period for foods to 15 days | 1998/2003 | Decreases poverty |
| Higher coverage of food consumption (from gifts) | 1998/2003 | Decreases poverty |
| More detailed consumptionschedule | all rounds | Decreases poverty |
| Expenditures on school uniforms only in 2003 | 2003 | Decreases poverty |
| **Changes in Methodology: Consumption Aggregate** | | |
| Durables annualized in 1998/2003 | 1998/2003 | Small decrease in poverty, increase in inequality |
| Seasonal inflation factors in 1998 | 1998 | Reduces poverty, strong impact |
| Rents imputed in 1994, self-reported after | 1998/2003 | Increases poverty and inequality |
| **Changes in Methodology: Poverty Line** | | |
| Different consumption basket | all rounds | Inconsistent poverty lines |
| Different inflation for the PL items compared to rest | all rounds | Inconsistent poverty lines |

## A Comparable Welfare Indicator

This section spells out the normative choices made in constructing the comparable welfare indicator and presents the rationale for these choices. Given the substantial changes operated in the design of the Priority Survey from 1998 to 2003, the authors place more trust in the relative comparison over time than in estimates of absolute poverty. This understanding should facilitate the comparison of the figures reported in this paper with other estimates reported in other studies on poverty in Burkina Faso.

## Proposed Welfare Indicator

There is no "best" welfare indicator, and there are many reasonable choices one can defend in constructing such indicator. In this paper, the authors decided to generate a comparable welfare indicator for the 1998 and 2003 surveys by adapting (changing as little as possible) the methodology used to derive the welfare aggregate constructed by INSD in 2003. The resulting welfare indicator, *real per capita consumption,* covers only the items recorded identically in the PSs 1998 and 2003. It is real consumption, as all its components have been expressed in Jun-2003 Ouagadougou constant prices by using both temporal and regional price adjustments.

## Coverage of the Indicator

Few consumption items were excluded from the comparable consumption aggregate for theoretical reasons, notably the purchase of durables, other household investments[22] and bulky expenditures associated with ceremonies. These items represent investments made in the current (recall) period that generate utility for the household during their lifetime; bulky expenditures made at one moment in time, but used for a longer period of time. The standard practice is to include only their rental value as component of current consumption, or—as in our case—to exclude them if the information needed to estimate this value is not available (Deaton and Zaidi 1999; Deaton and Grosh 2000). The exclusion of these items does not have a large impact on reported poverty, but reduces inequality.

The components of the consumption aggregate which were not collected identically in the 1998 and 2003 surveys were also excluded. The following items fall in this category: fish and fish products; other meats than poultry; vegetables; *prêt a porter;* textiles (see Table 4.7). By using only a subset of items recorded similarly in the two rounds there is little loss in precision, as this abbreviated consumption indicator still covers 84 percent of the food consumption and 88 percent of total consumption reported in 2003 (Table 4.8). The coverage of the partial indicator is higher in 1998 (93 percent of total consumption and 92 percent of food consumption), indicating that the 1998 questionnaire captured, ceteris paribus, relatively less consumption than in 2003. There are two main reasons for the underestimation of consumption in 1998. The 1998 questionnaire (a) does not record the consumption of some items, such as school uniforms; and (b) includes more aggregated items which trigger higher recall bias, and hence less consumption being reported, in the case of fish, meat, vegetables, *prêt a porter* and textile consumption.

---

22. Such as (i) purchases of cars, motorbikes or bikes (code 23 in 1998 and codes 225–227 in 2003); (ii) purchases of television sets, refrigerators or freezers (code 25 in 1998 and codes 229–231 in 2003); (iii) purchases of furniture or sanitary installations (code 27 in 1998 and 233 in 2003) and expenditures associated with ceremonies (code 22 in 1998 and 224 in 2003).

The remaining items were aggregated into nine commodity groups (separately for purchases and *autoconsomation* or gifts): (a) food, beverages and tobacco; (b) clothes and shoes; (c) rent and utilities; (d) house maintenance; (e) health; (f) transport; (g) leisure; (h) health; and (i) other items. These groups match the CPI sub-indices collected by INSD Price Department for Ouagadougou city (see Table 4.9, used in the next steps to correct the differences in the cost of living over time).

**Table 4.7. Items Recorded Differently in 1998 and 2003 Which Were Excluded from the Consumption Aggregate**

|  | PS II 1998 Code | CWIQ 2003 Code |
|---|---|---|
| Fish and other see products | 10 | 110,111 |
| Meat (except poultry) | 11 | 112, 113, 114 |
| Vegetables | 18 | 121, 122, 123, 124 |
| Pret a porter | 15 | 215, 216 |
| Textiles | 17 | 218, 219 |
| School unformes | not collected | 1.3 |

**Table 4.8. Coverage of the Partial But Comparable Consumption Aggregate in 1998 and 2003**

| Welfare Aggregate | % of Full/Non-Comparable Aggregate | | |
|---|---|---|---|
|  | Full/Non-Comparable | Partial/Comparable | Ratio |
| Year | (1) | (2) | (3)=(2)/(1) |
| | Per Capita Consumption | | |
| 1998 | 109,827 | 102,568 | 93% |
| 2003 | 130,734 | 114,846 | 88% |
| | Per Capita Food Consumption | | |
| 1998 | 59,753 | 54,992 | 92% |
| 2003 | 70,700 | 59,613 | 84% |

*Note:* The full/non-comparable aggregate is constructed using the same methodology as the partial/comparable one, without excluding any of the consumption items which were either added or disaggregated in 2003. Both indicators do not include durables or other household investments.

## Consumption Normalized

Each component of household consumption is normalized into annual consumption. Keeping with INSD practice, we multiply by a factor of 24 food consumption (purchases, *autoconsomation* and from gifts, with 15 days recall period), and by 12 all other elements (with 30 days recall period) except schooling (whose recall period is the current school year). Tobacco consumption was added to the food component after it was annualized, as we use the same CPI for the whole commodity group (food, beverages and tobacco).

**Table 4.9. Ouagadougou Consumer Price Inflators, by Commodity Group**

| Commodity Group | EP II | | | | EP III | | | |
|---|---|---|---|---|---|---|---|---|
| | May-98 | Jun-98 | Jul-98 | Aug-98 | Apr-03 | May-03 | Jun-03 | Jul-03 |
| Food, beverages and tobacco | 103.5% | 98.2% | 103.2% | 101.7% | 117.4% | 106.5% | 100.0% | 108.6% |
| Clothes and shoes | 113.6% | 113.8% | 113.8% | 113.7% | 99.8% | 100.0% | 100.0% | 100.9% |
| Rent and utilities | 111.3% | 112.4% | 112.5% | 111.4% | 101.3% | 99.7% | 100.0% | 101.3% |
| House maintenance | 101.6% | 101.1% | 101.0% | 100.4% | 99.9% | 99.9% | 100.0% | 99.9% |
| Health | 108.2% | 108.0% | 110.5% | 111.3% | 100.9% | 100.9% | 100.0% | 100.0% |
| Transport | 118.8% | 119.7% | 119.4% | 119.7% | 97.2% | 98.5% | 100.0% | 100.4% |
| Leisure | 103.2% | 103.2% | 103.2% | 103.2% | 100.0% | 100.0% | 100.0% | 100.0% |
| Education | 110.7% | 110.7% | 110.6% | 110.6% | 100.0% | 100.0% | 100.0% | 100.0% |
| Other goods | 113.6% | 113.5% | 113.5% | 113.2% | 100.0% | 100.0% | 100.0% | 100.1% |
| Total | 109.2% | 107.2% | 109.3% | 108.6% | 105.2% | 102.0% | 100.0% | 102.7% |

*Note:* The price inflators are derived from the official price statistics of INSD. They show by how much one should multiply consumption in a given month, to express it in June 2003 constant prices.

## Cost-of-Living Adjustment

As in many other countries, in Burkina Faso there are substantial differences in the cost of living both across space and time. Two adjustments are used to correct for such differences in the purchasing power:

(i) The regional price index constructed by INSD for each survey is used to transform household consumption from local to constant Ouagadougou prices (the Annex Tables present the value of the regional price indices used in each of the surveys), by dividing the value of consumption expressed (reported) in local prices by this index. The index was constructed using a basket of 10 staple goods, of which 6 foods and 4 non-foods.

(ii) Each of the nine components of household consumption are expressed in Jun-2003 constant prices using the corresponding price indices from Table 4.9. This method performs a more accurate adjustment than, for instance, the use of an unique CPI for total consumption, as it implicitly uses the observed, household-specific con-sumption shares instead of the CPI weights. The latter are computed from an older consumption survey, and are based on the shares of these commodity groups in total household purchases, not consumption. The most important implication is that the weight of food is lower in the CPI (as it includes only purchases, without taking into account *autoconsomation* and gifts), compared to our method. As food prices are a volatile element of household consumption, the use of commodity-group-specific price indices increases the accuracy of the adjustment.

The two adjustments described above implicitly assume that prices are changing, over time, proportionally with the changes observed (only) in Ouagadougou.

## Adjustments for Household Size

Keeping with INSD practice, there is no adjustment for household size, that is, for economies of scale in consumption or for differences in the needs of children versus adults. The welfare aggregate is expressed in per capita terms.

## The Welfare Aggregate

The formula used to construct the comparable consumption aggregate for 1998 and 2003 is:

Real per capita consumption =

$$[24 * F * F_{cpi} + 12 * (C * C_{cpi} + R * R_{cpi} + M * M_{cpi} + H * H_{cpi} + T * T_{cpi} + L * L_{cpi} + O * O_{cpi}) + S * S_{cpi}]/$$
$$[(\text{Regional price deflator/Household Size})]$$

where:

$F$ = food, beverages and tobacco consumption, and $F_{cpi}$ is the corresponding CPI index;
$C$ = consumption of clothes and shoes, and $C_{cpi}$ is the corresponding CPI index;
$R$ = rent and utilities payments, and imputed rents, and $R_{cpi}$ is the corresponding CPI index;
$M$ = articles for housing maintenance, and $M_{cpi}$ is the corresponding CPI index;
$H$ = consumption of health services and medicines, and $H_{cpi}$ is the corresponding CPI index;
$T$ = transport expenditures, and $T_{cpi}$ is the corresponding CPI index;
$L$ = expenditures for leisure activities, and $L_{cpi}$ is the corresponding CPI index;
$S$ = consumption of schooling, and $S_{cpi}$ is the corresponding CPI index;
$O$ = consumption of other goods or services, and $O_{cpi}$ is the corresponding CPI index.

## The Poverty line

The poverty line is determined endogenously from the 2003 survey using the comparable per capita consumption aggregate, to generate the same poverty head count as estimated by INSD using the 2003 CWIQ survey and the full consumption aggregate. A poverty line of 72,110 CFA Francs in June 2003 Ouagadougou prices replicates the poverty head count of 46.4 percent reported by INSD for 2003 (INSD, 2004).

# The Results: Quo Vadis Poverty?

Burkina Faso experienced substantial reduction in poverty, without significant changes in inequality, between 1998 and 2003 (Table 4.10). The poverty head count went down from an estimated 54.6 percent in 1998 to 46.4 percent in 2003. The reduction in poverty was more pronounced in rural areas, where the head count fell from 61.1 percent in 1998 to 52.4 percent in 2003. The reduction of poverty in urban areas was substantially smaller, and not statistically significant. Inequality remained unchanged between the two surveys (Gini Index of 0.444), and was systematically higher in urban (0.484) than in rural areas (0.376).

*These findings hold for a broad range of plausible poverty lines*, as illustrated in Figure 4.1 where we use 1st order stochastic dominance tests to investigate the trends in poverty. In

**Table 4.10. Poverty and Inequality Dynamics, 1998 versus 2003**

| | National | | Rural | | Urban | |
|---|---|---|---|---|---|---|
| | *Estimate* | *Std. Err.* | *Estimate* | *Std. Err.* | *Estimate* | *Std. Err.* |
| **Poverty Headcount (P0)** | | | | | | |
| 1998 | 54.6% | 1.1% | 61.1% | 1.1% | 22.4% | 1.9% |
| 2003 | 46.4% | 1.2% | 52.4% | 1.3% | 19.2% | 1.7% |
| **Poverty Gap (P1)** | | | | | | |
| 1998 | 0.183 | 0.005 | 0.208 | 0.005 | 0.057 | 0.006 |
| 2003 | 0.153 | 0.005 | 0.176 | 0.006 | 0.051 | 0.005 |
| **Poverty Severity (P2)** | | | | | | |
| 1998 | 0.082 | 0.003 | 0.094 | 0.003 | 0.022 | 0.003 |
| 2003 | 0.068 | 0.003 | 0.079 | 0.004 | 0.019 | 0.002 |
| **Gini Index** | | | | | | |
| 1998 | 0.444 | 0.013 | 0.349 | 0.011 | 0.499 | 0.027 |
| 2003 | 0.444 | 0.011 | 0.376 | 0.012 | 0.484 | 0.013 |

*Note:* Standard errors take into account the survey design.

---

**Box 4.5. Are the Observed Changes in Poverty Statistically Significant?**

*The Survey Design and the Precision of the Poverty Estimates*

The poverty and inequality figures published by INSD and quoted in most official documents of the Government, the World Bank or other donors are sample estimates. They are not derived from a census, or any other exhaustive research on household welfare. They are estimated from surveys, with some known (im)precision. This precision improves with the stratification of the survey, and worsens with the degree of clustering of the sampled households. Knowing the inverse of the probability of selection of each household in the sample, the survey strata and clusters, confidence intervals having a given statistical significance (typically 5%) can be constructed. A 95% confidence interval, for instance, guarantees that the true poverty rate or inequality index will be found in this range in 95 out of 100 trials, where by trials we mean a different survey implemented at the same time, under the same design, but on a different sample of households.

The sample size of the PSs is comparable with international practice. Given the population of Burkina Faso, around 10–12 million during 1998/2003, a sample of 8,500 households gives reasonable precision. We use the following survey design parameters to generate the standard errors (and hence, the confidence intervals) of the poverty and inequality statistics produced in this paper:

♦ the codes for the primary sampling units (425 in total) indicate the clustering of the survey; and

♦ the regions (10 in 1998 and 13 in 2003) indicate the stratification variables.

♦ we use the set of expansion weights produced by INSD to extrapolate the results from the sample to the total population.

# Figure 4.1. Poverty Incidence Curves

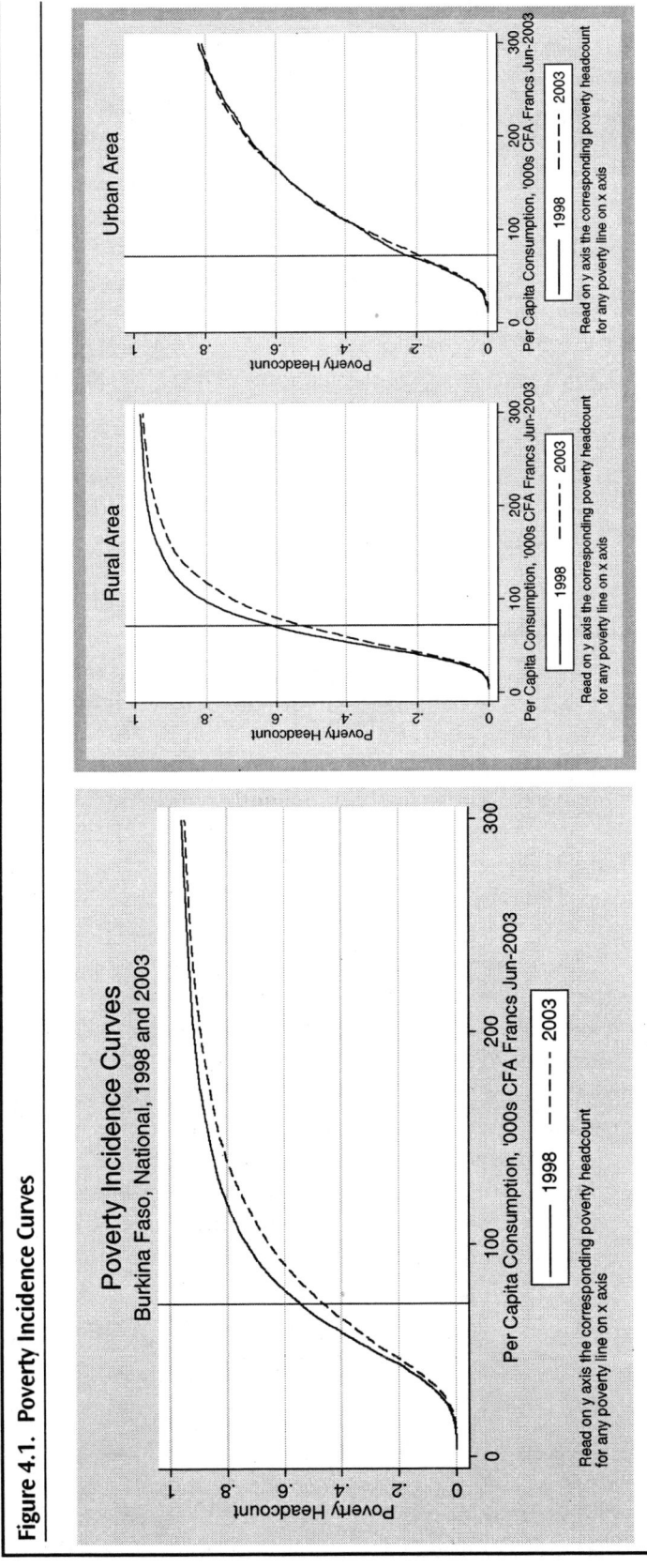

*Note:*
The three poverty incidence curves illustrate the relationship between a given (arbitrary) poverty line and the resulting poverty head count. The points along the horizontal axis can be considered as the complete set of poverty lines. The proportion of the poor can be found by reading off the proportion of the population on the vertical axis whose per capita consumption is less than a given level of per capita consumption. If, at any poverty line, one poverty incidence curve [1] is above the other [2], the amount of poverty in population [1] will be always greater than in population [2] for any given poverty line. In our case, the poverty rate would be lower in 2003 at any poverty rate, at the national level, as well as in rural and urban areas.

setting the poverty line there is a certain subjective element, the most important being the choice of the caloric requirement that would "anchor" the food component of the line. This raises the question: How robust are the poverty rankings across time to the choice of the poverty line? One way to make robust comparisons without choosing a particular poverty line is by testing for *stochastic dominance*, i.e. by comparing poverty incidence curves (or cumulative density curves) that summarize the distribution of per capita consumption. A poverty incidence curve has the cumulative share of population on the vertical axis, and the real per capita consumption on the horizontal axis. The points along the horizontal axis can be considered as the complete set of poverty lines. The proportion of the poor can be found by reading off the proportion of the population on the vertical axis whose per capita consumption is less than a given level. If, at any poverty line, one poverty incidence curve [1] is above the other [2], the amount of poverty in population [1] will be always greater than in population [2] for any given poverty line. If two poverty incidence curves intersect, then the comparisons will give different results for different ranges of poverty lines. However, this was not the case for Burkina Faso in 1998 and 2003, for any of the national, rural or urban samples.

*What can we say about the changes in poverty between 1994 and 1998?* Up to now, we argued strongly against the use of per capita consumption, affected by two opposite-sign factors whose amplitude is difficult to estimate (seasonality and different recall period for food consumption). However, the 1994 and 1998 surveys collect detailed information on household revenues, from agricultural sales, wages, profits, rents and other monetary transfers, using a similar schedule and the same recall period (revenues obtained during the last year). This comparison cannot be extended to 2003, when the recall period was shortened to 30 days.

Figure 4.2 presents a similar 1st order stochastic dominance test for a real per capita revenue aggregate constructed on the basis of the three surveys. The 1998 cumulative distribution curve lies below the 1994 one, suggesting a strong reduction in poverty between the two years.

The same trend is apparent from the comparison of the 2003 curve with 1998 for moderate poverty lines, but is no longer valid for extremely low levels of the poverty line. The later phenomenon is due to the shortening of the recall period in 2003 which increased the variance of the reported revenue, as many farmers or other seasonal workers who where unemployed during the month preceding the survey reported zero cash revenues. The same workers, if asked as in 1994/98 about their cash revenues during the previous year, would have reported positive amounts. The impact of a different recall period is similar here, for the comparison of real per capita revenues, as the one encountered earlier for the food consumption. The result is also similar: the welfare indicator constructed on the basis of revenues in 1998 and 2003 is not comparable.

## Conclusions and Recommendations

The intention of the authors is to facilitate a technical dialogue on the dynamics of poverty in Burkina Faso. The message of the paper—that substantial growth and unchanged inequality resulted in significant and important reductions in poverty over the last decade—contrasts with a more pessimistic picture given by unqualified comparisons of official statistics, but it is consistent with both macroeconomic statistics and other survey-based indicators of

**Figure 4.2. Cumulative Distribution of Per Capita Revenues**

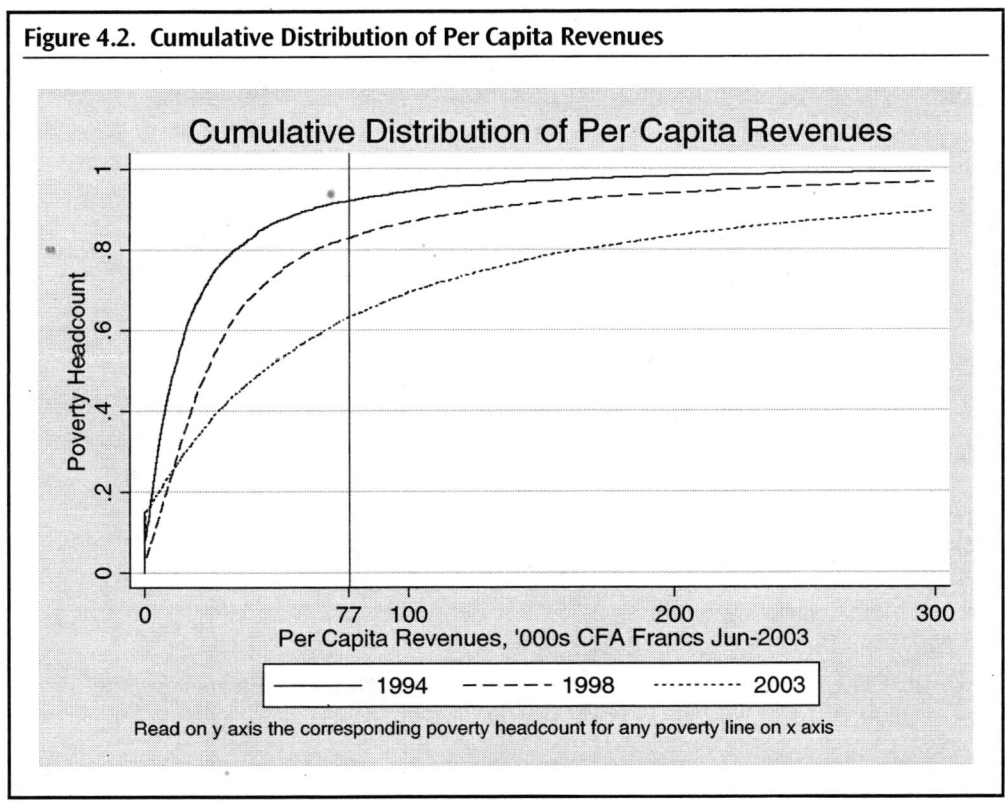

household welfare. Thus, the technical findings presented here have important implications for the assessment and formulation of the public policy in Burkina Faso.

To produce more reliable poverty indicators, comparable over time, the following is suggested:

- Improve the collection of price statistics, both outside and within the survey, by collecting information on both quantities consumed and the value of the respective purchases, or by administering price questionnaires at community level.
- Implement the survey in quarterly waves (quarterly panel), to eliminate the influence that seasonality and short-lived shocks have on reported consumption.
- Provide adequate financing for the survey, for an adequate monitoring of poverty and to ensure the comparability of the welfare indicators from micro and macro data sources.

The case of the poverty statistics in Burkina Faso is not singular, and seems to be more the rule than the exception. Almost all countries have improved their surveys over time, and placed most efforts in generating an improved poverty profile based on the most recent and reliable information. There was considerably less effort directed toward ensuring the comparability of those estimates with those derived from earlier surveys. Awareness of the fragility of poverty statistics derived from non comparable surveys is on the rise, as a number of recent studies have shown.

At the same time, the paper raises a red flag on the fragility of poverty estimates in Sub-Saharan Africa and possibly elsewhere, which are found to be extremely sensitive to changes in the recall period and the timing of survey. Apparently innocuous changes in survey design, such as the change in the recall period, have triggered substantial and spurious changes in reported consumption, and hence poverty. In addition, the timing of the survey has substantial impact on poverty trends, probably more so in the arid West African context than elsewhere, given the large differences in consumption in the lean (pre-harvest) and the post-harvest seasons.

## References

Deaton, A. 2003. *Measuring Poverty in a Growing World (or "Measuring Growth in a Poor World")*. NBER Working Paper 9822; RPDS Working Paper 222, Princeton University.

Deaton A., and Margaret Grosh. 2000. "Consumption." In Grosh and Glewwe, eds., *Designing Household Survey Questionnaires for Developing Countries: Lessons from Ten Years of LSMS Experience.*

Deaton A., and Salman Zaidi. 1999. *Guidelines for Constructing Consumption Aggregates for Welfare Analysis.* RPDS Working Paper 192, Princeton University.

Dercon S., and Pamela Krishnan. 2000. "Vulnerability, Seasonality and Poverty in Ethiopia." *The Journal of Development Studies* 36(6).

INSD. 1996. *Le Profil de Pauvreté au Burkina Faso—Etude Statistique Nationale.* Ouagadougou.

———. 2000. *Profil et Evolution de la Pauvreté au Burkina Faso—Etude Statistique Nationale.* Ouagadougou.

———. 2003. *Burkina Faso: La Pauvreté en 2003—version provisoire.* Ouagadougou.

Lanjouw, J. O., and Peter Lanjouw. 2000. *How to Compare Apples and Oranges: Poverty Measurement.*

Paternostro, S., Jean Razafindravonona, and David Stifel. 2001. "Changes in Poverty in Madagascar: 1993–1999." Africa Region Working Paper Series No. 19, The World Bank, Washington, D.C.

Ravallion, M. 1998. *Poverty Lines in Theory and Practice.* LSMS Working Paper 133. The Washington D.C.: The World Bank.

World Bank. 2004. "Burkina Faso: Risk and Vulnerability Assessment." Report No. 28144-BUR. Human Development Unit, Africa Region, The World Bank, Washington, D.C.

# Annex

## Table A4.1. Assignment of the PS II and III Non-Food Codes into the Nine Commodity Groups

| Commodity Group | PS II 1998 Included | PS II 1998 Excluded | PS III (CWIQ) 2003 Included | PS III (CWIQ) 2003 Excluded |
|---|---|---|---|---|
| Food, beverages and tobacco | 19+food | | 221 + food | |
| Clothes and shoes | c 15–18 | | 215–220 | |
| Rent and utilities | c 1–8 | | 201–208 | |
| Housing maintenance | c 9–14,26,28,29 | 25,27 | 209–214,232,234,235 | 229–231, 233 |
| Health | health | | health | |
| Transport | 20 | | 222 | |
| Leisure | 21 | 22 | 223 | 224 |
| Schooling | school | | school | |
| Other goods and services | 24, 30,31 | 23 | 228, 236, 237 | 225–227 |

## Table A4.2. Regional Price Deflators Used in 1994 by INSD

| Strate | Regional Price Deflator Total | Regional Price Deflator Food | Regional Price Deflator Non-Food | Weights Food | Weights Non-Food | Weights Rent | Weights Total |
|---|---|---|---|---|---|---|---|
| ouest | 0.842 | 0.804 | 0.936 | 0.54 | 0.39 | 0.07 | 1.00 |
| sud et sud ouest | 0.863 | 0.825 | 0.947 | 0.54 | 0.40 | 0.07 | 1.00 |
| centre nord | 0.888 | 0.890 | 0.927 | 0.55 | 0.34 | 0.11 | 1.00 |
| centre sud | 0.863 | 0.854 | 0.921 | 0.54 | 0.36 | 0.10 | 1.00 |
| nord | 0.979 | 1.004 | 0.973 | 0.66 | 0.30 | 0.04 | 1.00 |
| autres villes | 0.970 | 0.962 | 1.010 | 0.40 | 0.50 | 0.10 | 1.00 |
| ouaga bobo | 1.000 | 1.000 | 1.000 | 0.36 | 0.51 | 0.13 | 1.00 |

## Table A4.3. Regional Price Deflators Used in 1998 by INSD

| Region | Price Index |
|---|---|
| ouest | 0.83 |
| nord-ouest | 0.75 |
| sahel | 0.87 |
| est | 0.79 |
| sud-ouest | 0.69 |
| centre nord | 0.85 |
| centre-ouest | 0.74 |
| centre | 0.89 |
| nord | 0.78 |
| centre-est | 0.56 |

## Table A4.4. Regional Price Deflators Used in 2003 by INSD

| Région | Price Index |
|---|---|
| Hauts Bassins | 0.96 |
| Boucle du Mouhoun | 0.86 |
| Sahel | 1.01 |
| Est | 0.71 |
| Sud Ouest | 0.84 |
| Centre Nord | 0.80 |
| Centre Ouest | 0.82 |
| Plateau central | 0.97 |
| Nord | 0.91 |
| Centre Est | 0.84 |
| Centre | 1.00 |
| Cascades | 0.96 |
| Centre Sud | 0.89 |

**Table A4.5. Correspondence of the Codes of the Consumption Items in the Three Surveys**

| | PS I 1994 | PS II 1998 | PS III 2003 |
|---|---|---|---|
| *depenses scolaires* | l'annee scolaire passee | l'annee scolaire en cours | l'annee scolaire en cours |
| frais de scolarite | q10a11 (?) | N | N |
| livres et fournitures | q10a21(6) | N | N |
| frais transport scolaire | q10a31(6) | N | N |
| diverses contributions scolaires | q10a41 6 | — | — |
| cotisations des parents d'eleves | — | N | N |
| autres contributions scolaires | — | N | N |
| uniformes scolaires | — | | N |
| *depenses de sante* | 30 derniers jours | 30 derniers jours | 30 derniers jours |
| frais consultations | q10a51(6) | N | N |
| medicaments | q10a61(6) | N | N |
| hospitalisation | q10a71(6) | N | N |
| autres services medicaux | q10a81(6) | N | N |
| frais d'analyses medicales | — | N | N |
| *depenses alimentaires* | 30 derniers jours | 15 derniers jours | 15 derniers jours |
| 1 Riz | 1 | 1 | 101 |
| 2 Mil et sorgho | 2 | 2,3 | 102,103 |
| 3 Maïs | 3 | 4 | 104 |
| 4 Niébé | 4 | 5 | 105 |
| 5 Farines | 5 | 6 | 106 |
| 6 Igname,tuber. et plan | 6 | 9 | 109 |
| 7 Poisson et prod mer | 7 | 10 | 110,111 |
| 8 Viandes et oeufs | 8 | 11,12,26 | 112,113,114,115,132 |
| 9 Huiles | 9 | 13 | 116 |
| 10 Arach. et pâte d ara | 10 | 14,15 | 117,118 |
| 11 Tomate en pot | 11 | 16 | 119 |
| 12 Fruits | 12 | 17 | 120 |
| 13 Légumes | 13 | 18 | 121,122,123,124 |
| 14 Condiments et assais | 14 | 19,20,21,22 | 125,126,127,128 |
| 15 Pain, galettes, confis | 15 | 7,8 | 107,108 |
| 16 Sucre | 16 | 23 | 129 |
| 17 Café, thé, cacao | 17 | 24 | 130 |
| 18 Produits laitiers | 18 | 25 | 131 |
| 19 Boisson non alcoolis | 19 | 27 | 133, 136 |
| 20 Boissons alcoolisées | 20 | 28,29,30 | 134,135 |
| 21 Eau | 21 | 31 | 137 |
| 22 Cola | 22 | 32 | 138 |
| 23 Autres dép. aliment. | 23 | 33 | 139 |
| 24 Ensemble aliment. | 24 | | |
| (Ne peut pas detailler) | | 34 | 140 |

**Table A4.5.  Correspondence of the Codes of the Consumption Items in the Three Surveys**
           *(Continued)*

| depenses non-alimentaires | PS I 1994 30 derniers jours | PS II 1998 30 derniers jours | PS III 2003 30 derniers jours |
|---|---|---|---|
| 1 Charbon de bois | 1 | 1 | 201 |
| 2 Bois | 2 | 2 | 202 |
| 3 Gaz | 3 | 3 | 203 |
| 4 Electricité | 4 | 5 | 205 |
| 5 Bougie, pétrole | 5 | 6,7 | 206,207 |
| 6 Loyer | 6 | 8 | 208 |
| 7 Téléphone | 7 | 9 | 209 |
| 8 Domestique | 8 | 10 | 210 |
| 9 Equipement de ménage | 9 | 27,28 | 233,234 |
| 10 Savon,produits d ent | 10 | 11,12 | 211,212 |
| 11 Cosmétique,soin corp | 11 | 13 | 213 |
| 12 Habillem., cout., chauss. | 12 | 14,15,16,17,18 | 214–220 |
| 13 Cigarette-tabac | 13 | 19 | 221 |
| 14 Voyagestransport | 14 | 20 | 222 |
| 15 Loisirs | 15 | 21 | 223 |
| 16 Cérémonies diverses | 16 | 22 | 224 |
| 17 Matériel roulant | 17 | 23 | 225–227 |
| 18 Essence, lubrifiant | 18 | 24 | 228 |
| 19 Investissement | 19 | 25 | 229,230,231 |
| 20 Transferts versés | 20 | 30 | 236 |
| 21 Santé | 21 | — | — |
| 22 Autres dépenses | 22 | 31 | 237 |
| 4 Eau acheté (fontaine, facture et frais de branchement) | voire depense alimentaire | 21 | 204 |
| 26 Réparation d'équipement de ménage: radio, téléviseur, réfrigérateur, congélateur | | 26 | 232,235 |
| 31 Autres dépenses | | | 237 |

# CHAPTER 5

# Assessing Absolute and Relative Poverty Trends with Limited Data in Cape Verde

*By Diego Angel-Urdinola and Quentin Wodon*[23]

*Cape Verde shifted from a socialist to a capitalistic model in the late 1980s. This shift enabled the population to benefit from rapid economic growth, but concerns have been expressed about a potential increase in inequality. Two household surveys with consumption data implemented in 1988–89 and 2001–02 provide information that can be used to assess the impact on welfare of this policy shift. Initial estimates based on these two surveys suggested that there had been an increase in poverty over time, but this was mainly due to the adoption of a relative measure of poverty and to comparability issues between the surveys. The task of assessing the trends in poverty and inequality was also made more difficult because the unit level data of the first survey are not available. For the period 1988–89, the only information at our disposal consists of a number of tables on the distribution of income in the original report prepared 15 years ago on that survey. This makes it necessary to estimate poverty and inequality using group data. In this paper, we use the Poverty module of SimSIP in order to obtain new poverty and inequality trends over time with group data. We find that despite an increase in inequality over time, and thereby an increase in relative measures of poverty, absolute poverty measures have been reduced dramatically thanks to rapid growth.*

Cape Verde is a small country constituted by ten islands located 650 kilometers away from the coast of Senegal and with an area of 4036 square kilometers. Out of the ten islands, only nine are populated and more than half of the total population of

---

23.  Diego Angel-Urdinola and Quentin Wodon are with the World Bank. This paper was prepared as a contribution to the poverty assessment for Cape Verde prepared by the World Bank (see World Bank 2005; the previous poverty assessment dated back to 1994). The views expressed here are those of the authors, and they do not necessarily represent those of the World Bank, its Executive Directors, or the countries they represent.

434,625 people according to the 2002 census lives in the Island of Santigo. Due to the particularities of the country's Sahelian climate (dryness and lack of rain), only one tenth of the country's soil is arable. Persistent periods of drought and a shortfall of water supply from rivers and springs makes it difficult for the country to develop a stable agricultural production, and even in the best rain seasons, agricultural production is able to supply only part of the population's food requirements.

After independence in 1975, the economic model of Cape Verde relied on the government to assume a leading role of entrepreneurship in agriculture, industry, and services, giving low importance to the private sector, and creating public enterprises within the key sectors of the economy. These strategies lead to deterioration in competitiveness, low levels of foreign direct investment, and poor overall economic performance. In 1988, the post independence government adopted a new economic model with an outward oriented strategy consisting on privatizing public enterprises and promoting trade liberalization. Government spending shifted rapidly into building economic and social infrastructure, leaving private investment to take the lead in some industries, especially light manufacturing and fisheries.

High unemployment rates in the late 1980s and inequalities between the islands led to a switch in government in 1991. The incoming government continued to decrease the role of the state in the economy and set priorities towards improving education and reducing poverty and unemployment. Also, new legislation and reforms, that still need to be refined and implemented fully, were adopted on various aspects related to foreign investment, privatization, and offshore banking services. The new government also pursued multilateral and bilateral donor assistance in order to improve services for human and capital infrastructure.

As a result of these reforms, remarkable growth has been achieved since the late 1980s. Between 1988 and 2002, real GDP grew, on average, at 6.4 percent and inflation was contained at an average rate of 3 percent per annum. Most of the growth was generated within services, where private sector activities increased dramatically as the state withdrew from the sector following reforms implemented throughout the 1990s. Construction and trade are now the largest sectors of the economy. Together they constitute about 30 percent of GDP (each accounts for about 15 percent of GDP). The fastest growing sectors within services, however, are hotel and restaurant services, transport, and communications. These sectors owe much of their growth to a large expansion in tourism. In 2001, tourist arrivals increased by 50 percent, and the number of visitors has been growing by 10 to 20 percent in subsequent years.

The objective of this paper is to assess the impact of the reforms on poverty, in the specific sense of measuring the reduction in poverty that was achieved in parallel with the implementation of reforms. The shift in policy enabled the population to benefit from rapid economic growth, but concerns have been expressed about a potential increase in inequality. In order to assess the changes in poverty and inequality since the late 1980s, we rely on two household surveys with consumption data implemented in 1988–89 and 2001–02 (these are the IDRF surveys—Inquerito As Despensas E Receitas Familiares). Assessing the trends in poverty and inequality is however difficult because the unit level data of the first survey are not available. For the period 1988–89, the only information at our disposal consists of a number of tables on the distribution of income in the original report prepared 15 years ago on that survey. This makes it necessary to estimate poverty and inequality using group data, which is done using the Poverty module of SimSIP, a set of excel based tools for "Simulations for Social Indicators and Poverty." The advantage of using the SimSIP poverty module is that it enables the analyst to estimate poverty and inequality measures solely on the basis of grouped data. The next section provides our methodology. The second section describes the main results. We find that despite an increase in inequality over time, poverty has been reduced dramatically thanks to rapid growth. A brief conclusion follows.

## Methodology for Poverty Measurement

As noted in Coudouel and others (2002), in order to compute a poverty measure, three ingredients are needed. First, one has to select a relevant indicator of well-being. Second, one has to select a poverty line, that is, a threshold below which a given household or individual will be classified as poor. Finally, one has to select a poverty measure, which is used for reporting for the population as a whole or for a population subgroup only. In this paper, we will rely on the Foster-Greer-Thorbecke (1984) class of poverty measures. The general formula for this class of poverty measures depends on a parameter $\alpha$ which takes a value of zero for the head count, one for the poverty gap, and two for the squared poverty gap in the following expression:

$$P\alpha = \frac{1}{n}\sum_{i=1}^{q}\left[\frac{z-y_i}{z}\right]^{\alpha} \tag{1}$$

The headcount index gives the share of the population or households in poverty. The poverty gap takes into account the distance separating the poor from the poverty line. The squared poverty gap places a higher weight on the poorest households in the sample.

Two poverty lines for the 2001–02 household survey were obtained using INE's methodology. A household is considered as poor if its per capita consumption falls below a relative poverty line equal to 60 percent of the median household consumption per capita in the 2001–02 survey. That is, the method consists in ranking all households according to their per capita consumption, selecting the household at the 50th percentile of the distribution of household consumption, calculating a poverty line corresponding to 60 percent of the consumption level of that household, and considering all households with a lower per capita consumption as poor. For extreme poverty, we use a poverty line equal to 40 percent of the median per capita consumption at the household level. Using these definitions, the poverty and extreme poverty lines used in this note are respectively CV$43,250 and CV$28,833 (Escudos) per capita per year. At the current exchange rate of approximately 109 Escudos per U.S. dollar, this translates in poverty lines of about US$1.09 per day for poverty, and US$0.73 per day for extreme poverty.

Note that if the definition had been based on the level of consumption of the median individual in the population as a whole (instead of the median household), the method would have resulted in lower poverty lines (and thereby lower poverty measures) as poorer households tend to be larger in household size, so that the household in which the median individual is located is poorer than the median household.

In the terminology of poverty measurement, the approach adopted by INE is a relative approach (because the poverty line is defined relatively, in comparison to the standard of living in the country). An absolute approach to poverty measurement would have proceeded differently, by estimating a poverty line corresponding to the cost of basic food and non-food needs. However, even though poverty was measured by INE in relative terms in 2001–02, we can still obtain absolute trends in poverty over time by adjusting the poverty lines estimated in 2001–02, to reflect the inflation observed between 1988–89 and 2001–02. We can also obtain trends in relative poverty by applying the same method for estimating relative poverty lines using the 1988–89 data. In this paper, we will provide both absolute and relative poverty trends.

Following standard practice, the indicator of well-being is the per capita consumption of the household obtained by aggregating all sources of consumption in the survey and when needed, imputing additional sources of consumption. The estimation of per capita consumption for the 2001–02 survey was done by INE. A key problem was to obtain similar values for 1988–89. Because we did not have access to the unit level data from that survey, grouped data (mean values for different groups of households ranked by increasing consumption levels) had to be used. We used tabulations provided in a report written close to 15 years ago on poverty measurement with the 1988–89 survey. Yet the tabulations were not available in an appropriate format. Instead of providing data on per capita consumption, the only estimates available were in terms of total household consumption, without information on the mean household size.

Specifically, the information we have at our disposal is provided in the first column of Table 5.1. We know the share of total expenditure accruing to each of ten deciles of households (each deciles comprises of ten percent of households). Given that we also have the total level of consumption in the survey, this enables us to compute the total level of consumption in each household decile. What we need to do is estimate the number of individuals in each decile so that we can obtain an approximation of the level of per capita consumption by decile (by simply dividing household consumption by the estimated household size in each decile). Because we do not have access to the 1988–89 survey, we need to work from the mean household sizes in 2001–02, and make a number of assump-

**Table 5.1. Consumption Distribution in 1988/99 Based on Assumptions for Fertility Rates**

| Decile | Percent of total consumption by household decile (1) | Household consumption by decile (2) | Estimate of number of individuals by decile in 1988 (3) | Mean Consumption per capita by household decile (4) |
|---|---|---|---|---|
| 1 | 2.0 | 224,129,24 | 34,542 | 6,489 |
| 2 | 3.0 | 336,193,86 | 33,200 | 10,126 |
| 3 | 4.0 | 448,258,48 | 31,769 | 14,110 |
| 4 | 6.0 | 672,387,72 | 32,042 | 20,985 |
| 5 | 6.0 | 672,387,72 | 31,749 | 21,178 |
| 6 | 8.0 | 896,516,96 | 31,112 | 28,816 |
| 7 | 10.0 | 1,120,646,20 | 30,407 | 36,855 |
| 8 | 13.0 | 1,456,840,06 | 27,414 | 53,142 |
| 9 | 17.0 | 1,905,098,54 | 25,489 | 74,741 |
| 10 | 31.0 | 3,474,003,22 | 19,137 | 181,536 |
| Total | 100.0 | 11,206,462,00 | 296,860 | 37,750 |

*Source:* Authors using IDRF, 2001/02 and Inquérito as famílias, Cape Verde 1988–99.

tions in order to obtain estimates of the corresponding mean household sizes by household decile for 1988–89, taking into account demographic trends.

As shown in Table 5.2, data from recent demographic and health-type surveys are available on fertility rates in urban and rural areas for two periods of time: the period 1985–88, which precedes the first survey, and the period 1995–98, which precedes the second survey (INE, 1998). They show that fertility decreased faster in urban areas (from 5.24 to 3.14) than in rural areas (from 6.40 to 4.85). The issue is to find a realistic way to relate these fertility rates to expected changes in household size by consumption decile between both surveys.

**Table 5.2. Using Fertility Data to Estimate Normalized Populations by Decile in 1988–89**

| | Fertility Rates | | | |
|---|---|---|---|---|
| | 1995–1998 | | 1985–1988 | |
| Total | 4.030 | | 5.950 | |
| Urban (U) | 3.140 | | 5.240 | |
| Rural (R) | 4.850 | | 6.400 | |
| U / (U + R) | 0.393 | | 0.450 | |
| Decile | Share of population by household decile (2001 data) (5) | Share of population adjustment factor (6) | Share of population by household decile (2001 data) adjusted (7) | Estimate for population shares by household decile in 1988/89 * (8) |
| 1 | 14.26 | 1.00 | 14.26 | 11.64 |
| 2 | 12.93 | 1.06 | 13.71 | 11.18 |
| 3 | 11.71 | 1.12 | 13.12 | 10.70 |
| 4 | 11.21 | 1.18 | 13.23 | 10.79 |
| 5 | 10.57 | 1.24 | 13.11 | 10.69 |
| 6 | 9.88 | 1.30 | 12.84 | 10.48 |
| 7 | 9.23 | 1.36 | 12.55 | 10.24 |
| 8 | 7.97 | 1.42 | 11.32 | 9.23 |
| 9 | 7.11 | 1.48 | 10.52 | 8.59 |
| 10 | 5.13 | 1.54 | 7.90 | 6.45 |
| Total | 100.0 | - | 122.55 | 100.00 |

*Source:* Authors using IDRF, 2001/02 and Inquérito as famílias, Cape Verde 1988–99.

Consider first the 2001–02 survey. The urban ($U$) fertility rate as a share to the sum of the urban and rural rates was 39.3 percent in 1995–98. We also know that households are roughly evenly divided between urban and rural areas. If we assume that the top half of the distribution of households (the richer 50 percent) is somewhat representative of the urban areas because these are richer than rural areas, then we could conjecture on the basis of the independent information on fertility rates that the population share in the top half of the distribution according to household deciles will be equal to 39.3 percent. Luckily enough, this is what we observe in the data, as the actual population size in these five deciles is 39.3 percent.

$$\frac{F_U^{1995-98}}{F_U^{1995-98} + F_R^{1995-98}} = 0.393 = \sum_{i=6}^{10} Pop_i^{2001-02} \tag{2}$$

Then, our assumption will be that for the previous survey, the population share in the top five deciles should be roughly equal to 45.0 percent, which is the ratio of the fertility rate in urban areas divided by the sum of the fertility rates in urban and rural areas observed for the period 1985–88. In order to obtain this cumulative population share of 45.0 percent, we need to estimate "normalized population shares" by decile, denoted by $NPop_i^{1988-89}$, for each decile so that their sum for the top five deciles represent 45.0 percent of the total population, so that:

$$\frac{F_U^{1985-88}}{F_U^{1985-88} + F_R^{1985-88}} = 0.450 = \sum_{i=6}^{10} NPop_i^{1988-89} \tag{3}$$

As fertility rates decrease over time, household sizes also decreases, so that for any given household decile, the mean household size should be smaller over time, but the speed of the reduction in fertility is likely to be strongest for the richest deciles (or for the urban households, as noted above). We could assume for example that:

$$Pop_i^{1988-89} = \alpha_i \times Pop_i^{2001-02}, \text{with } \alpha_i = 1 + \rho(i-1). \tag{4}$$

The problem with (4) is that if we simply multiply the population shares in 2001–02 in each decile by the parameters, we will have a sum of population shares above 100 percent in the survey as a whole. In order to get back to 100 percent as the sum of the population shares in the various household deciles, we need to normalize the population shares as follows:

$$NPop_i^{1988-89} = \frac{1+\rho(i-1)}{N} \times Pop_i^{2001-02}, \text{ with } N = \frac{\sum_{j=1}^{10}(1+\rho(j-1))Pop_j^{2001-02}}{100} \tag{5}$$

As shown in the bottom part of Table 5.2, the value of the parameter $\rho$ that satisfies equations (3) and (5) turns out to be 0.06. Using this parameter, we can compute the population or alternatively the household sizes in each decile in 1998–89. The results are given in the third column of Table 5.1, which gives the estimated number of individuals in each decile, so that the per capita consumption can be computed in column 4. These are the values that we will use for estimating poverty and inequality measures. Note that by reconstructing the household size and population in the 1988–89 survey, we find in Table 5.3

| | Total Consumption in National Accounts (1) | Total Population (2) | Total Consumption in Survey (3) | Expanded Sample Size (4) | Ratio of Consumption per capita in survey versus National Accounts (5) |
|---|---|---|---|---|---|
| **Table 5.3. Consumption in National Accounts vs. Consumption in Surveys** | | | | | |
| 1988 | 19366000.0 | 328000.0 | 11206462.0 | 296860.0 | 0.6 |
| 2001 | 69934000.0 | 446000.0 | 46463000.0 | 470687.0 | 0.6 |

*Source:* Authors using 2001–02 and 1988–89 surveys. National Accounts data were provided by INE.

that the share of total consumption in the 1988–89 and 2001–02 surveys in proportion to total private consumption as registered in the national accounts is very similar, at roughly 60 percent, which gives us some confidence in comparing poverty and inequality estimates obtained from both surveys.

## Trend in Poverty

Having estimated poverty lines and levels of per capita consumption, we use the Poverty module of the SimSIP family of simulation tools (available at www.worldbank.org\simsip) to compute poverty and inequality measures (for a discussion of the poverty module of SimSIP, see Datt and others 2003). The data used in the simulator is in Table 5.4. To account for inflation (and use the 2001–02 poverty lines for both years), we multiplied the 1988–89 distribution by the national CPI deflator (cumulative inflation between 1989 and 2002 was 86.3 percent). The 1988–89 distribution corrected for inflation (in 2002 constant prices) is presented in Table 5.4, column 3. The distribution of per capita consumption by population decile for the year 2001–02 is directly obtained from the unit level data and presented in column 4 of Table 5.4. These are also the data entered in the SimSIP Poverty module, as shown in Figure 5.1 for 1988–89 (the population shares by household decile are taken from Table 5.2).

**Table 5.4. Distributions of Consumption Per Capita in 2001–02 Constant Currency**

| Decile | Mean consumption by decile in 1989 current prices (1) | Deflator (2) | 1988/89 Mean consumption per capita by household decile in 2001 prices (3) | 2001/02 Mean consumption per capita by population decile (4) |
|---|---|---|---|---|
| 1 | 6,489 | 1.8630 | 12,088 | 15,668 |
| 2 | 10,126 | 1.8630 | 18,866 | 25,316 |
| 3 | 14,110 | 1.8630 | 26,287 | 33,046 |
| 4 | 20,985 | 1.8630 | 39,095 | 41,775 |
| 5 | 21,178 | 1.8630 | 39,455 | 51,498 |
| 6 | 28,816 | 1.8630 | 53,684 | 64,035 |
| 7 | 36,855 | 1.8630 | 68,661 | 79,956 |
| 8 | 53,142 | 1.8630 | 99,003 | 103,241 |
| 9 | 74,741 | 1.8630 | 139,242 | 151,767 |
| 10 | 181,536 | 1.8630 | 338,202 | 421,257 |

*Source:* Authors using 2001–02 and 1988–89 surveys. Deflator was provided by INE.

Because for period 1 (1988–89) data on the distribution of consumption is available only at the national level and no other desegregation (such as urban/rural or by sector) is at hand, we leave blank the columns pre-designated for these data. Clicking the "Load Period 1 data" button enables the simulator to load the data. We repeat the same operation for period 2 (2001–02). After data for periods 1 and 2 has been entered, the user must

**Figure 5.1. Data Entry Window for SimSIP in Cape Verde, Period 1 (1988–89)**

| | | Time Period 1 | | | | | | | | | | |
|---|---|---|---|---|---|---|---|---|---|---|---|---|
| | | Urban | | Rural | | Group 1 | | Group 2 | | Group 3 | | National | |
| | | Percent of Population per interval | Mean income or Expenditures | Percent of Population per interval | Mean income or Expenditures | Percent of Population per interval | Mean income or Expenditures | Percent of Population per interval | Mean income or Expenditures | Percent of Population per interval | Mean income or Expenditures | Percent of Population per interval | Mean income or Expenditures |
| 4 | | | | | | | | | | | | 11.64 | 12,088 |
| 5 | | | | | | | | | | | | 11.18 | 18,866 |
| 6 | | | | | | | | | | | | 10.70 | 26,287 |
| 7 | | | | | | | | | | | | 10.79 | 39,095 |
| 8 | | | | | | | | | | | | 10.89 | 39,455 |
| 9 | | | | | | | | | | | | 10.48 | 53,684 |
| 10 | | | | | | | | | | | | 10.24 | 68,661 |
| 11 | | | | | | | | | | | | 9.23 | 99,003 |
| 12 | | | | | | | | | | | | 8.59 | 139,242 |
| 13 | | | | | | | | | | | | 6.45 | 338,202 |
| 14 | Poverty | z1(mod) | z2(ex) | z1 | z2 | z1 | z2 | z1 | z2 | z1 | z2 | z1 | z2 |
| 15 | Lines | 43250.00 | 28833.00 | | | | | | | | | 43250.00 | 28833.00 |

| | Intervals | | | | | | Populations Shares | | | | |
|---|---|---|---|---|---|---|---|---|---|---|---|
| | Urban | Rural | Group 1 | Group 2 | Group 3 | National | Urban | Rural | Group 1 | Group 2 | Group 3 |
| 19 | | | | | | 15,239 | | | | | |
| 20 | | | | | | 22,229 | | | | | |
| 21 | | | | | | 32,188 | | | | | |
| 22 | | | | | | 38,671 | | | | | |
| 23 | | | | | | 45,854 | | Load Period 1 data | | Return to Main Page | |
| 24 | | | | | | 60,232 | | | | | |
| 25 | | | | | | 82,543 | | | | Click for Time Period 2 | |
| 26 | | | | | | 117,291 | | | | | |
| 27 | | | | | | 235,052 | | | | | |
| 28 | | | | | | 568,054 | | | | | |

*Source*: Authors using 1988–89 survey.

click on the "Return to main page" button in order to see the simulation results. Results are automatically displayed, as shown in Figure 5.2, which provides measures of poverty and extreme poverty (head count, poverty gap, and squared poverty gap) as well as other statistics such the mean of the welfare indicator and the Gini coefficient. The simulator also presents the results of a growth and inequality decomposition of changes in poverty that will be discussed below. There are many cells marked "N/A" for not available in Figure 5.2 simply because we did not enter data for urban and rural areas separately, nor did we do this for various groups (groups 1 to 3 in the simulator).

Table 5.5 provides the key results in a more visible way. The share of the population in poverty (head-count index) in 2001–02 was 36.69 percent of the population. This implies that roughly 173,000 people were poor. Out of these, about 93,000 (20.50 percent of the population) lived in extreme poverty (their per capita consumption was below 28,833 Escudos per year).

If we adopt for 1988–89 a poverty line which corresponds to the same value in real terms as the 2001–02 poverty line (in order to compute a trend in terms of absolute poverty), we find that the share of the population living in poverty was reduced from 48.97 percent in 1988/89 to 36.69 percent in 2001/02 (a reduction of 12.28 points, one fourth of the initial level). The share of the population in extreme poverty was reduced from 32.34 percent to 20.50 percent. Other poverty measures such as the poverty gap (which takes into account the distance separating the poor from the poverty line) and the squared poverty gap (which takes into account the inequality among the poor) also decreased dramatically. For information, the survey data also suggest that the share of total consumption devoted to food (which can be considered to a large extent as consisting of basic necessities) was reduced from 50 percent to 35 percent, which is another indication of the large improvement in living standards observed between the two surveys.

## Figure 5.2.  SimSIP Results for Poverty Trends in Cape Verde, 1988–89 to 2001–02

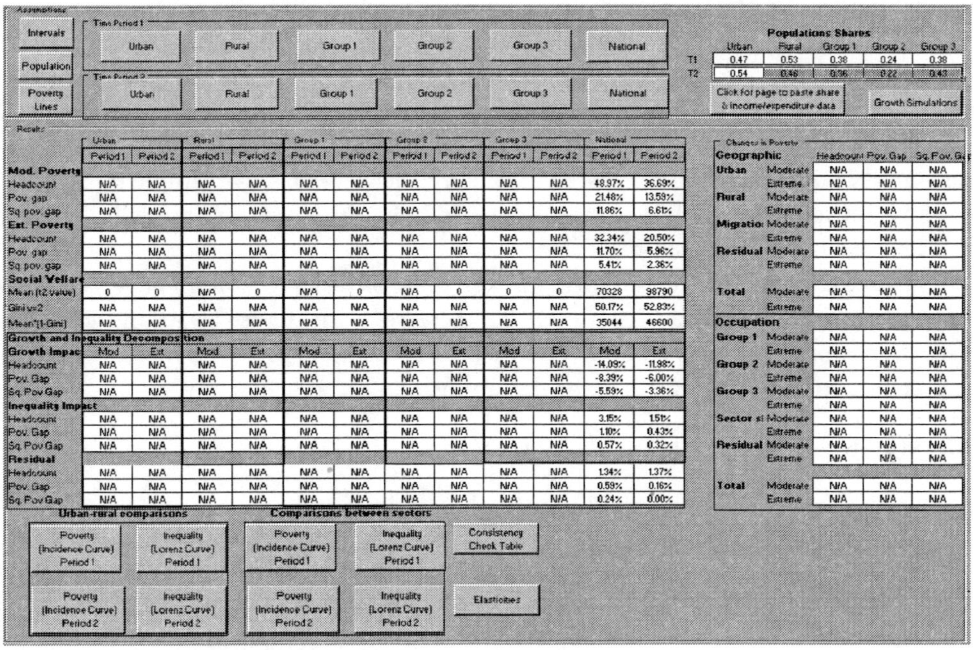

*Source*: Authors using 2001–02 and 1988–99 surveys. Deflator was provided by INE.

## Table 5.5.  Trend in Poverty and Inequality Measures, Cape Verde 1998–99 to 2001–02

| | 1998–99 Absolute poverty (with 2001–02 relative poverty line) | 1988–89 Relative poverty | 2001–02 Relative poverty |
|---|---|---|---|
| **Moderate Poverty** | | | |
| Head count | 48.97% | 31.15% | 36.69% |
| Poverty Gap | 21.48% | 11.06% | 13.59% |
| Squared poverty Gap | 11.86% | 5.02% | 6.61% |
| **Extreme Poverty** | | | |
| Head count | 32.34% | 17.32% | 20.50% |
| Poverty Gap | 11.70% | 4.36% | 5.96% |
| Squared poverty Gap | 5.41% | 1.40% | 2.36% |
| **Social Welfare** | | | |
| Mean consumption | 70328 | 70328 | 98790 |
| Gini index | 50.17% | 50.17% | 52.83% |
| Mean*(1-Gini) | 35044 | 35044 | 46600 |

*Source:*  Authors using SimSIP and 2001–02 and 1988–89 surveys.

If we adopt instead a relative poverty measurement approach for the 1988–89 survey, using an estimate of the median household per capita consumption of 46,570 Escudos, we find that the corresponding poverty lines are respectively 27,941.77 Escudos for poverty, and 18,627.84 for extreme poverty. As shown in Table 5.5, we find that relative poverty increased from 31.15 percent in 1988–89 to 36.69 percent in 2001–02, and relative extreme poverty increased similarly. This increase in relative poverty is due to an increase in inequality, as observed for example with the Gini index rising from 50.17 in 1988/89 to 52.83 in 2001/02. Despite the increase in inequality, social welfare, as captured by the mean per capita consumption times one minus the Gini index, increased substantially, by about a third versus the level in 1988–89.

The simulator also provides information on the changes in (absolute) poverty that are due to growth and those that are due to the increase in inequality (Datt and Ravallion 1992). Denoting by $P(\mu_t, L_t)$ the poverty measure corresponding to a mean income in period $t$ of $\mu_t$ and a Lorenz curve $L_t$, the decomposition is:

$$\Delta P = \left[ P(\mu_2, L_r) - P(\mu_1, L_r) \right] + \left[ P(\mu_r, L_2) - P(\mu_r, L_1) \right] + R_r \tag{6}$$

The first component is the change in poverty that would have been observed if the Lorenz curve had remained unchanged, while the second component is the change that would have been observed if mean income had not changed. The last component is a residual. As reproduced in Table 5.6, without the increase in inequality, the reduction in the share of the population in absolute poverty would have been larger (14.09 points for instead of 12.28 points).

| Table 5.6. Growth-Inequality Decomposition of Changes in Poverty, 1998–99 to 2001–02 | | |
| --- | --- | --- |
| | Mod. poverty | Extreme poverty |
| **Growth Impact** | | |
| Head count | −14.09% | −11.98% |
| Poverty Gap | −8.39% | −6.00% |
| Squared poverty Gap | −5.59% | −3.36% |
| **Inequality Impact** | | |
| Head count | 3.15% | 1.51% |
| Poverty Gap | 1.10% | 0.43% |
| Squared poverty Gap | 0.57% | 0.32% |
| **Residual** | | |
| Head count | 1.34% | 1.37% |
| Poverty Gap | 0.59% | 0.16% |
| Squared poverty Gap | 0.24% | 0.00% |

*Source:* Authors using SimSIP and 2001–02 and 1988–89 surveys.

The simulator also enables the user to predict future poverty based on growth assumptions. Here, we report only simulations based on a national growth rate (simulations with different growth rates for different sectors could also be provided). For example, if we wanted to be optimistic, we could first assume 13 years (from 2002 to 2015) of sustained growth at 5 percent per year per capita. If there is no change in inequality, the impact will be equivalent to multiplying the per capita consumption levels for all deciles by 1.89 [because $(1.05)^{13} = 1.885649$]. The share of the population in (absolute) poverty would then decrease from 36.69 percent to 13.11 percent, as shown in Figure 5.5 (the cells with N/A or #VALUE! in Figure 5.3 are again simply due to the fact that we did not enter in the simulator separate data for urban and rural areas or by sector or "groups").

**Figure 5.3. Future Poverty and Growth Simulation Results, Cape Verde**

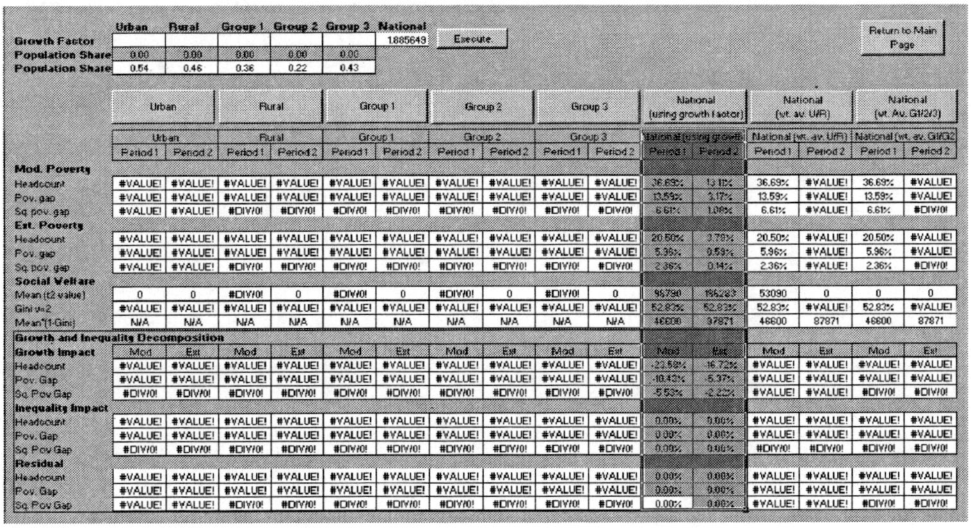

| | Urban | Rural | Group 1 | Group 2 | Group 3 | National |
|---|---|---|---|---|---|---|
| Growth Factor | | | | | | 1.885649 |
| Population Share | 0.00 | 0.00 | 0.00 | 0.00 | 0.00 | |
| Population Share | 0.54 | 0.46 | 0.36 | 0.22 | 0.43 | |

Execute

Return to Main Page

| | Urban | | Rural | | Group 1 | | Group 2 | | Group 3 | | National (using growth factor) | | National (wt. av. U/R) | | National (wt. Av. G1/2/3) | |
|---|---|---|---|---|---|---|---|---|---|---|---|---|---|---|---|---|
| | Urban | | Rural | | Group 1 | | Group 2 | | Group 3 | | National (using growth | | National (wt. av. U/R) | | National (wt. av. G1/G2 | |
| | Period 1 | Period 2 | Period 1 | Period 2 | Period 1 | Period 2 | Period 1 | Period 2 | Period 1 | Period 2 | Period 1 | Period 2 | Period 1 | Period 2 | Period 1 | Period 2 |
| **Mod. Poverty** | | | | | | | | | | | | | | | | |
| Headcount | #VALUE! | #VALUE! | #VALUE! | #VALUE! | #VALUE! | #VALUE! | #VALUE! | #VALUE! | #VALUE! | #VALUE! | 36.69% | 13.11% | 36.69% | #VALUE! | 36.69% | #VALUE! |
| Pov. gap | #VALUE! | #VALUE! | #VALUE! | #VALUE! | #VALUE! | #VALUE! | #VALUE! | #VALUE! | #VALUE! | #VALUE! | 13.59% | 3.17% | 13.59% | #VALUE! | 13.59% | #VALUE! |
| Sq. pov. gap | #VALUE! | #VALUE! | #DIV/0! | #DIV/0! | #DIV/0! | #DIV/0! | #DIV/0! | #DIV/0! | #DIV/0! | #DIV/0! | 6.61% | 1.08% | 6.61% | #VALUE! | 6.61% | #DIV/0! |
| **Ext. Poverty** | | | | | | | | | | | | | | | | |
| Headcount | #VALUE! | #VALUE! | #VALUE! | #VALUE! | #VALUE! | #VALUE! | #VALUE! | #VALUE! | #VALUE! | #VALUE! | 20.50% | 3.78% | 20.50% | #VALUE! | 20.50% | #VALUE! |
| Pov. gap | #VALUE! | #VALUE! | #VALUE! | #VALUE! | #VALUE! | #VALUE! | #VALUE! | #VALUE! | #VALUE! | #VALUE! | 5.96% | 0.59% | 5.96% | #VALUE! | 5.96% | #VALUE! |
| Sq. pov. gap | #VALUE! | #VALUE! | #DIV/0! | #DIV/0! | #DIV/0! | #DIV/0! | #DIV/0! | #DIV/0! | #DIV/0! | #DIV/0! | 2.36% | 0.14% | 2.36% | #VALUE! | 2.36% | #DIV/0! |
| **Social Welfare** | | | | | | | | | | | | | | | | |
| Mean (t2 value) | 0 | 0 | #DIV/0! | 0 | #DIV/0! | 0 | #DIV/0! | 0 | #DIV/0! | 0 | 95790 | 196283 | 53090 | 0 | 0 | 0 |
| Gini v=2 | #VALUE! | #VALUE! | #VALUE! | #VALUE! | #VALUE! | #VALUE! | #VALUE! | #VALUE! | #VALUE! | #VALUE! | 52.83% | 52.83% | 52.83% | #VALUE! | 52.83% | #VALUE! |
| Mean*(1-Gini) | N/A | N/A | N/A | N/A | N/A | N/A | N/A | N/A | N/A | N/A | 46600 | 87871 | 46600 | 87871 | 46600 | 87871 |
| **Growth and Inequality Decomposition** | | | | | | | | | | | | | | | | |
| **Growth Impact** | Mod | Ext | Mod | Ext | Mod | Ext | Mod | Ext | Mod | Ext | Mod | Ext | Mod | Ext | Mod | Ext |
| Headcount | #VALUE! | #VALUE! | #VALUE! | #VALUE! | #VALUE! | #VALUE! | #VALUE! | #VALUE! | #VALUE! | #VALUE! | -23.58% | -16.72% | #VALUE! | #VALUE! | #VALUE! | #VALUE! |
| Pov. Gap | #VALUE! | #VALUE! | #VALUE! | #VALUE! | #VALUE! | #VALUE! | #VALUE! | #VALUE! | #VALUE! | #VALUE! | -10.42% | -5.37% | #VALUE! | #VALUE! | #VALUE! | #VALUE! |
| Sq. Pov Gap | #DIV/0! | #DIV/0! | #DIV/0! | #DIV/0! | #DIV/0! | #DIV/0! | #DIV/0! | #DIV/0! | #DIV/0! | #DIV/0! | -5.53% | -2.22% | #VALUE! | #VALUE! | #DIV/0! | #DIV/0! |
| **Inequality Impact** | | | | | | | | | | | | | | | | |
| Headcount | #VALUE! | #VALUE! | #VALUE! | #VALUE! | #VALUE! | #VALUE! | #VALUE! | #VALUE! | #VALUE! | #VALUE! | 0.00% | 0.00% | #VALUE! | #VALUE! | #VALUE! | #VALUE! |
| Pov. Gap | #VALUE! | #VALUE! | #VALUE! | #VALUE! | #VALUE! | #VALUE! | #VALUE! | #VALUE! | #VALUE! | #VALUE! | 0.00% | 0.00% | #VALUE! | #VALUE! | #VALUE! | #VALUE! |
| Sq. Pov Gap | #DIV/0! | #DIV/0! | #DIV/0! | #DIV/0! | #DIV/0! | #DIV/0! | #DIV/0! | #DIV/0! | #DIV/0! | #DIV/0! | 0.00% | 0.00% | #DIV/0! | #DIV/0! | #DIV/0! | #DIV/0! |
| **Residual** | | | | | | | | | | | | | | | | |
| Headcount | #VALUE! | #VALUE! | #VALUE! | #VALUE! | #VALUE! | #VALUE! | #VALUE! | #VALUE! | #VALUE! | #VALUE! | 0.00% | 0.00% | #VALUE! | #VALUE! | #VALUE! | #VALUE! |
| Pov. Gap | #VALUE! | #VALUE! | #VALUE! | #VALUE! | #VALUE! | #VALUE! | #VALUE! | #VALUE! | #VALUE! | #VALUE! | 0.00% | 0.00% | #VALUE! | #VALUE! | #VALUE! | #VALUE! |
| Sq. Pov Gap | #VALUE! | #VALUE! | #DIV/0! | #DIV/0! | #DIV/0! | #DIV/0! | #DIV/0! | #DIV/0! | #DIV/0! | #DIV/0! | 0.00% | 0.00% | #VALUE! | #VALUE! | #DIV/0! | #DIV/0! |

*Source*: Authors using SimSIP and 1988–89 surveys.

One question is whether the country is likely to achieve the Millennium Development Goal target or reducing poverty by half versus its 1990 level (for which the poverty measures obtained in 1988–89 can be used as proxy). Given the progress achieved so far, the results in Figure 5.4 suggest that if GDP continues to grow rapidly as in the previous years, poverty could easily be reduced by half in 2015 versus the 1990 level. Assuming that growth is evenly distributed among all individuals—assuming no future change in inequality, a possibly optimistic scenario given the mild increase in inequality in Cape Verde between 1988/89 and 2001/02—under a constant growth rate in GDP per capita of 3, 4, and 5 percent per year, Cape Verde would be able to achieve the target of reducing poverty by half set in the Millennium Development Goals by the years 2011, 2009, and 2008 respectively. Even if inequality were to continue to increase a bit, the target of reducing poverty by half in 2015 would still be achieved under these growth assumptions.

## Conclusion

Estimating trends in poverty in any country is often a difficult exercise. In Cape Verde, the exercise is made even more difficult than elsewhere because of comparability issues between surveys, and because of the fact that the unit level data for the 1988/89 survey are

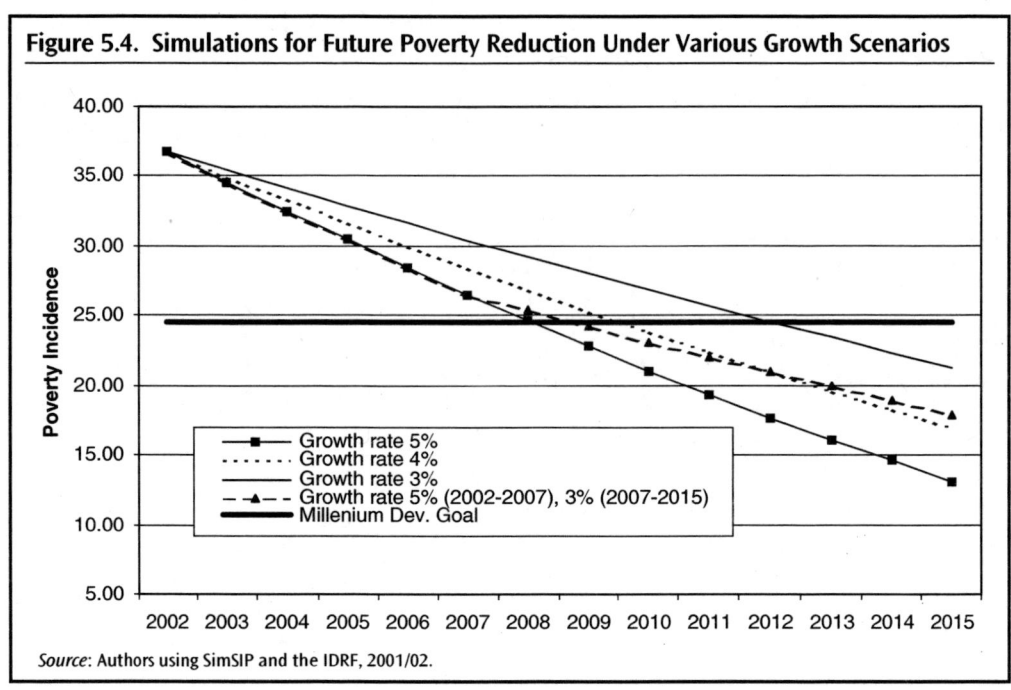

Figure 5.4. Simulations for Future Poverty Reduction Under Various Growth Scenarios

*Source*: Authors using SimSIP and the IDRF, 2001/02.

not available. At the time of the preparation of Cape Verde's PRSP (Poverty Reduction Strategy Paper), concerns were raised regarding the fact that despite substantial growth in the 1990s, poverty apparently had increased according to data from the household surveys implemented in 1998–99 and 2001–02. This was a puzzling result, which put in doubt the contribution of growth to poverty reduction, but was due to the use of relative poverty comparisons as well as issues of comparability between the two surveys.

The analysis provided in this paper confirms that there has been an increase in inequality over time in the country, and thereby an increase in relative poverty, but it also suggests that absolute (as opposed to relative) poverty measures have been reduced substantially. Specifically, the strong economic performance observed in the 1990s (as a result of the implementation of market-oriented reforms and political stability) contributed to reduce the share of the population in absolute poverty from 49 percent in 1988–89 to 37 percent in 2001–02. If GDP were to continue to grow rapidly, the country would easily be able to achieve the Millennium Development Goal of reducing poverty by half in 2015 versus the 1990 level.

## References

Coudouel, A., J. Hentschel, and Q. Wodon. 2002. "Poverty Measurement and Analysis." In J. Klugman, editor, *A Sourcebook for Poverty Reduction Strategies, Volume 1: Core Techniques and Cross-Cutting Issues*. Washington, D.C.: The World Bank.

Datt, G., K. Ramadas, D. van der Mensbrugghe, T. Walker, and Q. Wodon. 2003. "Predicting the Effect of Aggregate Growth on Poverty." In F. Bourguignon and L. Pereira da Silva, editors, *The Impact of Economic Policies on Poverty and Income Distribution: Evaluation Techniques and Tools.* Washington, D.C.: The World Bank.

Datt, G., and M. Ravallion. 1992. "Growth and Redistribution Components of Changes in Poverty Measures: A Decomposition with Applications to Brazil and India in the 1980s." *Journal of Development Economics* 38:275–95.

Foster, J. E., J. Greer, and E. Thorbecke. 1984. "A Class of Decomposable Poverty Indices." *Econometrica* 52:761–66.

INE. 1998. *Inquérito Demográfico de Saúde Reproductiva.* Praia, Cape Verde.

———. 2002. *Carácterísticas Económicas de la Populaçao –Censo 2000.* Praia, Cape Verde.

World Bank. 1994. "Poverty in Cape Verde: A Summary Assessment and a Strategy for Its Alleviation." Report No. 13126-CV. Washington, D.C.

———. 2005. "Cape Verde: Poverty Diagnostic." Report No. 32826-CV. Washington, D.C.

# CHAPTER 6

# Conflict, Growth, and Poverty in Guinea-Bissau

*Boubacar-Sid Barry and Quentin Wodon*[24]

*Conflicts and political instability have been serious constraints to growth in Guinea-Bissau. Of special concern was the civil war of 1998, which lasted 11 months and led to substantial loss of life as well as to a massive decrease in GDP per capita. Based on research on the economic cost of conflicts in Sub-Saharan Africa conducted by Lopez and Wodon (2005) and using a technique to identify outliers in time series and to correct the series for such outliers, this chapter estimates that GDP per capita today could have been more than 40 percent higher if there had been no conflict in 1998. In turn, one in three persons living in poverty today might not be poor had it not been for the conflict.*

Conflicts have had a devastating impact on the economies of affected countries in Sub-Saharan Africa (Yartey 2004, World Bank 2000a, Easterly and Levine 1999, Rodrick 1999). In Guinea-Bissau, conflicts and political instability have been the main constraints for growth and poverty reduction over the past three decades. Rather than being massive and pervasive, conflicts and instability in Guinea-Bissau have become cyclical events confined, to some extent, to the capital, but with economic and social conquences for the country as a whole. While the continued instability has not often caused a significant loss of human life and physical destruction (with the notable exception of the 1998 conflict, as discussed below), the instability has been detrimental to institution building and has not produced an environment conducive to investment, growth, and poverty reduction. As many as six major military-related incidents concerning political power have taken place since independence in 1974. Thereafter, the country experienced two decades of a state-controlled system before organizing its first democratic elections in 1994. The fledgling democratic process was halted by the 1998 civil conflict that led

---

24. The authors are grateful to Humberto Lopez for help in estimating the impact of Guinea-Bissau's conflict on per capita GDP.

to a drop in GDP per capita of roughly 30 percent, and to the displacement of up to 350,000 people—or about one-fifth of the population.

A state of persistent political instability prevailed after the war, and it was only in 2001 that new democratic elections brought a new civilian government to power. However, the democratic process stalled again as the elected government failed to restore political stability and good governance. Following several cabinet reshuffles, alleged coup attempts, and the dissolution of the parliament during 2001–02, the military staged a bloodless coup d'état in September 2003, and a civilian transition government was charged with restoring order and rebuilding the public administration. Since mid-2004, the authorities have made significant progress in restoring fiscal discipline despite the highly polarized and still fragile political environment.

The objective of this chapter is to measure the impact of the conflict on per capita GDP in Guinea-Bissau. This was done using a technique developed by Tsay (1988, 1986) and Gomez, Maravall, and Peña (1997) that identified and corrected outliers in time series. This was then applied to the assessment of the impact of conflicts on GDP per capita in Sub-Saharan African countries by Lopez and Wodon (2005).[25] The estimates suggest that GDP per capita would be roughly 42 to 43 percent higher today if the conflict had not occurred. In turn, assuming that the conflict had no impact on inequality (we don't have data on that potential impact), we found that about one-third of people now in poverty can be said to be poor because of the conflict.

The chapter is organized as follows: the first section briefly reviews the political context and recent economic performance of the country, including a discussion of the various impacts of the conflict; and the second section provides econometric estimates of the loss in per capita GDP attributed to the conflict and the likely impact that this economic loss has had, in turn, on poverty. A brief conclusion follows.

## Guinea-Bissau's Conflict and Economic Performance: A Brief Review

### Political Context

Guinea-Bissau has experienced a long history of conflict and political instability. Following a decade-long freedom war with Portugal, Guinea-Bissau became independent in 1974. As noted in Chapter 1, the government of Luis Cabral was overthrown in a bloodless coup led by the prime minister and former armed forces commander, João Bernardo "Nino" Vieira, in 1980. There were several coup attempts against the Vieira government in 1983, 1985, and 1993. In 1994, the country's first multiparty legislative and presidential elections were held. President Vieira, of the ruling Party for the Independence of Guinea-Bissau and Cape-Verde (PAIGC), was re-elected with a slight margin over Kumba Yala of the Party of Social Restoration (PRS). An army uprising against the Vieira government in June 1998 triggered a bloody civil war that displaced over 300,000 members of the civilian population. Failed

---

25. Lopez and Wodon (2005) noted that this approach differs from that used by Murdoch and Sandler (2001) who used cross-country panel data to measure the average effect of conflicts on growth. The main issue with cross-country results is that indices of war tend to be discrete variables with low cross-country variability. As a result, the averaging involved in estimating the impact of conflicts may under- or overestimate impacts where conflicts are particularly severe or instead relatively mild, respectively.

governance, breakdown of the rule of law, and limited accountability and transparency of public sector management were among the causes of this conflict, which lasted nearly a year.

Following the conflict, attention was turned to the task of reconciliation and rehabilitation. By June 1999, the situation, although still fragile, calmed down and improved steadily. A Government of National Union (GNU) was put in place and charged with the tasks of preparing a National Reconciliation and Rehabilitation Program (NRRP) and organizing elections. Free and fair parliamentary elections were held on November 28, 1999, and a presidential runoff vote took place on January 16, 2000. Opposition parties scored a landslide victory in both elections. President-elect Kumba Yala of the PRS took office on February 17, 2000. Shortly after, a broad coalition cabinet, including members of various parties in the national assembly, was appointed.

The task of national reconciliation and reconstruction was, however, undermined by the lack of political consensus. Following the elections, the parliament approved a new constitution in April 2001, which was neither vetoed nor promulgated by the president. The resulting ambiguity undermined the rule of law, and a prolonged friction developed between the executive and the legislative branches of the government over the choice of the new cabinet chief. As a result, the country operated without an effective government for several weeks, and the announcement of yet another foiled coup attempt in mid-April 2001 demonstrated once again the fragility of the political and democratic processes. The prevailing political instability, which affected all institutions, was not conducive to economic recovery and postconflict reconstruction. In December 2001, the government allegedly thwarted a coup attempt by army officers.

Delays in holding parliamentary elections led to a military coup and the appointment of a transition government in September 2003. Between December 2001 and December 2002, President Yala carried out two cabinet reshuffles, dissolved the parliament, and called for legislative elections, which were repeatedly postponed. The ensuing discontent among the population led the army to seize power in a bloodless coup in September 2003. President Yala announced his resignation and was placed under house arrest. The military, led by the chief of defense, Gen. Verrisimo Seabra (who was later killed along with other officers during the October 6, 2004 mutiny), quickly restored power to civilian control, and a civilian caretaker government was appointed with the objective of restoring the rule of law and reasserting control over public finances. In this context, the businessman Henrique Rosa was sworn in as interim president, with the support of almost all political parties as well as that of the civil society. By the end of 2003, the newly appointed government prepared an Emergency Economic Management Plan (EEMP) and a budget for 2004 with the support of the international community.

Parliamentary elections were successfully organized in early 2004, and the postelection government endorsed the EEMP reform agenda. Legislative elections were held in March 2004 and an orderly transition to a government elected on the basis of a broad reform platform took place in May 2004. The transition government, led by the leader of the PAIGC, Carlos Gomes Júnior was appointed with the objective of ensuring the functioning of the public administration and preparing presidential elections by mid-2005. Despite the difficult economic situation, the government prepared a draft of the country's PRSP and significantly improved budgetary discipline during the second half of 2004. The government also endorsed the reform program, which was agreed to by the international community; prepared the 2005 budget; and successfully organized a free, fair, and transparent presidential election that was won by the independent candidate and former president, João Bernardo "Nino" Vieira.

Recurrent military interventions on the political scene, as experienced in the recent past, still remain a major obstacle to stability and democracy. So far, the military has kept their promise not to intervene in the political process during and after the presidential elections. However, the widespread poverty in the barracks and the highly polarized political environment remain ingredients for future interventions of the military. Moreover, the majority of soldiers in Guinea-Bissau's army are from the *Balante* ethnic group. There is a critical need for reforming the security sector to prevent further instability and conflict.

### Consequences of the 1998 Conflict

The human losses and economic disruption created by the 11-month conflict that took place in 1998 were widespread. Between 2,000 and 6,000 lives were lost and up to 350,000 persons were internally displaced, including 7,000 who were generally better educated and sought refuge in Senegal, Cape Verde, the Gambia, Guinea, and Portugal, thereby depleting Guinea-Bissau's limited human capital. While solidarity within the population helped to avoid a major humanitarian crisis, deprivation increased dramatically and food stocks were depleted (on vulnerability in Guinea-Bissau, see for example Lourenço-Lindell, 2002, and World Bank 2000b and 2006).

Real GDP declined by 28 percent because of a sharp decline of production in all sectors. A significant deceleration in the production of cashew nuts and cereals probably helped cause a 17 percent decline in agriculture production. Most of the formal industrial, trade, and service activities were interrupted in the last seven months of 1998. The closing of banks and nonpayment of most wages repressed the impact of the war on prices. However, the armed conflict adversely affected the country's fiscal position and its balance of payments. Marketing of cashew nuts, the main source of public revenue, was severely disrupted and merchandise exports and imports (in U.S. dollars) decreased by about 45 and 30 percent, respectively, over the period 1997–98. As a result, the external current account deficit (excluding official transfers) remained at a high of nearly 16 percent of the GDP, and the current primary budget balance moved from a surplus of about 5 percent of the GDP in 1997 to a deficit of about 7 percent of the GDP in 1998. After June 1998, external debt service arrears piled up that were equivalent to almost 10 percent of the GDP. Arrears on salaries, goods and services, pensions, and transfers also represented 5 percent of the GDP.

Apart from a reduction in income flows as represented by the GDP, capital destruction was also widespread. Damages to public infrastructure (including the airport, energy and water systems, health and education facilities, roads, markets, public enterprises, and administrative buildings) amounted to $25–$30 million. Some 5,000 houses were damaged in the capital city of Bissau, and losses of up to $90 million were incurred by businesses because of destruction, requisition, confiscation, and looting. As the private sector was hit, the banking system was also weakened from an already fragile position. Investor confidence faded, leading to a reduction in investments (both foreign and domestic). Furthermore, the implementation of necessary reforms in the areas of taxation, civil service, public enterprises, and the social sectors were interrupted as the administration could not implement the 1998–2001 Policy Framework Paper that had been agreed upon in May 1998, and the conflict led to a temporary halt in donor funding.

## *Postconflict Economic Performance*

The economy bounced back during 1999–2000 because of a return to peace and good agricultural performance. During the two years following the conflict, economic performance improved as a result of the enhanced security situation and gradual resettlement of displaced populations. Nearly all of the 300,000 to 350,000 persons initially displaced by the conflict in 1998 returned to their homes. Agricultural production, which represents nearly 60 percent of the GDP, grew on average by 6 percent in real term per annum during the period 1999–2000. Cashew nut production, the leading agricultural subsector, averaged 70,000 metric tons over the indicated period (compared to 50,000 metric tons in 1997). Performance in agriculture had positive spillover effects on the economy as a whole (as evidenced by the close correlation between trends of real GDP growth and cashew nut production). Services grew on average by 15 percent in real terms, largely because of the close interrelationship between transportation activities and the boom in the cashew sector. Industrial activities suffered from heavy damage in infrastructure and electricity supply. Industrial growth first decelerated by 1 percent in 1999 and then picked up by 10 percent in the following year, thanks to donor support to the government's reconstruction program.

Real annual GDP grew by an average of nearly 8 percent from 1999 to 2000, leading to a growth in per capita GDP of close to 10 percent over two years. At the same time, government revenue reached 18 percent of the GDP, and the overall budget deficit (excluding grants) increased from 14 percent to 25 percent of the GDP as a result of increased postconflict reconstruction activities. Late in 1999, the government and the International Monetary Fund agreed upon a macroeconomic framework for the period 2000–01 that would consolidate and sustain economic performance, reduce inflation, and limit fiscal and external gaps to financially sustainable levels. Progress continued to be encouraging on the macroeconomic front through December 2000, and the country completed its interim PRSP, reached the decision point under the HIPC Initiative, and agreed to a three-year PRGF program with the IMF for the period 2001–03.

However, inadequate public policies prevented the conclusion of the IMF's first PRGF review in 2001, resulting in payment difficulties. Early in 2001, the macroeconomic program was found to be substantially off track owing to large unbudgeted expenditures mainly on defense that were financed by credit from the banking system and promissory notes. Late in 2001 a string of political crises at the northern border with Senegal in the Casamance region added to the worsening security situation. Military crackdowns ordered by the authorities led to a significant expenditure overrun, and the primary fiscal deficit reached 3.7 percent of the GDP in 2001 compared with the targeted surplus of 0.8 percent under the PRGF program. Consequently, the first review of the PRGF by the IMF was not concluded as scheduled in 2001, and the program was declared off track. After two unsuccessful short-term, staff-monitored programs, efforts to revive the program were abandoned by mid-2002, and the arrangement expired at the end of 2003 without the completion of a review. In view of the disappointing developments, the IMF established that it would be unlikely that Guinea-Bissau would be able to meet PRGF standards in the near future.

Under these conditions, donor support (equivalent to 4 percent of the GDP) did not materialize as expected, causing severe payment difficulties. External budgetary supports decreased from $12 million in 2000 to $1 million in 2001. The balance of payment and fiscal difficulties were further fueled by a record 37 percent decline in world market prices of cashew nuts in 2001. Consequently, export volume growth plummeted from 26 percent to −1 percent between 1999 and 2002, and government budgetary revenues as a share of GDP decreased from 19 percent to 15 percent during the same period. In this context, the external account and budget deficits (excluding external grants) reached 13 percent and 26 percent of the GDP, respectively, by the end of 2001.

The economy became recessionary in 2001 and further stagnated through 2002–03. Real GDP grew at a minor rate of 0.2 percent by the end of 2001, and contracted by 7.2 percent by the end of 2002. The main contributing factors to the economic contraction in 2002 were the 15 percent fall of the production of cashew nuts, a lower than expected agricultural performance due to unfavorable weather conditions, and the continued suspension of donor-funded policy lending representing about 7 percent of the GDP. The fiscal situation continued to be precarious because of the sharp decline in economic activity and the implementation of a number of policy decisions outside the emergency financial management framework that was agreed upon with the IMF and the Bank.

Economic performance remained sluggish in 2003. Although the agriculture sector grew by about 5 percent, real GDP grew by only 0.6 percent because of a significant contraction in the other sectors of the economy. Simultaneously, fiscal management further deteriorated when a substantial diversion of resources to expenditures took place outside the legally established budgetary procedures. A key issue in public finance management was the decision by President Yala to increase the salaries of the military in 2003 by more than tenfold. Consequently, the public sector wage bill increased from 8 percent of GDP in 2003 to about 11 percent in 2004.[26]

Thanks to an enhanced fiscal management and increased donor support to the EEMP, economic performance started to recover in 2004. During the second half of 2004, the transition government formed after the September 2003 military coup took decisive measures aimed at restoring fiscal discipline. The treasury committee, established in 2003, was reinstated and tasked with implementing a strict cashflow management system. As a result, budgetary revenues increased from 15.5 percent in 2003 to 17.5 percent by the end of 2004. It is worth noting that this performance was largely attributed to improved tax collection in the informal sector and illegal fishing activities. The government, however, continued to rely on external assistance for the implementation of the EEMP in 2004. The economy started to recover in 2004 with real GDP growth reaching 2.2 percent by the end of 2004. While growth was not expected to change substantially in 2005 because of capacity constraints and continued political uncertainties, performance was expected to improve in the medium term if adequate fiscal and capacity building reforms were carried out (for a recent review of developments in Guinea-Bissau, see Economist Intelligence Unit, 2005).

## Impact of the Conflict on GDP Per Capita and Poverty

### Impact of the Conflict on Per Capita GDP

This section assesses the impact of the conflict on per capita GDP using a procedure proposed by Tsay (1988, 1986) for detecting outliers in time series. The basic idea is to empirically test and correct the data for the presence of outliers in the GDP per capita time series.

---

26. Most public sector wages remained unpaid in the first nine months of 2003 prior to the military coup.

If the outliers are observed at the time of conflicts (for example, the year 1998 for Guinea-Bissau), then the corrected series for GDP per capita can be assumed to represent the counter-factual path that the economy would have followed if there had been no conflict. Details on the estimation methodology are provided in Lopez and Wodon (2005) who conducted similar work on Rwanda. Here we provide the basic estimation strategy and the key empirical results. The results for Guinea-Bissau are compared to a broader set of results for Sub-Saharan countries that had a recent conflict.

The variable e(t) can be understood as a white noise sequence with a zero mean and constant variance $\sigma^2$. L is the lag operator (i.e., Le(t) = e(t−1)), and $\varphi$ (L) is a polynomial in L with $\Sigma_j |\varphi_j| < \infty$ and roots of $\varphi(z) = 0$ outside the unit circle. GDP per capita, denoted by Y(t), is represented through a univariate time series with:

$$Y(t) = X(t) + Z(t), \text{ with} \tag{1}$$
$$X(t) = \mu + \varphi(L)e(t), \text{ and} \tag{2}$$
$$Z(t) = w(L)o(t) \tag{3}$$

In the above, X(t) is a stationary and invertible series for which the polynomial $\varphi(L)$ can be approximated by $\varphi(L) = \theta(L)/\phi(L)$, with $\theta(L)$ and $\phi(L)$ finite order polynomials in L (that is, X(t) would follow an ARMA process). Z(t) is defined so that o(t) = 1 at t = s, if at time s an outlier occurs and o(t) = 0 otherwise. The structure of w(L) defines various potential types of outliers, which are represented visually in Figure 6.1. If w(L) = $\omega$, Z(t) defines an additive outlier (AO), which accounts for a "one shot" change in GDP in a given year. If w(L) = $\omega/(1−L)$, we obtain a level shift (LS), which implies a permanent impact on the series. Finally, if w(L) = $\omega/(1−\delta L)$, the estimation suggests a transitory change (TC), which vanishes over time. The empirical strategy to estimate these equations is discussed in Lopez and Wodon (2005). The method can be generalized to control for additional variables that may affect the GDP per capita, which is done here to consider the potential impact of changes in terms of trade.

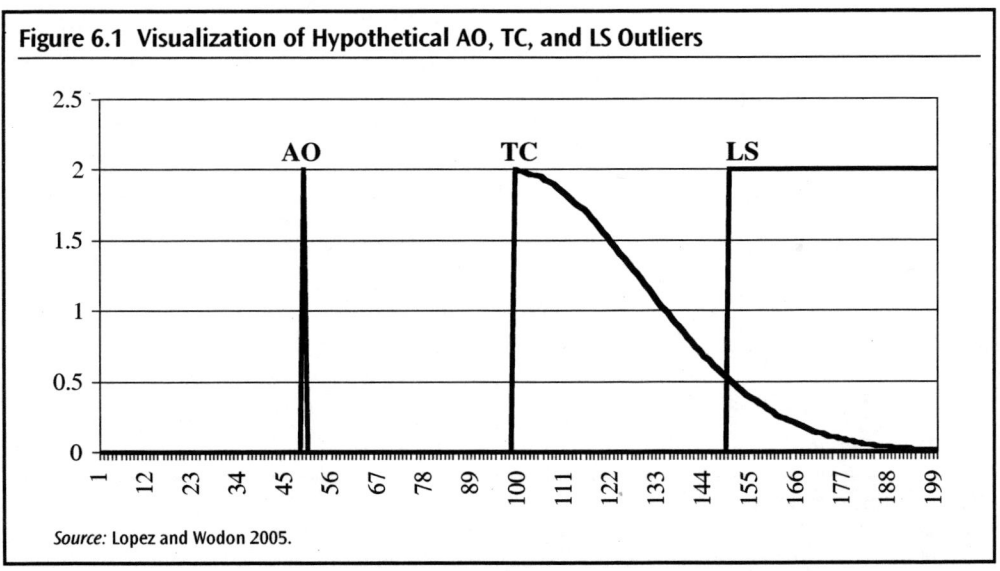

**Figure 6.1  Visualization of Hypothetical AO, TC, and LS Outliers**

*Source:* Lopez and Wodon 2005.

The procedure applied to Guinea-Bissau using the data on GDP per capita in constant local currency units as well as data on the changes in the terms of trade reveals the existence of a single additive ("one shot") outlier for the year 1998, which corresponds to the civil war. The estimates provided here are from comparative data for Guinea-Bissau and various other Sub-Saharan African countries that a conflict.

According to Table 6.1, GDP per capita would have been 42 or 43 percent higher in 2004 (depending on the model) than it actually was if there had been no conflict, which is a very large impact (also see Figure 6.2). As a point of comparison, in Rwanda, where the human, social, and economic costs of the genocide have been staggering, the estimates suggest that the per capita GDP would be between 25 and 30 percent higher today than if the genocide had not taken place (Lopez and Wodon 2005), which suggests a smaller economic impact than in Guinea-Bissau. Much of the difference between the impacts observed in Guinea-Bissau and Rwanda stems from the fact that two outliers were identified in Rwanda. First, in 1994, the year of the genocide, there was a loss of about 40 percent of the GDP. In the following year, however, there was a rebound (another additive, but this time a positive outlier) so that part of the negative impact of

**Table 6.1  Impact of the Conflict on Per Capita GDP**

| Year | GDP per capita index | GDP Per capita Index, controlling for the conflict | GDP per capita index, controlling for the conflict and terms of trade |
|---|---|---|---|
| 1970* | 100.0 | 100.0 | 100.0 |
| 1980* | 80.9 | 80.9 | 80.9 |
| 1990 | 102.6 | 102.6 | 102.6 |
| 1991 | 104.1 | 104.1 | 104.1 |
| 1992 | 101.8 | 101.8 | 101.8 |
| 1993 | 100.9 | 100.9 | 100.9 |
| 1994 | 101.0 | 101.0 | 101.0 |
| 1995 | 102.4 | 102.4 | 102.4 |
| 1996 | 111.0 | 111.0 | 111.0 |
| 1997 | 115.1 | 115.1 | 115.1 |
| 1998 | 80.6 | 114.7 | 115.2 |
| 1999 | 84.5 | 120.3 | 120.8 |
| 2000 | 88.3 | 125.7 | 126.2 |
| 2001 | 86.0 | 122.4 | 122.9 |
| 2002 | 77.6 | 110.4 | 110.9 |
| 2003 | 75.8 | 108.0 | 108.4 |
| 2004 | 76.8 | 109.3 | 109.8 |
| GDP cost (%) in 2002 | — | −42.3 | −42.9 |

*Source:* Authors' estimates.
*Note:* The value of 42.4 percent is obtained as (109.3/76.8) − 1. While estimates are only provided for 1970 and 1980, the actual estimations were done using annual GDP data from before 1990.

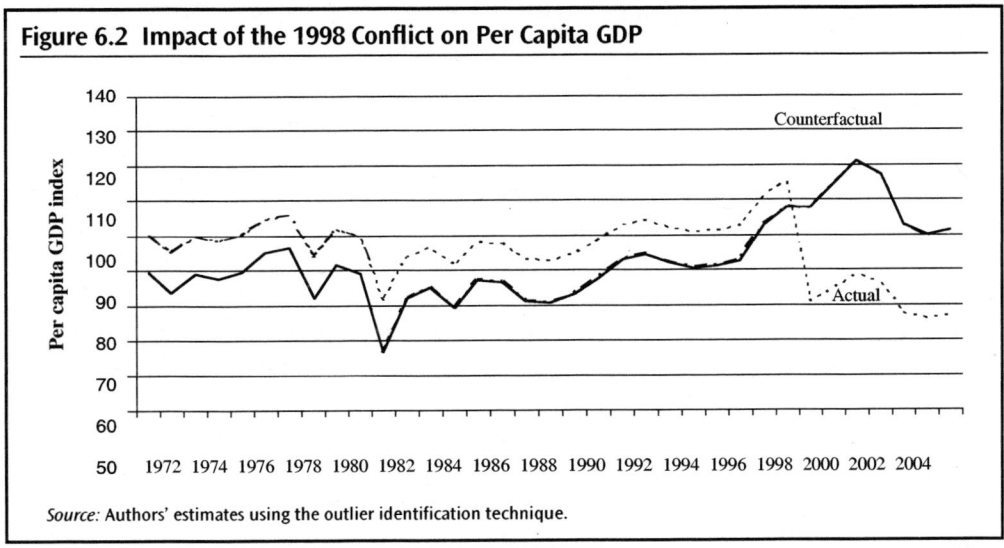

**Figure 6.2  Impact of the 1998 Conflict on Per Capita GDP**

*Source:* Authors' estimates using the outlier identification technique.

the conflict was offset. Such a rebound was not observed in Guinea-Bissau, leading to a larger economic impact of the conflict even though the loss in human life was substantially less severe.

It is also important to note that losses in GDP were observed in Guinea-Bissau as in Rwanda, but the conflicts did not seem to have a negative impact on the growth rate of GDP per capita. These results could be interpreted as an indication that these conflicts generated a reduction in the stock values of key economic variables, such as human and physical capital, without changing the returns on these stocks.

## *Impact of the Conflict on Poverty*

Once we have estimated what level of GDP per capita would have been achieved without the conflict, it is straightforward to estimate what the poverty level would have been without the conflict, provided we are willing to make a number of (rather strong) assumptions. In the absence of good information on the distributional consequences of a conflict (that is, who gets affected most and why), these assumptions are necessary to translate our estimate of the impact of the conflict on GDP per capita into an estimate of how consumption per equivalent adult may have changed as measured in household surveys. To explain these assumptions, it is useful to briefly review how poverty was estimated in Guinea-Bissau within the framework of the Poverty Reduction Strategy prepared by authorities.

The official estimates of poverty for Guinea-Bissau are based on a somewhat ad hoc methodology, in part because of weaknesses in the scope of the data collected in the household survey used to measure poverty. The only available nationally-representative survey is the 2002 ILAP, a light household survey that was implemented following the core welfare indicator survey (CWIQ) methodology. The survey includes a consumption module, but this module is not very detailed, making it difficult to properly estimate poverty lines based on traditional approaches, such as the cost of basic needs framework. Instead, the authorities adopted an extreme poverty line of $1 per person per day after adjusting for purchasing power parity (Sylla 2004). This resulted in a unique extreme poverty line for the country as a whole (without adjusting for differences in the cost of living between urban and rural areas, for example) of CFAF 108,000 per person per year. A second poverty line of CFAF 216,000 per person per year was obtained, which corresponded to $2 per person per day. An estimate of the consumption of households per equivalent adult was then derived from the survey data to identify those in poverty and compute a range of poverty and extreme poverty measures.

The results from our GDP per capita simulations for poverty measurement assumes that the GDP per capita growth, as measured in the national accounts, is essentially perfectly correlated with the average growth in the consumption per adult equivalent at the household level. That is, we will use our estimates of the impact of the conflict on per capita GDP as our best guess for the impact of the conflict on the mean adult equivalent per household consumption. A second assumption is that we can rely on the poverty lines used for measuring poverty in the 2002 household survey to assess the impact of the conflict. We do not change the poverty lines for our counterfactual poverty measures without the conflict because we assume that the conflict did not affect relative prices and consumption patterns in such a way that other poverty lines would have had to be used in the absence of conflict. A third assumption is that inequality in per adult equivalent consumption was not affected by the conflict, so that we only need to incorporate the impact of the conflict on mean consumption for our poverty simulations. We only have one survey in Guinea-Bissau that does not have comparable preconflict household level data, so we simply cannot assess the impact of the conflict on inequality. It is best to assume that the inequality has remained unchanged.

If we accept these assumptions, the procedure for assessing the impact of the conflict on poverty is very simple. We first compute poverty using the 2002 household survey data, and then we compute our counterfactual poverty measures after scaling up the adult equivalent consumption aggregate for all households in the survey by a factor equal to the ratio of the estimated per capita GDP without the conflict to the observed per capita GDP at the time of the survey.

The poverty measures used here are the standard first three poverty measures of the so-called FGT class (Foster and others, 1984), namely the head count, the poverty gap, and the squared poverty gap. Denoting the poverty line by $z$, the number of households (population weighted) by n, the number of poor households by $q$, and the adult equivalent consumption aggregate of household $k$ by $c_k$, then the three measures are defined, taking a value of zero for the head count, one for the poverty gap, and two for the squared poverty gap in the following expression:

$$P_a = \frac{1}{n}\sum_{k=1}^{q}\left[\frac{z-c_k}{z}\right]^{\alpha} \tag{4}$$

Today, as shown in Table 6.2 and following the methodology used in the PRSP for poverty measurement, we find that 65.7 percent of the population is poor; that is, with a level of consumption per equivalent adult below the $2 poverty line in purchasing power parity terms, with 21.6 percent being the extreme poor. If the conflict had not taken place, so that per capita GDP today would be 42.3 percent higher than actually observed (the results would be very similar after correcting for terms of trade, hence are not provided here),

**Table 6.2  Impact of the 1998 Conflict on Poverty**

|  | Poverty observed in 2002 survey (1) | Poverty without the conflict (2) | Poverty reduction in percentage points (2)–(1) | Poverty reduction, percentage versus baseline [(2)–(1)]/(1) |
|---|---|---|---|---|
| **Poverty** | | | | |
| Head count index | 65.7 | 43.0 | −22.7 | −34.6% |
| Poverty gap | 25.7 | 13.2 | −12.5 | −48.6% |
| Squared poverty gap | 12.9 | 5.7 | −7.2 | −55.8% |
| **Extreme poverty** | | | | |
| Head count index | 21.6 | 7.6 | −14.0 | −64.8% |
| Poverty gap | 5.5 | 1.8 | −3.7 | −67.3% |
| Squared poverty gap | 2.2 | 0.7 | −1.5 | −68.2% |

*Source:* Authors' estimates using 2002 ILAP.

poverty would be much lower. Table 6.2 suggests that the share of the population in poverty today could be around 43.0 percent instead of 65.7 percent, while the share of the population in extreme poverty could be at 7.6 percent instead of 21.6 percent. Note that the percentage reduction in poverty following the 42.3 percent reduction in GDP per capita suggests that the elasticity of poverty reduction to growth is roughly around one (it is lower for some poverty measures, and higher for others), which is a reasonable estimate according to international experience.

As expected, the corresponding elasticities for the extreme poverty measures are larger, (these elasticities are a function of the poverty lines—the higher the poverty line, the lower the elasticity). Overall, one in three persons is in poverty today in Guinea-Bissau because of the conflict, with an even higher share for extreme poverty measures.

## Conclusion

This paper has estimated the economic cost of the 1998 Guinea-Bissau conflict on poverty. Following previous work by Lopez and Wodon (2005), a methodology for the identification and correction of outliers in time series was used to estimate the counterfactual GDP per capita that would have been observed in 2002 if the conflict had not taken place. The results suggest that the per capita GDP could have been between 42 to 43 percent higher in 2002 than it was without the conflict, assuming that the trend in GDP as available in national accounts statistics adequately represents changes in economic activity. Next, relying on a number of (admittedly) strong assumptions, we estimated the counterfactual poverty measures that would have prevailed in the absence of the conflict. Our estimates suggest that one in three persons today in poverty might not have been poor if the conflict had not taken place, and the proportion is even higher for extreme poverty. While all these results could be sensitive to some of our assumption, they do provide an idea of the large impact that the conflict has had on poverty in Guinea-Bissau.

## References

Economist Intelligence Unit (EIU). 2005. *Country Report—Guinea-Bissau, April 2005.* London: EIU.

Easterly, W., and R. Levine. 1997. "Africa's Growth Tragedy: Policies and Ethnic Divisions." *Quarterly Journal of Economics* 112 (November):1203–50.

Foster, J., J. Greer and E. Thorbecke. 1984. A Class of Decomposable Poverty Measures." *Econometrica* 52(3): 761–66.

Gomez, V., A. Marvall, and D. Peña. 1997. "Missing Observation in ARIMA Models: Skipping Strategy versus Additive Outlier Approach." Working Paper no. WP9701, Bank of Spain.

Lopez, H. and Q. Wodon. 2005. "The Economic Impact of Armed Conflict in Rwanda." *Journal of African Economies* 14(4):586–602.

Lourenço-Lindell, I. 2002. *Walking the Tight Rope: Informal Livelihoods and Social Networks in a West African City.* Stockholm: Stockholm University.

Murdoch, J. and T. Sandler. 2001. "Economic Growth, Civil Wars, and Spatial Spillovers." University of Texas.

Rodrick, D. 1999. "Where Did All the Growth Go? External Shocks, Social Conflict, and Growth Collapses." *Journal of Economic Growth* 4:385–412.

Sylla, M. B. 2004. Evaluation de la pauvrete en Guinée Bissau (2001–2002). Bissau.

Tsay, R. S. 1986. "Time Series Model Specification in the Presence of Outliers." *Journal of the American Statistical Association* 81: 132–141.

———1988. "Outliers, Level Shifts, and Variance Changes in Time Series." *Journal of Forecasting* 7:1–20.

World Bank. 2000a. *Can Africa Claim the 21st Century?* Washington, D.C.: The World Bank.

———. 2000b. *Report and Recommendation of the President of the International Development Association to the Executive Directors on a Proposed Economic Rehabilitation and Recovery Credit in an Amount of SDR 18 Million to the Republic of Guinea-Bissau.* World Bank, Washington, D.C.

———. 2006. "Guinea-Bissau: Integrated Poverty and Social Assessment." World Bank Report No. 34553-GW.

Yartey, C. 2004. "The Economics of Civil Wars in Sub-Saharan Africa." In Jean A. P. Clément, ed., *From Conflict to Reconstruction—Main Lessons and Challenges for Sub-Saharan Africa—The Case of the Democratic Republic of Congo.* Forthcoming, Washington D.C.: International Monetary Fund.

# CHAPTER 7

# Macroeconomic Volatility, Private Investment, Growth, and Poverty in Nigeria

*By Douglas Addison and Quentin Wodon*[*]

*At the time when this paper was written, the latest nationally representative survey implemented in Nigeria dated back to 1996, and the available estimations suggested that two thirds of the population was poor. This high level of poverty was due in large part to macroeconomic volatility that depressed private investment and growth. Using cross-sectional data for 87 countries, we show that real per-capita growth over the period 1980–1994 was a function of productivity growth and investment rates, both of which were negatively effected by volatility (in terms of trade, real exchange rate, and public investments). When comparing Nigeria to high growth nations, we find that most of the growth differential can be attributed to Nigeria's higher macroeconomic volatility. Simulations suggest that if Nigeria had had lower levels of volatility and better macroeconomic policies, poverty would have been much lower than observed.*

Accrding to Nigeria's Federal Office of Statistics (1999), 66 percent of Nigeria's population was poor in 1996, the latest year for which a nationally representative household survey with consumption information was implemented at the time this paper was written.[27] This paper argues that this high level of poverty was due

---

[*]The authors are with the World Bank. This work was completed for recent World Bank (2003, 2004) studies respectively on policy options for growth in Nigeria, and on poverty and vulnerability in Nigeria. The views expressed here are those of the authors and need not reflect those of the World Bank, its Executive Directors or the countries they represent.

27. A new household survey has been implemented since then (in 2004) and the data have been made available for analysis in 2006. New measures of poverty are now available for that survey. However, there are important issues of comparability between these measures and the measures of poverty obtained for 1996, so we do not make reference in this paper to the new estimates of poverty for 2004. On poverty measurement and growth in Nigeria, see also Canagarajah and Thomas (2001), Aigbokhan (2000), Ali (2000), Amaghionyeodiwe and Osinubi (2004), and Canagarajah and Thomas (2001).

to poor growth performance, itself resulting in large part from high macroeconomic volatility.

Recent empirical and theoretical research has established that macroeconomic volatility can have an adverse impact on growth. Easterly, Kremer, Pritchett, and Summers (1993) find, for example, that country characteristics alone are not sufficient to explain cross-country growth patterns, with external shocks being an important part of the story. Similarly, Bleaney and Greenaway (2002) find that real growth is negatively affected by terms of trade volatility. As shown by Bleaney and Greenaway (2000) and Serven (2002), one of the channels through which macro shocks affect growth is through a negative impact on private investment, as firm managers are hesitant to invest if future economic conditions are uncertain (on Nigeria, see Marchat and others 2001).[28]

The impact of macroeconomic volatility is especially important for relatively poor countries such as Nigeria which are exposed to terms of trade and exchange rate shocks due to their dependence on basic commodities such as oil. Nigeria ranked among the most volatile countries in the world, especially over the period 1980–94 which preceded the 1996 survey on which official poverty measures are based. Since achieving higher growth in Nigeria is an urgent priority in order to reduce poverty, an understanding of the impact of macroeconomic volatility on growth is needed.

The objective of this paper is two-fold. In the first section, we use cross-sectional data for 87 countries to analyze the impact of volatility on private investment and growth over the period 1980–1994, which corresponds to the most volatile period in terms of the behavior of Nigeria's macroeconomic indicators. Nigeria's private sector invested an average only 7 percent of GDP per annum between 1980 and 1994[29], which is well below the average of 20 percent invested by the world's fastest growing economies, leading to an average year-to-year growth in per capita GDP of only 0.2 percent, and a drop in GDP over the period as a whole due to severe losses in the early 1980s. Our empirical framework consists of two regression equations. The first seeks to explain real per-capita growth as a function of productivity growth and investment rates where the former is a function of volatility and the latter are given. The second equation seeks to explain the private investment rate as a function of openness to trade, institutional quality and volatility. Our key findings are that volatility indeed is detrimental for growth, with both direct negative effects on growth, and indirect negative effects through a dampening impact on private investment.

---

28. This is especially true when the financial system is weak. One explanation for the ability of a strong financial system to reduce the negative impact of volatility is provided by Acemoglu and Zilibotti (1997), who suggest that there is a virtuous circle whereby risk is reduced by wealth and portfolio diversification while the investment needed for diversification is encouraged by falling risk and rising wealth. In a related paper, Denizer and others (2002) find empirical support for the positive effect that financial systems have in reducing macroeconomic volatility. It is important to note here that Nigerian firm managers complain about inadequate access to finance more often than any other problem except uncertainty and poor infrastructure (Marchat and others 2001). Lack of credit forces enterprises to rely on internally generated funds both for working capital and for investment. This hampers firms' ability to manage their working capital, making it difficult for them to increase sales and operate at full capacity. The shortage of finance also limits investments to improve technology, to lower costs and to expand output. The high cost and limited availability of credit is thus a major factor that raises the cost of doing business and lowers competitiveness in Nigeria.

29. The Federal Office of Statistics does not divide investment into government and private contributions. This estimate is from a World Bank database where private investment equals total investment less government investment.

Next, in the second section, we use the results from the first section to measure what poverty might have been in 1996—the latest year for which a nationally representative survey with consumption data is available in Nigeria—if the country had not suffered from high macroeconomic volatility. For this, four scenarios are considered, with each scenario resulting in progressively higher levels of private investment and growth. Apart from providing an indication of what counterfactual poverty measures might have been observed in 1996 under these alternative macroeconomic scenario, we also look at the magnitude of progress that the country could achieve by 2015 in terms of poverty reduction if it were able to implement policies that would lead to such macroeconomic outcomes.

## Assessing the Cost of Macroeconomic Volatility

### Macroeconomic Volatility and Growth

To model the determinants of growth, including the impact of macroeconomic volatility, we start with the basic Mankiw-Romer-Weil (hereafter MRW, 1992) model. Growth in GDP per worker depends on the savings rates $s_k$ and $s_h$ for physical and human capital, as well as on labor force growth $n$ and capital decay $\delta$, and productivity growth $g$. In MRW, $s_k$ is proxied by the period average investment-to-GDP ratio, $I/Y$. Here, to see the relative impact of both public ($I_g$) versus private ($I_p$) investment, the variable $s_k$ will be divided into private and government sector investment ratios. Because public investment may have a lower impact in countries with the least stable public investment rates, we also include a variable that interacts the logged government investment rate with the standard deviation of the government investment rate. Next, while in MRW $s_h$ is proxied by the product of the secondary enrollment rate times the population of school aged children, we follow Benhabib and Spiegel (1994) who show that population multiplied by average educational attainment in years of schooling may be a better measure for $s_h$ (again, we use period averages for each country). As in MRW, we assume an exogenous and constant rate of decay $\delta$ for both physical and human capital, and the labor force is proxied by population. Denoting the error term by $\mu$, and accounting for baseline per capita GDP, we have:

$$\Delta\ln\left(\frac{Y}{L}\right)=\beta'Z_t+\alpha_1\ln\left(\frac{IP}{Y}\right)+\alpha_2\ln\left(\frac{IG}{Y}\right)+\alpha_3\ln\left(\frac{IG}{Y}\right)\sigma\left(\frac{IG}{Y}\right)+\alpha_4\ln s_h-\alpha_5\ln(n+\delta)-\alpha_6\ln\left(\frac{Y_0}{L_0}\right)$$

$$+\mu, \text{ with } Z'=\left(\sigma(TOT), OECD\_Growth, (X+M)/Y, Governance\right) \quad (1)$$

In (1), a key modification versus MRW's model is that we will let productivity growth vary across countries through a vector of variables **Z**. This vector includes the standard deviation of the terms of trade, following Bleaney and Greenaway (2002) who find real growth is negatively affected by TOT instability. The average growth rate of each nations' OECD trade partners is also included following Easterly (2001) who finds that OECD recessions contributed to slower growth in the rest of the worlds' economies. Likewise, openness to trade (as measured by share of the sum of exports and imports in GDP), is included following Edwards (1998) and others who found openness contributes to growth.[30] Finally, we include

---

30. This remains the subject of debate. Rodriguez and Rodrik (1999), for example, agree that there is no credible evidence that trade restrictions contribute to growth, but disagree that trade openness unambiguously contributes to growth. They argue the contribution from openness is contingent upon other variables.

a measure of good governance and respect for property rights following Hall and Jones (1999) who find this is an important determinant of productivity. Similarly, Kaufmann, Kraay, and Zoido-Lobaton (1999) show that countries scoring higher on indices of rule of law, graft, voice and accountability tend to have lower infant mortality and higher literacy rates, as well as higher per capita incomes.[31]

The regression is estimated using a cross-country sample of 87 countries for the period 1980–94. Table 7.1 shows the results. Three variables appear to be insignificant at the 10 percent confidence level: the stock of human capital, the trade share and the quality of governance. Further testing of the results suggests only the latter two can be eliminated. The modified results are shown in column B. The regression results required the addition of three dummy variables for Botswana, Ghana and Uganda in order to make the error term (residual) normally distributed. The conclusion that none of the remaining variables can be rejected is not altered when the dummies are removed. This regression passes the RESET test for mis-specification but does display some heteroskedasticity corrected by using White's heteroskedastic-consistent estimators.

Note that if volatility in public investment is driven by TOT volatility, collinearity between the interactive public investment term and TOT volatility could weaken the statistical significance of, and/or change the sign of, the coefficient for TOT volatility. The results in Table 7.1 suggest, however, that both types of volatility—in TOTs and in public investment—have a negative impact on growth. In column C, human capital is eliminated since it is not statistically significant (this does not imply that there is no benefit from schooling: the public investment term continues to capture the beneficial impact of investments in schooling and other services).

Two more tests were made on the results in column C. The first uses the Hausmann test for contemporaneous correlation between the private sector investment rate and the error term. This could occur either due to omitted variables or endogeneity. The instruments used for this test come from the investment equation described below where the measurement of volatility is based on the real exchange rate.[32] The results failed to reject the null hypothesis of no contemporaneous correlation. The second test uses Bayesian Averaging of Classical Estimates as documented in Dopplehofer et al. (2000) to reveal weaknesses in the choice of variables when there are many regressors with collinearity, so that the sign and significance of one or more variables may not be stable when other variables are added to, or subtracted from, the regression. Column D of Table 7.1 reports that most of the variables are robust to the inclusion or exclusion of the remaining variables in the equation. The exceptions, when significance is conditional upon other variables, are the stock of human capital, the trade share and the measure of governance.

---

31. There are debatable assumptions in this model. In particular, one might question whether all countries are in fact converging to their steady-states as is assumed in the MRW formulation. The main utility of the augmented Solow model is its widespread acceptance and good results in terms of fit. One can also debate the choices of variables used. The final and authoritative word on what drives growth, and what does not, has yet to be spoken (see Soludo and Kim [2002] for a provocative survey of the current state of play in growth theory). Growth researchers are particularly vexed by the way many different variables tend to cluster together. For example, the wealthiest nations tend to have more open economies, low tariffs, low inflation, strong adherence to the rule of law and, often, practice democracy. This can lead to the conclusion that 'everything counts' with little guidance on what a nation's priorities should be.

32. The results do not change when the measure of volatility is based on the TOT.

## Table 7.1. Determinants of Growth in Real GDP Per Capita, 1980–94, OLS

| | A[a] | B[a] | C[a] | D[g] |
|---|---|---|---|---|
| **Constant** | | | | |
| Coefficient | 0.45 | −0.68 | 3.38 | |
| Probability | 0.92 | 0.86 | 0.39 | |
| **Initial GDP per Capita[b]** | | | | |
| Coefficient | −0.92 | −0.46 | −0.42 | |
| Probability | 0.01 | 0.10 | 0.10 | Robust |
| **Private Investment Rate[b]** | | | | |
| Coefficient | 1.59 | 1.91 | 2.22 | |
| Probability | 0.00 | 0.00 | 0.00 | Robust |
| **Gov't Investment Rate[b]** | | | | |
| Coefficient | 0.78 | 0.92 | 1.37 | |
| Probability | 0.06 | 0.01 | 0.00 | Robust |
| **Gov't Investment Rate·SD Gov't Investment Rate** | | | | |
| Coefficient | | | −2.12 | |
| Probability | | * | 0.00 | Robust |
| **Stock of Human Capital[b]** | | | | |
| Coefficient | 0.25 | 0.27 | | |
| Probability | 0.19 | 0.03 | | Conditional |
| **Labor Growth & Depreciation[b]** | | | | |
| Coefficient | −3.96 | −5.06 | −4.81 | |
| Probability | 0.01 | 0.00 | 0.00 | Robust |
| **OECD Partner Growth** | | | | |
| Coefficient | 2.58 | 2.55 | 2.09 | |
| Probability | 0.00 | 0.00 | 0.00 | Robust |
| **Trade Share (% of GDP)** | | | | |
| Coefficient | 0.00 | | | |
| Probability | 0.87 | | | Conditional |
| **Governance & Property Rights** | | | | |
| Coefficient | 2.68 | | | |
| Probability | 0.19 | | | Conditional |
| **Standard Deviation in TOT Growth Squared** | | | | |
| Coefficient | −0.08 | −0.09 | −0.07 | |
| Probability | 0.00 | 0.00 | 0.00 | Robust |
| Observations | 87 | 87 | 87 | |
| Adjusted R-squared | 0.55 | 0.64 | 0.66 | |
| Hausmann (Probability)[c] | 0.45 | 0.30 | 0.26 | |
| Normal residual rejected ?[d] | No | No | No | |
| White (Probability)[e] | 0.44 | 0.26 | 0.00 | |
| RESET (Probability)[f] | 0.04 | 0.17 | 0.14 | |

a. Calculated with White's heteroskedastic-consistent estimators.
b. In natural logs.
c. Probability refers to the significance of the fitted variable version of Ip/Y.
d. Requires Jarque-Bera statistic smaller than critical value calculated by Deb and Sefton (1996).
e. No cross terms.
f. Probability refers to the significance of one fitted variable (squared).
g. Bayesian Averaging of Classical Estimates. Based on the prior expectation that 10 out of
   14 variables should be significant.
*Source:* Authors' estimations.

## Macroeconomic Volatility and Private Investment

Apart from its direct effect on growth, macroeconomic volatility may also have indirect effects through some of the variables that affect growth. In this section, we also analyze the extent to which macro volatility dampens private investment, itself a key determinants of growth as demonstrated in the previous section. Following Bleaney and Greenaway (2000), we would expect that RER volatility/uncertainty depresses investment. Serven (2002) also found a negative impact of RER, especially at high levels, possibly implying a thresh-hold effect, with the impact depending upon the degree of openness to trade and the strength of the financial system. Private investment is reduced by RER uncertainty in nations with low trade openness and/or weak financial systems. Conversely, RER uncertainty appears to encourage private investment in nations with a high degree of openness and strong financial systems. Finally, we would also expect that good governance and respect for property rights will encourage private investment.

In our specification, the logged private investment rate is a function of the Hall and Jones (1999) measure of the quality of governance and respect for property rights, the degree of openness proxied by the sum of exports and imports as a share of GDP, the strength of the financial system proxied by domestic credit to the private sector as a share of GDP, real exchange rate uncertainty proxied either by RER or TOT volatility (that is, the standard deviation in the growth rate of the RER or TOT), the interaction between RER or TOT volatility and trade and, lastly, the interaction between RER or TOT volatility and our measure of financial system strength. We thus have:

$$\ln\left(\frac{IP}{Y}\right) = \eta_0 + \eta_1 Gov + \eta_2\left(\frac{X+M}{Y}\right) + \eta_3\frac{DCp}{Y} - \eta_4\sigma(TOT) + \eta_5\sigma(TOT)\frac{X+M}{Y}$$
$$+ \eta_6\sigma(TOT)\frac{DCp}{Y} + \varepsilon \tag{2}$$

Table 7.2 provide the regression results. The regression requires dummies for Hungary and Madagascar to make the residual normally distributed, but it passes the heteroskedasticity and misspecification tests. Private investment is higher with good governance and trade openness, and lower under RER volatility. The negative impact of volatility is, however, reduced for nations with strong financial systems. In fact, the impact of low to moderate RER volatility is positive for nations with sufficiently strong financial systems. When volatility in TOT is substituted for volatility in RER as the proxy for uncertainty, the results are similar, except that the proxy for openness no longer remains significant. The main conclusion remains intact: the impact of uncertainty (proxied by volatility) is negative for nations with weak financial systems.

## Summary Results: Comparing Nigeria to High Growth Economies

In Table 7.3, the regression results have been transformed to provide a simple account of the contribution of various variables to growth. Nigeria's performance is recorded in column A while the average outcomes for a group of 15 high growth countries is in column B. Column C shows the differential between the two. Row 1 of the top part of the table give the observed growth rates. Rows 2 through 11 show contributions to growth from var-

**Table 7.2. Determinants of the Logarithm of Private Sector Investment as a Share of GDP, 1980–94, OLS**

| | RER Volatility | | TOT Volatility | |
| --- | --- | --- | --- | --- |
| | A | B | C | D[d] |
| **Constant** | | | | |
| Coefficient | 1.91 | 1.88 | 1.96 | 2.03 |
| Probability | 0.00 | 0.00 | 0.00 | 0.00 |
| **Governance & Property Rights** | | | | |
| Coefficient | 0.74 | 0.98 | 0.73 | 0.97 |
| Probability | 0.00 | 0.00 | 0.00 | 0.00 |
| **(X+M)/Y** | | | | |
| Coefficient | 0.29 | 0.20 | 0.22 | |
| Probability | 0.02 | 0.06 | 0.14 | |
| **DCp/Y** | | | | |
| Coefficient | 0.21 | | 0.24 | |
| Probability | 0.27 | | 0.26 | |
| **Volatility** | | | | |
| Coefficient | −4.46 | −6.95 | −5.14 | −8.87 |
| Probability | 0.05 | 0.00 | 0.19 | 0.01 |
| **Volatility · (X+M)/Y** | | | | |
| Coefficient | −5.37 | | −7.38 | |
| Probability | 0.24 | | 0.44 | |
| **Volatility · DCp/Y** | | | | |
| Coefficient | 34.56 | 35.50 | 37.86 | 36.07 |
| Probability | 0.00 | 0.00 | 0.01 | 0.01 |
| Observations | 85 | 85 | 85 | 85 |
| Adjusted R-squared | 0.59 | 0.59 | 0.54 | 0.53 |
| Normal residual rejected ?[a] | No | No | No | No |
| White (Probability)[b] | 0.63 | 0.53 | 0.50 | 0.04 |
| RESET (Probability)[c] | 0.10 | 0.61 | 0.52 | 0.30 |

a. Requires Jarque-Bera statistic smaller than critical value calculated by Deb and Sefton (1996).
b. No cross terms.
c. Probability refers to the significance of one fitted variable (squared).
d. Calculated with White's heteroskedastic-consistent estimators.
*Source:* Authors' estimations.

ious variables. There are three major sources of discrepancies between the Nigerian growth experience and the outcomes in the fastest growing nations. First, the private sectors in the fast growing nations tend to contribute roughly 2.1 percent per-annum more in growth than the Nigerian private sector (row 4). Second, the positive effect of demand induced by OECD trading partner growth is higher for the fast growing nations than for Nigeria, with the difference at 0.8 percent of growth per year (row 8). Third, volatility in the terms of trade (row 9) and instability in the government investment rate (row 6) both adversely affect growth, with a combined growth loss to Nigeria of 2.8 percent per annum.

The simultaneous, negative impact of TOT volatility and instability in the government investment rate raises a question. If a major source of macroeconomic volatility in most nations is the TOT (another being capital flows, especially in Latin American countries), then less TOT volatility should be associated with less government investment volatility.

**Table 7.3. Explaining the Growth and Investment Differentials for Nigeria, 1980–94**

| | | Nigeria | 15 High Growth Countries | |
| | | | Outcome | Differential |
| | | A | B | C |
|---|---|---|---|---|
| 1 | Real Growth per Capita | 0.24 | 4.07 | 3.83 |
| 2 | Initial Income per Capita, 1979 | −3.08 | −3.30 | −0.22 |
| 3 | Investment Rates | 6.39 | 8.42 | 2.03 |
| 4 | Private | 4.39 | 6.48 | 2.09 |
| 5 | Government | 3.25 | 2.90 | −0.35 |
| 6 | Government · (Volatility of Gov't Inv. Rate) | −1.24 | −0.96 | 0.28 |
| 7 | Population Growth & Capital Decay | −9.79 | −9.54 | 0.25 |
| 8 | Real Growth, OECD Partners | 3.35 | 4.11 | 0.76 |
| 9 | Terms of Trade Volatility | −1.57 | −0.43 | 1.14 |
| 10 | Errors and Omissions | 1.56 | 1.43 | −0.13 |
| 11 | Constant | 3.38 | 3.38 | 0.00 |

| | | Nigeria | 15 High Growth Countries | |
| | | | Outcome | Differential |
| | | A | B | C |
|---|---|---|---|---|
| 1 | Private Sector Investment Rate | 4.39 | 6.48 | 2.09 |
| 2 | Governance and Property Rights | 0.93 | 1.41 | 0.48 |
| 3 | Openness to Trade | 0.25 | 0.41 | 0.16 |
| 4 | RER Volatility | −1.99 | −0.09 | 1.90 |
| 5 | RER Volatility · (Dom. Credit as % GDP) | 1.39 | 0.22 | −1.17 |
| 6 | Error | −0.37 | 0.36 | 0.73 |
| 7 | Constant | 4.17 | 4.17 | 0.00 |

a. All investment shares have been logged and converted to GDP growth contributions.
*Source:* Authors' estimations.

The data appear to support this. In our sample of 87 countries, most of the high TOT volatility countries displayed a lot of instability in the rate of government investment while most low TOT countries were also stable government investors. Ideally then, Governments would aim to reduce TOT volatility, thus making it easier to reduce instability in the government investment rate. However, it is quite possible for governments to make expenditure decisions independently of TOT volatility—and the data show that 23 out 87 countries did exactly that. Six of the high TOT volatility countries managed to reduce the instability in their rates of government investment while 17 low TOT volatility countries displayed high levels of volatility in their rates of government investment. This suggests that fiscal policy choices count, even in the face of strong TOT volatility.

The bottom part of Table 7.3 provides the interpretation of the results for the determinants of private investment. The first row provides the contribution to growth from private investment. Rows 2 through 7 show impacts on investment from various variables. Row 2 indicates that Nigeria loses almost half of a percent of growth relative to the performance of the fastest growing nations due to the poor quality of governance and respect for property rights. The country loses another 0.2 percent per annum in growth relative to the fastest growing nations due to the latter's greater openness to trade. Rows 4 and 5 indicate that RER volatility also has a negative impact on private investment led growth, unless the financial sector is sufficiently strong. Unfortunately, net credit flows to the private sector for the period 1980–94 were worth an average of 2.6 percent of current price GDP in Nigeria, versus 6.6 percent of GDP in high growth countries. This means that Nigeria's financial sector was weak to overcome the impact of deep RER volatility. Taken together, rows 4 and 5 show that Nigeria loses another 0.6 percent per annum in growth through the private investment channel. Similar results are obtained when TOT volatility is used instead of ROR volatility to capture uncertainty.

## From Higher Private Investment and Growth to Poverty Reduction

### Methodology

A reduction in macroeconomic volatility in Nigeria would help to achieve higher rates of growth, and thereby lower rates of poverty. The objective of this section is to quantify this gain, using a number of macroeconomic scenarios and assumptions to relate the scenarios to poverty reduction.

To construct the macroeconomic scenarios, we assume that the parameter estimates obtained from the regressions in the previous section apply to the specific case of Nigeria. This means that we can use those parameters to simulate various economic scenarios for the country. Since we don't have enough (time series) data on Nigeria to test this hypothesis, it must be acknowledged that our scenarios are indicative only, that is, they are not meant to be predictions. Each scenario is based on targets for economic, social and institutional outcomes. These targets are all plausible in the sense that many other nations have already achieved them. The precise policies needed to achieve these outcomes in Nigeria, however, are not articulated here, although several key issues are identified. Again, this exercise is meant only to provide some indications as to how poverty reduction could be accelerated through higher per-capita growth under lower levels of macroeconomic volatility.

Next, in order to make the link between growth and poverty reduction, additional assumptions are needed. A first assumption is that growth in per capita GDP in the National Accounts is perfectly correlated with growth in per capita consumption as would be measured in household surveys. A second assumption is that growth in real terms, and the changes in policy that would enable the country to reach a higher level of growth, do not change the estimation of the poverty lines used for measuring poverty in Nigeria's 1996 survey. This means, for example, that relative prices and consumption patterns are not affected by policy changes implemented in order to reduce macroeconomic volatility. A third assumption is that inequality in per consumption also does not change with growth' and under alternative macro-scenarios, so that growth is enough to project poverty measures. Under all these assumptions, assessing the impact of alternative growth scenarios on poverty is very simple since the procedure simply consists in multiplying the per capita consumption in the 1996 household survey by various factors reflecting different growth rates, and re-computing the poverty measures with the new vector of household consumption.

We use the first three poverty measures of the FGT class (Foster and others 1984), namely the head count (share of the population in poverty), the poverty gap (share of the population in poverty times the income gap for the poor which depends on the average distance separating the poor from the poverty line), and the squared poverty gap (which takes into account the square of the distance separating the poor from the poverty line). If we denote by z the poverty line, n the number of households (population weighted), q the number of poor households, and $c_k$ the per capita consumption of household k, the first three FGT poverty measures are defined for $\alpha$ equal to zero (head count), one (poverty gap), and two (squared poverty gap) in the following expression:

$$P_\alpha = \frac{1}{n}\sum_{k=1}^{q}\left[\frac{z-c_k}{z}\right]^\alpha. \qquad (3)$$

Four different scenarios are used to assess the impact that a reduction in volatility and other reforms could have had on growth and thereby poverty. For each scenario, we provide counterfactual measures for the value that the FGT poverty measures could have taken in 1996 if macroeconomic volatility had been lower and growth higher during the preceding sixteen years.

In addition to these four scenarios, we also provide baseline poverty estimates, which are based on the average year-to-year per capita GDP growth observed over the period 1980–1994. The rationale for this baseline case can be seen in Figure 7.1, which shows the counterfactual growth paths from 1980 onwards for the various scenarios and the baseline case. Apart from the actual trend in per capita GDP, there are five lines in the Figure starting from 1980 onwards. The baseline case corresponds to an average growth rate of 0.2 percent per year, which is the historical average over the period 1980–1994. However, while the average growth rate was indeed positive over that period, GDP per capita decreased substantially, because Nigeria's economy collapsed in the early 1980s (a few years of sharp decrease in GDP per capita followed by a slow recovery may indeed lead to a positive year-to-year average annual growth rate despite an overall decrease in GDP per capita). When we assess the impact of reduced volatility and better macroeconomic policies on poverty using scenarios one to four, it is best to compare the poverty measures obtained under these scenarios to the baseline case rather than to the actual measures of poverty in 1996, in order not to

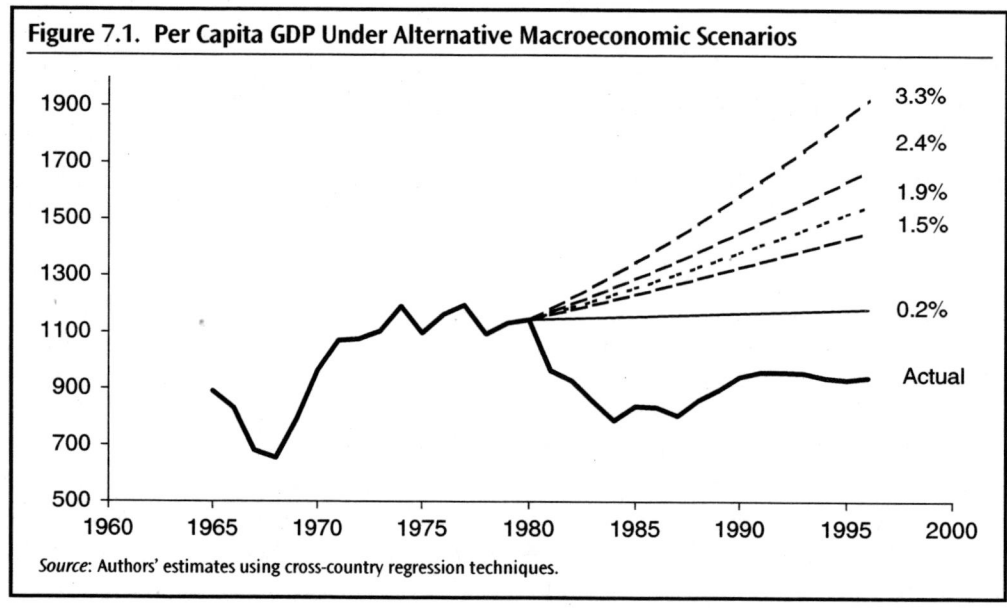

**Figure 7.1. Per Capita GDP Under Alternative Macroeconomic Scenarios**

*Source*: Authors' estimates using cross-country regression techniques.

overestimate the reduction in poverty that can be achieved through lower volatility. If we were comparing the counterfactual macroeconomic scenarios from 1980 onwards with the actual GDP trend and related poverty in 1996, we would get a very large difference in GDP and poverty versus 1996, which would overstate the findings from the regression analysis.

## Scenarios and Results

The baseline case is obtained by assuming a year-to-year historical average growth rate of 0.2 percent per year from 1980 until 1996 (although our historical average is based on data from 1980 to 1994, we continue the simulations up to 1996 which corresponds to the household survey data year). This results in a baseline poverty head count of 54.9 percent, versus the 65.6 percent actually observed in the survey. The difference in GDP and poverty levels between our baseline case and the actual 1996 values is due to the especially sharp drop in GDP per capita in the first half of the 1980s, which can be attributed to a Dutch disease effect[33]— an issue that was in part related to macroeconomic volatility, but was not captured as such in our regression analysis, so that is better to not include this effect in our estimates of the GDP and poverty gains that could have been achieved under lower volatility and better macroeconomic management in Nigeria.

The first scenario corresponds to the implementation of ambitious macroeconomic reforms. This includes an expenditure smoothing fiscal rule leading to substantial reductions in the volatility of public expenditures and the real exchange rate. We assume that average RER volatility is reduced to one third the level observed in 1980–94. Such an outcome is possible though challenging: only a handful of countries with high TOT volatility were able to achieve this over the period 1980–94. We also assume also that the volatility in the public investment rate is reduced to 0.16 (the same as in fast growing nations) from the Nigerian historical average of 0.25. In addition, we assume that the stock of net domestic credit to the private sector grows to 20 percent of GDP (which is still far below the average of 44 percent of GDP achieved by the fast growing nations.) In this first scenario, private investment reaches 9.3 percent of GDP and real growth per-capita increases to 1.5 percent per annum. If this growth rate is applied from 1980 onwards up to 1996, the poverty head count obtained for 1996 is 45.5 percent, instead of the baseline case of 54.9 percent.

The second scenario maintains the policy targets set in the first scenario and adds two more. It is assumed that openness to trade is increased by 10 percent of GDP to a period average of 65 percent of GDP. At the same time, it is assumed that TOT volatility is reduced by 2015 to almost the same level already achieved by the fast growing nations. In this scenario, private sector investment reaches 9.5 percent of GDP and real per capita growth increases to 1.9 percent per year. Applying this growth from 1980 to 1996 yields a poverty head count in 1996 of 42.4 percent, equivalent to a decrease in head count of 12.5 points versus the baseline case of 54.9 percent.

---

33. The Dutch disease refers to the experience of the Netherlands during the 1970s, when natural gas exports led to an appreciation of the Dutch currency, thereby making other exports less competitive and leading to unemployment. The Nigerian story of the early 1980s is similar: as both the volume of oil exports and oil prices increased in the 1970s, Nigeria's real exchange rate appreciated by 83 percent over the decade. High inflation fueled by heavy government spending induced the real exchange rate to appreciate further between 1980 and 1984 even though oil prices were gradually falling. Urban consumers initially benefited from cheaper imports, but agricultural production and exports fell. This led to a loss in GDP and higher dependency on oil. This ultimately led to a devaluation and fiscal austerity measures.

In a third macroeconomic scenario, in addition to the targets set in scenarios 1 and 2, it is also assumed that the quality of governance and the defense of property rights are improved. The effect of this policy is another substantive boost in the rate of private investment to 11.9 percent of GDP. As a consequence, real per capita growth increases to 2.4 percent per annum. This reduces the poverty head count in 1996 to 39.4 percent when the scenario is applied from 1980 onwards.

In a fourth and last scenario, it is assumed that aggressive measures are taken to boost real per-capita growth to 3.3 percent per annum. First, in addition to the targets set in the scenarios above, it is assumed that Nigeria moves closer to the financial outcome of the fast growing nations, with the result that the stock of domestic credit to the private sector is increased to 30 percent of GDP. Second, TOT volatility in this scenario is reduced to half the 1980–94 average. As a result of these measures, the private sector investment rate is increased to an average of 12.7 percent of GDP and the real per capita GDP growth rate rises to 3.3 percent. The counterfactual head count of poverty is 33.2 percent in 1996 when the scenario is applied from 1980 onwards, leading to a reduction of poverty of almost 40 percent versus the baseline case of 54.9 percent of the population in poverty.

The results are summarized in Table 7.4 and Figure 7.2, where the first vertical bar provides the actual poverty measures observed in Nigeria, and subsequent vertical bar refer to

**Table 7.4. Per Capita GDP Growth and Poverty Scenarios, 1980–96**

| | Outcomes | | | | | Policy Targets | | | | | |
|---|---|---|---|---|---|---|---|---|---|---|---|
| | Growth Rate | Private Investment Rate | Poverty Head Count | Poverty Gap | Squared Poverty Gap | RER Volatility | Gov't Inv. Rate Volatility[b] | Private Sector Domestic Credit (% GDP) | Trade Openness (% GDP) | TOT Growth Volatility | Governance |
| **Benchmarks, 1980–94[a]** | | | | | | | | | | | |
| Nigeria (baseline case) | 0.2 | 7.2 | 54.9 | 25.3 | 14.8 | 0.36 | 0.25 | 14 | 55 | 0.23 | 0.43 |
| High growth economies[b] | 4.2 | 20.4 | — | — | — | 0.07 | 0.16 | 44 | 90 | 0.06 | 0.65 |
| **Macroeconomic scenarios** | | | | | | | | | | | |
| Scenario 1 | 1.5 | 9.3 | 45.5 | 19.5 | 10.9 | 0.12 | 0.16 | 17 | — | — | — |
| Scenario 2 | 1.9 | 9.5 | 42.4 | 17.9 | 9.9 | 0.12 | 0.16 | 17 | 65 | 0.17 | — |
| Scenario 3 | 2.4 | 11.9 | 39.4 | 16.0 | 8.7 | 0.12 | 0.16 | 17 | 65 | 0.17 | 0.65 |
| Scenario 4 | 3.3 | 12.7 | 33.2 | 12.9 | 6.8 | 0.12 | 0.16 | 30 | 65 | 0.12 | 0.65 |

a. Benchmarks for fiscal data are based on averages for 1993–2001. All others are based on averages for 1980–94.
b. Average for volatility of public investment rate excludes outlier observations for Lesotho and Singapore.
*Source:* Authors' estimations.

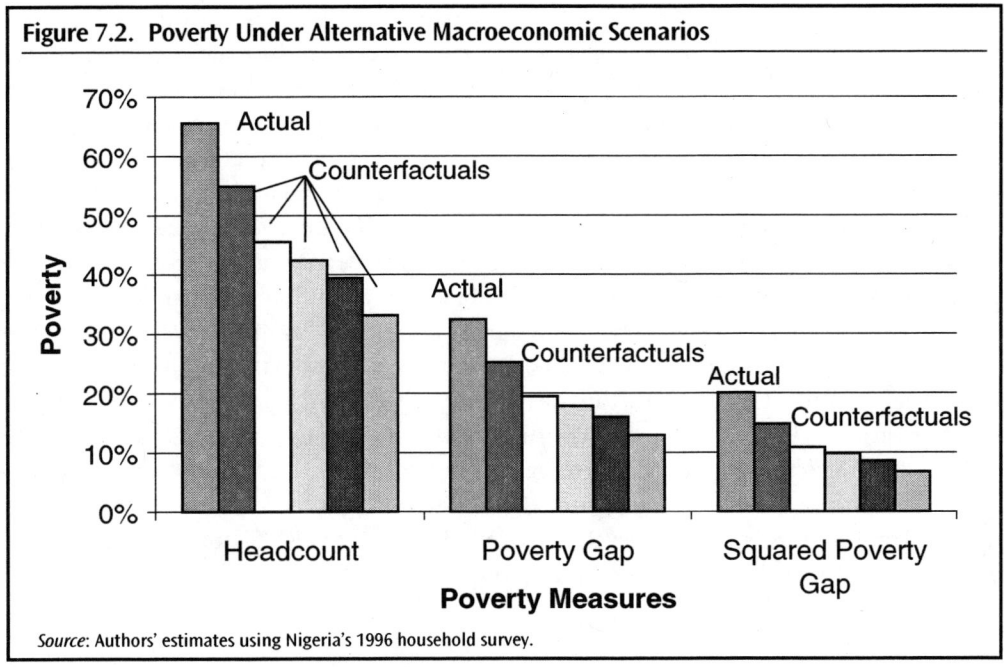

**Figure 7.2. Poverty Under Alternative Macroeconomic Scenarios**

*Source*: Authors' estimates using Nigeria's 1996 household survey.

the baseline case and the four scenarios. The impact of the alternative scenarios on poverty for the poverty gap and squared poverty gap measures is very similar to that observed for the headcount, as expected.

## Conclusion

Policymakers seeking growth have faced strong challenges over the course of Nigerian history. Among these have been deep losses from a civil war, drought, disease and pests, and extremely volatile terms of trade due to oil price shocks. The war appears to have caused the deepest losses, both in terms of lives lost and in terms of economic losses. Yet, the economy rebounded when the war ended. However, oil volatility and real exchange rate uncertainty have continued to penalize growth and private investment, and thereby to lead to high levels of poverty.

While our results indicate a large negative impact of volatility on private investment and growth over the period 1980–94, and thereby a large negative impact on poverty, which was captured in Nigeria's 1996 household survey, the subsequent period has been one of substantive changes. Some of the key events include: the transition from military to civilian rule in 1999, the change from a fixed official exchange rate for government use to a more market determined exchange rate system in 1999, and the end of a drought, but also sharp fluctuations in the price of oil and escalating government expenditures especially at the local government level. A new household survey being implemented in 2004 in Nigeria should tell us whether these changes have been important and positive enough led to a reduction in poverty.

Finally, although we have not discussed this here, it is worth pointing out that volatility is detrimental for what has been referred to as the risk-adjusted standard of living of the poor, which is simply a measure of welfare that adjusts nominal income or consumption for their variability, on the basis of assumptions regarding the degree of risk aversion of households (see, for example, Makdissi and Wodon 2003). In simpler terms, most households would prefer to avoid large fluctuations in income or consumption over time. The consequences for the poor of income (or consumption) volatility over time can be especially negative as they may be forced to make decisions to survive that can be detrimental in the long run, such as selling assets or curtailing food intake. Said differently, standards of living would be higher, and poverty lower in a country with a similar mean level of income or consumption as Nigeria, but with lower volatility. Volatility, apart from having a negative impact on investment and growth, thus has a direct negative impact on households through a higher variation in their income or consumption from year to year. If we had taken into account these effects in the analysis, the negative impact of volatility on poverty would have been even stronger, because apart from the impact of volatility on growth and thereby mean income and consumption levels, we would have had to also factor in the direct negative impact of volatility in itself on households.

## References

Acemoglu, D., and F. Zilibotti. 1997. "Was Prometheus Unbound by Chance? Risk, Diversification and Growth." *Journal of Political Economy* 105(4):709–51.

Aigbokhan, B. E. 2000. *Poverty, growth and inequality in Nigeria: A case study.* AERC Research Paper, no. 102. Nairobi: African Economic Research Consortium.

Ali, A. G. 2000. "The Evolution of Poverty in Nigeria 1985–92." *African Development Review/Revue Africaine de Developpement* 12(2):206–20.

Amaghionyeodiwe, L. A., and T. S. Osinubi. 2004. "Poverty Reduction Policies and Pro-poor Growth in Nigeria." *Brazilian Electronic Journal of Economics* 6(1):1–25.

Benhabib, J., and M. Spiegel. 1994. "The Role of Human Capital in Economic Development: Evidence from Aggregate Cross-Country Data." *Journal of Monetary Economics* 34:143–173.

Bleaney, M., and D. Greenaway. 2001. "The Impact of Terms of Trade and Real Exchange Rate Volatility on Investment and Growth in Sub-Saharan Africa." *Journal of Development Economics* 65(2):491–500.

Canagarajah, S., and S. Thomas. 2001. "Poverty in a Wealthy Economy: The Case of Nigeria." *Journal of African Economies* 10(2):143–73.

Cashin, P., and C. Patillo. 2000. "Terms of Trade Shocks in Africa: Are They Short-lived or Long-lived?" Working Paper WP/00/72, International Monetary Fund, Washington, D.C.

Deb, P., and M. Sefton. 1996. "The Distribution of a Lagrange Multiplier Test of Normality." *Economics Letters* 51:123–130.

Denizer, C., M. Iyigun, and A. Owen. 2002. "Finance and Macroeconomic Volatility." *Contributions to Macroeconomics* 2(1).

Doppelhofer, G., X. Sala-i-Martin, and R. Miller. 2000. "Determinants of Long-run Growth: A Bayesian Averaging of Classical Estimates (BACE) Approach." Working Paper 7750, Cambridge, Mass.: National Bureau of Economic Research.

Easterly, W. 2001. "The Lost Decades: Developing Countries' Stagnation in Spite of Policy Reform 1980–1998." *Journal of Economic Growth* 6(2):135–57.

Easterly W., M. Kremer, L. Pritchett, and L. Summers. 1993. "Good Policy or Good Luck? Country Growth Performance and Temporary Shocks." *Journal of Monetary Economics* 32(3):459–83.

Easterly, W., and S. Rebelo. 1993. "Fiscal Policy and Economic Growth: an Empirical Investigation." *Journal of Monetary Economics* 32(3):417–58.

Edwards, S., 1998. "Openness and Productivity Growth: What Do We Really Know?" *Economic Journal* 108:383–98.

Federal Office of Statistics. 1999. *Poverty Profile for Nigeria 1980–1996.* Abuja.

Foster, J. E., J. Greer, and E. Torbecke. 1984. "A Class of Decomposable Poverty Measures." *Econometrica* 52:761–66.

Hall, R., and C. Jones. 1999. "Why Do Some Countries Produce So Much More Output Per Worker Than Others?" *Quarterly Journal of Economics* 114(1):83–116.

Kaufmann, D., A. Kraay, and P. Zoido-Lobaton. 1999. "Governance Matters." World Bank Policy Research Working Paper 2196, The World Bank, Washington, D.C.

Mankiw, N., D. Romer, and D. Weil. 1992. "A Contribution to the Empirics of Economic Growth." *Quarterly Journal of Economics* 107(2):407–37.

Makdissi, P., and Q. Wodon. 2003. "Risk-Adjusted Measures of Wage Inequality and Safety Nets." *Economics Bulletin* 9(1):1–10.

Marchat, J., J. Nasir, V. Ramachandran, M. Shah, G. Tyler, and L. Zhao. 2001. "Results of the Nigeria Firm Survey." Regional Program on Enterprise Development, The World Bank, Washington, D.C.

Rodríguez, F., and D. Rodrik. 1999. "Trade Policy and Economic Growth: A Skeptic's Guide to the Cross-National Evidence." CEPR Discussion Paper No. 2143, London: Centre for Economic Policy Research. http://www.cepr.org/pubs/dps/DP2143.asp.

Servén, L. 2002. "Real Exchange Rate Uncertainty and Private Investment in LDCs." *Review of Economics and Statistics* 85(1):212–18.

World Bank, 2003. "Nigeria: Policy Options for Growth and Stability." Report No. 26215-NGA, Washington, D.C.

———. 2004. "Nigeria: Poverty and Vulnerability." The World Bank, Washington, D.C. Processed.

# Eco-Audit

## Environmental Benefits Statement

The World Bank is committed to preserving Endangered Forests and natural resources. We print World Bank Working Papers and Country Studies on 100 percent postconsumer recycled paper, processed chlorine free. The World Bank has formally agreed to follow the recommended standards for paper usage set by Green Press Initiative—a nonprofit program supporting publishers in using fiber that is not sourced from Endangered Forests. For more information, visit www.greenpressinitiative.org.

In 2006, the printing of these books on recycled paper saved the following:

| Trees* | Solid Waste | Water | Net Greenhouse Gases | Total Energy |
|---|---|---|---|---|
| 203 | 9,544 | 73,944 | 17,498 | 141 mil. |
| '40" in height and 6-8" in diameter | Pounds | Gallons | Pounds $CO_2$ Equivalent | BTUs |